Anthony Bourdain
and Philosophy

Pop Culture and Philosophy®

General Editor: George A. Reisch

For full details of all Pop Culture and Philosophy® books, and all Open Universe® books, visit www.carusbooks.com

Pop Culture and Philosophy®

Anthony Bourdain and Philosophy

An Appetite for Life

Edited by
SCOTT CALEF

OPEN UNIVERSE
Chicago

Volume 12 in the series, Pop Culture and Philosophy®, Series Editor George A. Reisch

To find out more about Open Universe and Carus Books, visit our website at www.carusbooks.com.

Anthony Bourdain and Philosophy: An Appetite for Life

ISBN: 978-1-63770-039-6

This book is also available as an e-book (978-1-63770-038-9).

Library of Congress Control Number: 2022951773

For Sean Kay

The Menu

The Last Supper Game

Anthony Bourdain often played a game with his chef pals and culinary associates in the high-end world of Michelin-starred restaurants. It's called "The Last Meal" game. Everyone has to imagine they're on Death Row and about to die and that they have the chance to choose their last meal. Tony often observed that almost no one answers, "I'd love to try a forty-course tasting menu from The French Laundry or NOMA." Instead, the answer is almost always some variation on "Mama's meatloaf" or "My grandmother's pasta" or "Birds-in-the-nest the way my dad used to make it on weekends when we didn't have to get up early for school."

Sometimes, it seems, less is more, and what really makes a meal memorable is not how artfully and intricately decorated the small plates are or how crisply the wait staff snaps to attention the second your wine glass gets low, but who you're with, the intimacy of connection with those around you, and the way a lovingly-prepared meal transports you back to your childhood or more innocent and carefree times. That, and lots of alcohol.

I sometimes imagine myself playing a variation on the Last Meal game, only instead of asking, "What would your last meal be if you knew you were about to die?" the question is, "If you could share a meal with any one person on Earth, from any historical period, who would it be?" Now, I assume that if you've lost a loved one—a child or spouse or beloved relative—that that person would be chosen. But bracket that for a second. Suppose that you couldn't choose someone you're related to, or someone that you've known well, like a best friend who has died or whom you haven't seen for the last ten years. If you could only choose one person, who would you most like to meet, converse with, and break bread?

- Gandhi? Probably wouldn't be much of a meal. Half a chapati, a couple of olives and a glass of goat's milk.

- A prophet, avatar, or religious leader? Someone like Jesus? While it would be interesting to meet the man behind the myth, and Jesus liked hanging out with people who drank a lot of wine, Jesus was pretty hard on hypocrites and made a lot of people very uncomfortable. Divine love notwithstanding, spending several awkward hours with someone whose omniscient gaze suggests he knows all of my deepest, darkest and most shameful secrets runs the risk of being too intense to actually be enjoyable. Salvific, perhaps, but fun?

- What about Churchill or Lincoln or Queen Elizabeth or somebody like that? While dining with any of these esteemed personages would no doubt be memorable, I'm assuming I've only got one shot at this and that it's a once-in-a-lifetime opportunity. The problem with selecting any intriguing historical or political figure is that there are so many of them. How to choose?

- Socrates? Hell no! That's definitely a hard pass. Although he's probably my favorite philosopher, if I want to be totally humiliated by someone way out of my league, I can just go to a nightclub and ask someone to dance. Besides, Socrates doesn't speak English (and, according to Alcibiades in Plato's *Symposium*, he doesn't get drunk, either).

- Maybe a rock star? Angus Young or Keith Richards or Jerry Garcia would have oodles of highly entertaining and amusing stories to tell. That would be fun. But again, how to choose? The one who has done the most drugs? The one who had the most raunchy sex? The miscreant who busted up the most hotel rooms? The one with enough brain cells left to actually remember the 60s and 70s?

I choose Anthony Bourdain over all of these people, and let me tell you why:

- First, unlike dinner with Gandhi, the food would probably be great.

- Unlike Jesus, Saint Anthony was a sinner, and so I should feel right at home. No moralizing sermons making me squirm in my seat.

- Though not a Churchill, a Lincoln, or even a MacArthur, Tony impressed everyone who knew him with his erudition and general knowledge of history, literature, art, and film. He was a writer and a storyteller and a damn good one. So if you're tempted by Kennedy or Warhol or Dostoevsky or somebody like that because you want to talk about history or politics or culture or literature, Bourdain's actually not a bad choice. Others undoubtedly had more knowledge than Anthony Bourdain on particular topics, but Bourdain had breadth. He was complex. I like that in a dinner companion.

● Despite being impressively well-read, however, beyond the TV bluster Bourdain was reportedly humble, self-effacing, and acutely aware of how much he didn't know. He wrote that enlightenment is realizing "that there is no final resting place of the mind; no moment of smug clarity. Perhaps wisdom . . . is realizing how small I am, and unwise, and how far I have yet to go." This sounds just like Socrates. If philosophy is the love of wisdom, Bourdain was a philosopher. He grappled with profound and existential questions: What is happiness? How can we attain it? (Or, more pertinent, why can't we for more than about two minutes at a time?) What makes us human? How can we right the many evils and injustices of the world? Why in the hell would a loving God create clowns, mimes, and karaoke? Anthony Bourdain was a deep individual.

● Finally, Kerrang called him "the world's most rock'n'roll chef" and the Smithsonian dubbed him "the Elvis of bad boy chefs." Although the guy wasn't literally a rock star, he sure hung out with a lot of them—Iggy Pop, Alice Cooper, Alison Mosshart, the Black Keys, Jack White, Josh Homme, Serj Tankian. I mean, come on! He dedicated *The Nasty Bits* to the Ramones! Tony Bourdain's done all the drugs, had the girlfriends, gone on tour, traveled the world and partied hard.

So go ahead. Slurp your noodles with Obama or Einstein or Frida Kahlo. I'm not judging you. But Bourdain's a bad ass. He's my guy.

Unfortunately, I can't offer you a last meal with Anthony Bourdain, but the philosophical spirits who have written for this volume are almost guaranteed to give you plenty of food for thought and topics for a lively dinner conversation. They, too, would make pretty memorable dining companions and each of them brings a lot to the table. Like Bourdain himself, they don't shy away from the tough questions—and even offer a few answers: Who *was* Anthony Bourdain, and why do we care? What does it mean to praise him for his "authenticity"? What can he show us about how better to live our lives? Was Bourdain a hedonist? An Epicurean? What can an addictive personality like Bourdain's teach us about true freedom? Are addicts always irrational or irresponsible? How could such a surly, snarky, overbearing boss bring folks together in a sense of community? How could someone who, early in his career, exemplified machismo and toxic masculinity become one of the

#MeToo movement's most passionate and ardent allies? What makes someone a more expert taster than someone else? Is taste purely subjective? How could Bourdain actually *enjoy* "disgusting" food? Is it ethical to dine in expensive, fancy restaurants? Do standards of taste help maintain class distinctions and social hierarchies, and if so, how? What's up with the graphic novels and the jiu jitsu? Why would the man with "the best job in the world" kill himself? Thanks to the miracle of AI, can Anthony Bourdain speak to us from beyond the grave? And how can we best carry on his work, honoring *it* while remembering *him*?

Anthony Bourdain loved to write, and he loved to read. I hope this book brings you pleasure, and at least a few morsels of wisdom. Anthony Bourdain and Philosophy? They belong together. Like hot dogs and papaya drinks. Cream cheese and bagels. Beer and . . . everything Bourdain ever ate, or smoked, anywhere in the world!

I

Taste

1
A Man for All Seasonings

MICHAEL SHAFFER

And now I'm ready to close my eyes
And now I'm ready to close my mind
And now I'm ready to feel your hand
And lose my heart on the burning sand.

—THE STOOGES, "I Wanna Be Your Dog" (1969)

Many of our hearts burned with sadness on June 8th 2018. That is the day that Anthony Bourdain passed away in a hotel room in Kaysersberg France, after missing dinner with his great friend and fellow gastronome Éric Ripert.

Beginning with his incredibly witty exposé *Kitchen Confidential* and continuing in his written and television work, Anthony Bourdain made many of us pay attention to food, to culture, and to our experiences of food. But his perspectives on food and culture were never simplistic and naive. Bourdain himself was a man who was complex, and he embodied many contradictions.

He was a chef, but he insisted that he was merely a cook. He was an Epicurean possessed of extensive knowledge of the most exquisite culinary fare and yet he was simultaneously an aficionado of the simplest foods of so very many cultures. He loved classical French cuisine and dirty water hotdogs with equal zeal. He loved the pastoral beauty of nature and the cacophonous chaos of punk rock. He was both judgmental and tolerant. He was a champion of the common people and a friend of the culinary elite. He was kind and he was acerbic. He was the human equivalent of Agrodolce, both sweet and sour at once. To many of us, he was a friend we never had the luck to have met.

These contradictions are, in part, what made him such a compelling cultural figure and what gave him, in the best sense, the power to transcend social strata. He brought cuisine, both fancy and pedestrian, both worldly and local, to so very many people in a way which worked. We are all better for his work, and it was indeed work. Bourdain made no bones about it. He hated provincialism and small-mindedness and devoutly believed that wide-scoped experiences of food made people more humane. So, while he was extremely knowledgeable about the foods of the world, he was not a food snob as a result of his extensive experience. Moreover, he wanted us to be with him in his quest for food and cultural experience. He cared that others have such opportunities as well.

Bourdain's TV shows and writings raise interesting questions about the nature of taste, the aesthetics of food, and the moral implications of taste. It's easier to understand the various connections he drew between culinary experience, gastronomic expertise, and his respect for food and people of all sorts if we compare them to Jean Anthelme Brillat-Savarin's classic work, *The Physiology of Taste*. Brillat-Savarin's crucial distinction between the subjective and objective aspects of taste illuminates Bourdain's complex feelings about food and culture and explains how someone as sophisticated as Bourdain managed to retain a down-to-earth respect for the commonplace that avoided aesthetic elitism. The view which emerges exemplifies Bourdain's mission to guide us to what tastes good and to make us appreciate the people of many cultures.

A Taste of Things to Come

Relativism about taste is a familiar theme in aesthetics, especially when it comes to the faculty of tasting itself. Most people are relativists or subjectivists—they believe that, when it comes to matters of taste, we're each authoritative. You're entitled to your judgments about your tastes, and I'm entitled to mine. Subjectivists maintain that no one person's judgment(s) are superior to anyone else's. You can prefer chocolate ice cream, while I prefer vanilla and neither preference is better than the other.

However, somewhat inconsistently, we also believe that some people are experts when it comes to matters of taste and that there's something objective and authoritative about the expert's judgments. We seem to believe both that it's okay to prefer street fish tacos to a fancy French dish like Sole à la Normandie, while also believing that an expert refined French gastronome is authoritatively correct when he or she tells us that the Sole is better than the tacos. This observation raises tricky questions about the relationship between truth, expertise, and taste that help us understand what was so special about Anthony Bourdain's work.

In accordance with the 'objectivist' idea of expertise, it's often supposed that gastronomes possess knowledge that others lack. This is because many forms of expertise involve abilities or knowledge not possessed by the rest of us. An expert mechanic has certain abilities (such as skill at repairing the brake system on a car), and certain knowledge (such as that the timing belt connects the crankshaft and the camshaft together to control the valve operation) that are lacked by non-experts. These are objective aspects of the mechanic's expertise. So, when a mechanic asserts that the timing belt connects the crankshaft and the camshaft together to control the valve operation, we ought to believe it and when a literary critic tells us that Tolstoy's *War and Peace* is a better book than Bourdain's *Bone in the Throat,* we should believe that too. We often suppose that gastronomes are also experts whose judgments about taste are to be accepted and when a gastronomic expert claims that a food tastes good or that a particular cheese or wine has a flinty taste, we ought to accept these judgments as true.

However, in accordance with the 'subjectivist' idea of taste, we also often suppose that matters of taste are entirely personal and individualistic. In "Of the Standard of Taste" David Hume tells us that

> a thousand different sentiments, excited by the same object, are all right: Because no sentiment represents what is really in the object, It only marks a certain conformity or relation between the object and the organs or faculties of the mind . . . Beauty is no quality in things themselves; It exists merely in the mind which contemplates them; and each mind perceives a different beauty. One person may even perceive deformity, where another is sensible of beauty; and every individual ought to acquiesce in his own sentiment, without pretending to regulate those of others. To seek real beauty, or real deformity, is as fruitless an enquiry, as to pretend to ascertain the real sweet or real bitter. According to the disposition of the organs, the same object may be both sweet and bitter; and the proverb has justly determined it to be fruitless to dispute concerning tastes. (p. 230)

According to *this* 'Humean' view of taste there is no objective component in taste experience on the basis of which one could be a gastronomic expert. After all, how can one be more expert at discriminating the genuine taste of things if things really have no true taste qualities? So, is 'subjectivism' the right account of gastronomic expertise or is 'objectivism' the right account of taste? Or, is there some way to reconcile these two views?

I maintain that gastronomic expertise is nothing more than an ability to describe fundamental taste experiences more eloquently (Shaffer, "Taste, Gastronomic Expertise and Objectivity"). It is an acquired ability to use subjective concepts to describe more basic tastes that arise in virtue of our physiological abilities to taste. This is just the ability to do things like noting that a particular red wine that tastes a little sweet, quite bitter, and rather sour is reminiscent of the taste and smell of tobacco and blackberries.

So, it turns out that there is nothing especially profound or objective about the specific judgments of gastronomical experts. Gastronomic experts don't possess special abilities to taste things that non-experts can't, and the abilities they do have are just reflections of their personal experiences that are accessible to everyone willing to put in the work. As it turns out, this view of gastronomic expertise fits spectacularly well with Bourdain's approaches to food and culture, and it shows what was so special about his life's mission to get us to eat just about everything everywhere.

The clash of objectivity and subjectivity with respect to taste is clarified when we distinguish between the direct and the reflective aspects of taste (*The Physiology of Taste*, pp. 40–41). Direct taste experiences are experiences of taste properties at the most basic level using our tongues, mouths, and innate physiological abilities to detect sweetness, sourness, saltiness, bitterness, and savoriness. Such experiences are uninterpreted and not yet thought about.

Reflective taste experiences, on the other hand, are direct tastes conceptually interpreted using taste concepts present in the brain. This allows for interpretation of direct tastes in terms of concepts like 'flintiness', 'oakiness', and so on. The application of these sorts of concepts and the connections they involve are subjective in a way that the detection of sourness or saltiness using one's tongue is not. To make this distinction clearer let's consider a typical review offered by the gastronomic expert Judy Ridgway. She offers the following account of the taste of Langres, a cheese from the Champagne region of France:

> The rind is the typically bright orange color of washed rind cheese and this gives it its pungent farmyard-like aroma. The paste is very creamy with a pretty pale yellow color and a sweet aroma of lemons

and a touch of bacon. The flavor is strong but creamy. There is a definite suggestion of old socks but this is balanced by a lovely lemony tang. (*The Cheese Companion*, p.126.)

Similarly, Bourdain himself describes the taste of haggis as follows:

Peppery, hot, meaty-it didn't taste of anything you might expect in a dish cooked in a stomach. Not really tasting organlike at all, no bittery liver taste, no chewy mysterious bits, no wet-dog taste of tripe. It was in no way offensive to even the most pedestrian American tastes, but subtle and rich in a boudin noir sort of way. *(A Cook's Tour,* p. 256.)

What are we to make of these kinds of descriptions? Notice first that there is almost no reference to direct taste qualities in these descriptions, and that the taste descriptions used are almost exclusively of the reflective sort. These include the tastes of lemon, old sock, and bacon, farmyard odors, and creaminess in the Ridgeway case. In Bourdain's description we have appeals to tastes including their being organlike, livery, and reminiscent of wet dog. So, as is typical, Ridgeway and Bourdain draw a host of analogies between their direct tasting and their past taste experiences. This points to the fact that reflective tasting involves processing in the parts of the brain that allow for higher-level cognitive functioning and not just the physiological events that happen in the mouth and tongue.

Reflective tasting involves sophisticated description and drawing connections to past experiences. The complex reflective concepts that we acquire and use to interpret direct taste experiences are imposed on direct taste experiences so that we can think about them in a richer manner. This allows such direct experiences to be integrated into our broader perspective on the world and it involves a host of connections to ideas that go far beyond tasting sweetness, saltiness, and the like. Such conceptualization involves connections to other people and their cultural contexts.

So, it should be clear that the judgments of gastronomic experts almost exclusively concern reflective tasting. It is the more florid and rich kinds of description of direct tastes and their relations to our broader experiences that are the content of gastronomic expertise. This ability is grounded in using our reflective taste concepts to draw analogies between direct taste experiences and past experiences of all sorts of things. Where do these concepts come from? They are learned through experience, and having a richer set of reflective taste concepts to draw on allows for the ability to describe taste experiences in a more sophisticated manner. Claiming that a cheese tastes like old socks is saying nothing more than that the taste of the cheese is, in some way, *like* the taste/smell of old socks. The one is reminiscent of the other. But this connection cannot be made without the previous experience of old socks, and each of us has a unique collection of such previous experiences. Nevertheless, this ability to draw connections between experiences also makes such experiences richer and more complex and offers us a window into the complex lived experiences of others. But this is all there is to gastronomic expertise, and, despite the simple nature of this account of taste, it is nonetheless deeply important and Bourdainian. He understood that there is no contradiction in respecting gastronomic expertise and in embracing the beauty of simple and pedestrian foods.

The upshot here is that gastronomic expertise is not a sort of rational and objective expertise, because it involves nothing more than the ability to apply our own high-level experiential concepts to direct tastes reflectively, and this is essentially subjective in nature. What is objective about taste according to our current physiological understanding of taste perception is simply the shared innate physiological capacity to taste directly (despite some smallish variations in such abilities). We have very good scientific reasons to believe that any properly functioning human can detect real, objective tastes such as saltiness, sourness, bitterness, and so on. But you could only get so far in describing the taste of a cheese or a wine in terms of sweetness, saltiness, bitterness, and so forth, and such descriptions would be boorishly uninformative.

There are, however, good reasons to suppose that there are real differences in capacities when it comes to reflective taste, the real content of gastronomic expertise. While Brillat-Savarin was ironically correct in making his aphoristic claim that "The pleasures of the table are for every man, of every land, and no matter of what place in history or society," there is more to the story (*The Physiology of Taste*, p. 3). Essentially, we can all directly taste the same things, but we are not all on an equal footing when it comes to reflective tasting. We do not all have the same set of reflective taste concepts, in part because they are acquired via wide-scoped personal experience that essentially varies from person to person. So, how does this relate to the work of Anthony Bourdain?

Plato and the Perils of Provincialism

It is remarkable that there has been an upsurge in xenophobic sentiments in the last twenty years, a time when it has become increasingly easy to engage with people of other cultures through television, the internet in general, and through social media in particular. Moreover, the pandemic years aside, actual physical travel to other countries is easier, more convenient, and cheaper than ever before. It is then a bit of a mystery why, given the ease of cultural engagement, it seems that a debilitating kind of provincialism has become more common in our culture. But perhaps we should not be surprised by this phenomenon in light of the recent resurgence of political populism and the casual, low-brow, dismissal of expertise in the US (Tom Nichols, "How America Lost Faith in Expertise"). However, there is no better example of opposition to this sort of myopia in recent times than Anthony Bourdain. It is crucial to understanding both gastronomic expertise and Bourdain's enduring legacy that we appreciate his linking such expertise to cultural experience and thereby to cultural tolerance, and we can see this Bourdainian insight through Plato's allegory of the cave. We shall see that Bourdain's mission regarding taste and tolerance mirrors Plato's understanding of the role of the philosopher in helping others to grasp the truth.

In *Republic* Books VI and VII, Plato discusses the relationship between knowledge, the forms (the objective, eternal, unchanging, and non-physical essences of things), and inquiry. The allegory of the cave is a richly symbolic thought-experiment that is supposed to inform us about the human condition and how we can escape our most dangerous illusions. In the allegory a group of men is chained in the bottom of a dark cave so as to only be able to see the cave's back wall. Behind them objects sit upon a wall and behind the wall is a fire. Owing to the light of the fire, these objects cast flickering shadows on the back wall of the cave.

So, the men who are chained up for their entire lives naturally believe that the images on the wall are true reality. That is the limit of their awareness. But there is a path beyond the wall behind them that leads out into the light of the outside world, that leads to true reality. The central idea of the allegory is that real knowledge concerns the "forms" (the truth), but most people are badly deceived into thinking that the physical world is real and knowable. So, as Plato sees it, most people are ignorant, but do not *know* that they are ignorant. On the other hand, Socrates—Plato's main spokesperson in the *Republic*—is ignorant and knows that he is ignorant. This puts Socrates in a crucially better position than most of us, for he can proceed to inquire into the truths he does not know. He can do the hard work of ascending the path out of the cave and into the light. Those who are ignorant, but do not know that they are ignorant, cannot do so, for they believe they already know. They are ignorant both of the path and the outside world and this is what keeps them chained. So, breaking the chains of unacknowledged ignorance and leaving the cave represents the process of replacing our unacknowledged false and biased opinions with true knowledge, and this requires first that we acknowledge our ignorance.

However, it's nearly impossible to accomplish this task on our own. We need help to free ourselves from the bonds of our engrained and unacknowledged ignorance. We need to be *led to the truth* by a knowing chaperone, but the chaperone cannot know for us. The chaperone can only show us how to free ourselves and inquire into the truth. It's also crucial to the Platonic and Socratic view that coming to see the truth in the form of the good, in fact, makes us good. It is then one of Plato's most personal homages to his mentor Socrates that it is the critical philosopher who can break the chains that bind us, so that he can then take our hands and help us to ascend out of the cave by our own hard work. So, it's with Socrates's help that we ascertain the truth and become morally good. It is Socrates who can lead us out of the darkness of our unacknowledged ignorance and into the light of truth and goodness, but only if we learn these lessons and do the work.

What then does this have to do with Anthony Bourdain's legacy and the theory of gastronomic expertise introduced here? Well, since gastronomic expertise has nothing to do with acquired or innate variations in the ability to directly taste things, gastronomic expertise only involves employing reflective concepts learned via experience. We are (almost) all on a level playing field when it comes to direct tasting; variations in expert ability to taste involve the possession of more-or-less rich bodies of reflective concepts that are acquired by having wider cultural experiences. The gastronomic expert directly tastes the same thing that the non-expert does when they eat Langres, but the expert can describe that direct taste experience in a more florid manner using a wider palate of references to reflective concepts gleaned through their richer experiences. These reflective concepts are subjective, personal, and acquired in our broad experience of complex physical and social things. But everyone can develop such concepts through the pursuit of wider and more varied experiences.

What then makes Bourdain's work special? I believe that it is his role as the gastronomic equivalent of Socrates. Anthony

Bourdain did not *accidentally* link food and culture immersion. His expertise as a gastronome was dependent on his wide experience of and appreciation for culture, for it is the cultural experiences we each have that provide the reflective concepts available to us to frame our direct taste experiences and to make them richer. Those experiences cannot be transmitted to others, but we can be led to them. Bourdain then, in essence and like Socrates, returned to the cave to remind us that we need to have wide cultural experience in order to appreciate what we directly taste and that this makes us better people, for such experience improves our tasting, makes us more expert in our taste judgments, and engenders cultural tolerance. Bourdain had nothing good to say about picky eaters and closed-minded provincialists.

Bourdain also did not despise common food and he did not love food snobbery, but this makes sense when we understand that what he prized were the food *experiences* which transcend and augment the purely objective taste qualities of things. They make us individually richer and collectively more humane. Indeed, the closed-minded champions of provincialism then are simply ignorant denizens of the cave who unwittingly embrace limited experience and cultural intolerance by eschewing wide gastronomic experience. They both deprive themselves of better taste experiences and of the cultural understanding that makes us better people who possess a better and more diverse understanding of others.

But you don't need to be a food snob in order to have wide taste experiences either. They are available to us all. This is the crux of Bourdain's view. We can then have our cake and eat it too! We should see that Anthony Bourdain was the living embodiment of the idea that taste incorporates objective components that are subjectively contextualized and which, in being conceptualized, allow us a window into the cultural worlds of others. Having expansive experiences of this sort makes us better people and Bourdain knew this all too well.

I Wanna Be Your Guide Dog

So, Bourdain's lessons can be captured in a telling re-write of Iggy Pop's seminal Stooges era song referenced above:

> And now I'm ready to open my eyes
> And now I'm ready to open my mind
> And now I'm ready to take your hand
> And lead you through this culinary land.

Many of us miss Anthony Bourdain (even if we did not know him personally), but his lessons remain clear and Socratic: neither an elitist snob, nor a closed-minded provincialist be. Rather, what we should be are the kinds of seekers of diverse gastronomic experience and lovers of the cultural diversity that makes us all human. He showed us the way.

So, eat a cheese steak in Philly and a Chicago hot dog covered in green relish and sport peppers in the Chi. Order the Hiramasa at Le Bernardin in New York and the Nova Scotia Lobster Galette at the French Laundry in Yountville.

All of it adds up. All of it enriches us. All of it makes us appreciate the humanity in everyone. There are so very many foods that taste delicious and help us to understand others, even Bourdain's stinky durian. Thanks, Tony.

2
To Eat or Not to Eat?

WALTER BARTA AND CANDACE MIRANDA

When you get hungry for dinner tonight, should you eat at your local dive bar for the fifth time in a row, or try someplace new? And when you sit down with the menu, should you order your go-to dish or the chef's special? Should you play it safe or take the risk? Anthony Bourdain, in his first book, *Kitchen Confidential*, claims that "good food, good eating is all about risk" (p. 6) but what does he mean?

Any time you try a new thing whether it's food or drink or travel, you're taking a risk. Because it's your first time, you don't know if the benefits of the experience will outweigh the costs. Will it be delicious or dangerous? Bourdain believed that risk was the core of his culinary and cultural project—the cooking and writing and traveling that defined his life—even to the extent of fetishizing risk as a good in itself. As Bourdain himself puts it in the introductory segment to his first television show, *A Cook's Tour*:

> As a cook, tastes and smells are my memories, and now I'm in search of new ones, so I'm leaving New York City and hope to have a few epiphanies around the world, and I'm willing to go to some lengths to do that. I'm looking for extremes of emotion and experience. I'll try anything. I'll risk everything. I have nothing to lose.

Like someone who plays an extreme sport, Anthony Bourdain played extreme spoon, daring us to partake along with him. And yet, Bourdain's struggles with addiction and his untimely death also give us hesitation before taking a bite: perhaps some risks are worth taking and others not. So, should we try new things? And how do we make that decision? Or, to rephrase Shakespeare's *Hamlet*: *To Eat or not to Eat: that is the question.*

This is a culinary question but also a philosophical question, in that it deals with fundamental considerations about how we should live our best lives. In order to explore Bourdain's dare, we can look at different philosophies, specifically schools of hedonism, the belief in the goodness of pleasure. Each school of hedonism may offer a different way of prioritizing pleasures and approaching dangers, illuminating Bourdain's life choices and our own.

Cost-Benefit Analysis

Like Bourdain himself, many philosophers have been students and teachers of the pleasures. Perhaps most infamous amongst them, Jeremy Bentham, the father of Utilitarian philosophy, believed that all of our actions are "under the governance of two sovereign masters, pain and pleasure" (*The Principles of Morals and Legislation*, p. 6). As a Utilitarian, Bentham believed that actions should be chosen for their utility. He was both a consequentialist and a hedonist, someone who believed that our decisions should be motivated by their consequences and that the best consequences were pleasures and the worst consequences pains.

Even if we're not purely hedonistic, we can see Bentham's point because almost everyone can admit that pleasures are good and pains bad, even if not the only good or bad. Accordingly, we can judge actions in terms of how much they increase or decrease pleasure and pain. Anthony Bourdain would surely be sympathetic to Bentham's hedonism. Indeed, one might suggest that Bourdain was the hedonist par excellence, making his life's work the discovery and experience of pleasures.

But what about those risky situations, like trying new things, that Bourdain was so fond of: situations that involve mixtures of pleasures and pains—as most do? Cost, sacrifice, and risk are themselves not considered goods by most, but hedonists generally think costs can be instrumental means to pleasurable ends. According to Bentham, cases involving mixtures of good and bad should be decided according to a cost-benefit analysis with calculated risks and rewards. When deciding to do something or not, the good brought about should be weighed against the bad brought about. Indeed, several factors regarding the benefits and costs should be considered, including the intensity, duration, certainty, and nearness of the pleasures and pains (*Principles*, p. 22). This method of calculating the expected utility of an action is actually fairly close to a method encountered by Bourdain in his travels, that used by the Bhutanese government, which employs a "Happiness Index" to attempt to measure the country's net happiness for the sake of policy decisions (*Parts Unknown*, "Bhutan").

In cost-benefit analysis, considering various factors, we must weigh outcomes against each other to compare them. For example, if we want to visit some of Anthony Bourdain's favorite countries and restaurants, we might make an itinerary, weighing options against each other to plan our trip, budgeting money, time, and effort against the sights, sounds, tastes, and general experiences. Further, in the spirit of Anthony Bourdain, applying this logic to gastronomic adventures, we might assess whether or not we should try new experiences based on the pleasures and the pains of consuming them. What benefits do they bring: what do they smell/taste/feel like, how full do they make us, what knowledge do they give us? What costs do they incur: food poisoning, allergic reaction, social stigma, not to mention monetary expense? Unlike Bourdain, we may not have access to a television show's budget and a French chef's palate, so the answers to these questions may be different for each of us; but, regardless, when the waiter hands over the menu and asks what we will be eating, there may in fact be better and worse choices, depending upon factors like taste, budget, appetite, and so forth.

According to this model, we might imagine at least four distinctly different categories of risk and reward outcomes, and each of these categories have had their philosophical advocates:

- High-Cost/Low-Benefit: The Ascetics
- Low-Cost/Low-Benefit: The Epicureans
- High-Cost/High-Benefit: The Cyrenaics
- Low-Cost/High-Benefit: The Utilitarians

As Bentham and the Utilitarians would say, the first category, high-cost/low-benefit, should be avoided and the fourth category, low-cost/high-benefit, should be pursued; whereas their opponents, the Ascetics, would say the opposite (*Principles*, p. 10). Of the middle categories, low-cost/low-benefit and high-cost/high-benefit—advocated by the Epicurean and Cyrenaic schools of hedonism, respectively—Bentham would have less certainty; each choice might be equally reasonable and neither could be dismissed as obviously irrational. That is because both offer similar net rewards to risks ratios, albeit drastically different lifestyles. We might examine each of these different categories of cost/benefit and their respective philosophical advocates to see where we might fit Bourdain's predilections.

The Ascetics (High-Cost/Low-Benefit)

Few consider sacrifice, cost, and pain to be goods in themselves, though some do. Jeremy Bentham calls these philosophers "Ascetics," and he defines their philosophy as the rejection of pleasure and acceptance of pain as a value, the opposite of Utilitarianism. To a hedonist like Bentham, Asceticism is nonsense because there is nothing intrinsically valuable about suffering, and life without pleasure is not worth living. Thus, to Bentham, Asceticism only becomes coherent if its practitioners believe in a heavenly afterlife where their suffering and sacrifice will be rewarded, which gives greater pleasure after death. But ironically, if they only suffer to get into heaven, then the Ascetics are hedonists themselves, because they are ultimately trying to maximize pleasure—eternal pleasure.

Anthony Bourdain surely would not have characterized himself as an Ascetic. As he says of the matter, "If you're not listening to pain, you're doing something wrong" (*Parts Unknown*, "Bhutan"). However, some of Bourdain's behaviors seem Ascetic at first glance; Bourdain sometimes seems to valorize danger for danger's sake. For example, in Japan, in the pilot episode of *A Cook's Tour*, Bourdain eats fugu, a Japanese pufferfish which is delicious prepared as a sushi and deadly if prepared incorrectly. That is because certain parts of its body contain a toxin, for which there is no antidote (*A Cook's Tour*, "A Taste of Tokyo"). Similarly, in a later escapade, Bourdain tries live octopus, sannakji chulpan, which comes with some not-inconsiderable risk of suffocation (*No Reservations*, "New York: Outer Boroughs"). However, as Bentham's analysis might suggest, most if not all of Bourdain's ascetic tendencies prove hedonistic upon inspection. For example, in the fugu episode, Bourdain explains that he is taking the risk for a reward, hedonistically:

> For me, [fugu]'s kind of like climbing culinary Everest. It's an obstacle to be surmounted. If people are willing to risk death, it must taste phenomenal; and I'm guessing if maybe you have a bit of the poison, you might get a nice buzz.

As his intention shows, in this instance, Bourdain is not being truly ascetic, seeking a painful death for its own sake, but being hedonistic, taking a risk in the pursuit of pleasure.

However, in such instances, we might still suggest that Bourdain is being irrational because he seems willing to face risks that do not seem worth the rewards; Bourdain is making an error of cost-benefit analysis. Bentham and Bourdain would certainly disagree regarding these high-risk and low-reward adventures; Bourdain would seemingly eat the fugu and die smiling, saying "I want to try everything once", whereas Bentham would pass the plate along and perhaps have some well-done fried rice (*Kitchen Confidential*, p. 74). Of course, we do not know what the fugu tastes like until we try it, so it is hard to judge the reward; however, we do know that pufferfish toxin is extremely deadly, so we can judge the risk (let's say $x\%$ deadly, where x is some number). So, fugu must literally be worth dying for (or dying for $x\%$ of the time) to be worth trying. In prospect a taste worth dying for seems fairly unlikely; and, in retrospect, Bourdain admits that "fugu actually tastes rather bland" and is further disappointed that he did not even feel any "numbness around the lips." Indeed, through the experience Bourdain determines that "the thrill of eating fugu is all in the risk." This "thrill" is a pleasure uniquely attendant to risk, perhaps making a risk worth taking hedonistically—like in cases of skydiving, bungee-jumping, or zip-lining. And yet, with fugu or other such cases, thrill alone may not necessarily be worth the danger.

All this considered, the cost-benefit analysis of eating fugu ultimately depends upon the probability of death per serving. If the probability is low enough, then the risk is minimal, perhaps like eating any other fish. If the probability is high enough, then we could argue that Bourdain is probably not being rational when he eats the pufferfish: if Bourdain reflected upon his actions, he could not justify them because no single pleasure is worth the risk of death (even a $x\%$ risk).

Eating fugu is not nearly the worst case of Bourdain's miscalculated cost-benefit analysis. In an even more extreme example featured in his memoir *Medium Raw*, Bourdain confesses to driving drunk night after night down the winding roads of a Caribbean island and recklessly deciding whether or not to drive off the nearest cliff based on what song the DJ played next on the radio—a vehicular version of Russian Roulette. Like with fugu, this behavior involves high risk; unlike with fugu, which involves some reward, this behavior seems to have no reward at all: all downside; no upside— besides, perhaps, the thrill of the risk itself and the cessation of the depression Bourdain was feeling at the time. In this case and others, Bentham would warn Bourdain not to take risks senselessly, to make cost-benefit analyses, to take no risks without rewards, and ultimately to not emulate such behavior. Upon sober reflection, Bourdain agrees that this was indeed not a "smart, savvy, well-considered decision-making process" (p. 27). These risks were clearly not worth taking. However, the circumstances of Bourdain's death make us wonder whether these miscalculations eventually overcame him.

The Epicureans (Low-Cost/Low-Benefit)

The word "Epicurean" has come to be associated with foodies, the kinds of people who buy top shelf wines and eat smelly cheese and throw soirees serving hors d'oeuvres; however, the word actually derives from a very old philosophy that was popular in ancient Greece (*Lives and Opinions of the Eminent Philosophers*, pp. 424-480). Epicurus was the founder of this school of thought, for which his philosophy is named. Epicurus was a hedonist, like Bentham and Bourdain, and believed that pleasure and pain were the primary considerations in life. However, far from advocating the type of avocado-toast indulgences that characterize modern Epicureans, the founder of Epicureanism believed in the simple life. According to him, the ideal actions were those of moderation and the best state of being was "tranquility." Thus, Epicurus would have shunned binge-eating and binge-drinking because, while pleasurable today, they are all the more painful tomorrow. Epicurus even eschewed romance as, for all its pleasures, more trouble than it was worth; he preferred the peaceful company of old friends. The Epicurean might recommend that if it's not broken, don't fix it: the act of improvement might make things worse. This makes the Epicureans good exemplars of the low-risk/low-reward way of life.

Anthony Bourdain, perhaps surprisingly, would almost assuredly not have been an Epicurean. While Bourdain might believe in the pursuit of pleasure that Epicurean hedonism entails, he would have suggested that moderation is not the way to the good life. As producer, Tom Vitale, said of him, "Everything in moderation was not something Tony ever mastered" (*Bourdain: The Definitive Oral Biography*, p. 217). But Bourdain was not immune to the simple pleasures. As a connoisseur of all cultures and modes of being, Bourdain had his Epicurean proclivities from time to time.

Indeed, throughout his oeuvre, like an Epicurean, Anthony Bourdain often retreads his own comfort zones, including comfort foods. For most of us, there is no meal that is quite as dependable and comforting as our childhood favorite, and this is no different for Bourdain. While visiting his ancestral home of Archachon, France, he makes all the pit stops to revisit all the favorites of his youth—baguette, saucisson a l'ail, gaufres, and, of course, the notorious oyster (*A Cook's Tour*, "Childhood Flavors"). Similarly, when in New York, although it is not the fanciest of foods, like Russian caviar, there is nothing quite like Bourdain's local favorite, the Papaya King's classic combo of a simple frankfurter accompanied with a cup of papaya juice—something to satiate the palate of both adults and children alike (*A Cook's Tour*, "Hometown Favorites"). And, once the long day of a chef is done, Bourdain often likes to hang out with his fellow comrades sharing a cocktail and "humble soul food type stuff" (*A Cook's Tour*, "My Life as a Cook"). Furthermore, Bourdain, a renowned French chef, also partakes in the guilty pleasures most of us partake in like Los Angeles's In-N-Out burgers 'animal style' (smothered in grilled onions and a sauce akin to Thousand Island dressing), KFC's neon yellow macaroni and cheese, and the Frito pies found in Santa Fe's Five and Dime. In one characteristic example of Epicureanism, when in Rome, Italy, Bourdain and his girlfriend, Asia Argento, are spectators at a brutal boxing match while enjoying a pleasant meal of pasta and wine ringside. As Bourdain describes it: "These people are fighting their hearts out, getting brain damage, and I'm, like, eating spaghetti." This is a cathartic event for the spectator but is importantly low risk. There is the ability to release the rage within your heart of hearts vicariously through the boxers within the ring all while enjoying the pleasantries of a delightful meal, a relaxing glass of wine, and the safety of a candlelit table, risk free (*Parts Unknown,* "Rome").

However the ancient Epicurean lifestyle is less exemplified by Bourdain himself than by Bourdain's viewers, sitting comfortably on their couches, not risking the taxi-waits, the upset traveler's guts, and the airplane-seat cramps of an actual traveler. Ironically, watching Bourdain's TV shows may even make a viewer complacent and content, living vicariously through Bourdain, satisfied to watch TV instead of getting out of the house and doing things. Of course, the upside of Epicureanism is pleasure with high certainty, and since you don't even know what you're missing by staying at home, the loss is not perceived as painful. The downside is that such pleasures are low intensity, and you might be missing out. Such are the lifestyle tradeoffs of the Epicurean.

The Cyrenaics (High-Cost/High-Benefit)

The Cyrenaics, hedonists of another school, also believed that pleasure is the utmost good, but that one should seek all pleasures that can be acquired instantaneously, especially those of the body, due to their vivid and consistent nature (*Lives*, pp. 82–97). Following Aristippus of Cyrene, the Cyrenaics thought this type of instantaneous gratification should be sought in copious amounts with little to no regard for future consequences. True to his word, Aristippus was said to attend feasts of the wealthy as an eminent philosopher and honored guest, then eat and drink them bankrupt, much to the chagrin of his hosts. This behavior makes the Cyrenaics good exemplars of the high-risk/high-reward way of life.

In many ways, Anthony Bourdain was the embodiment of the teachings of the Cyrenaics, regarding himself as "a thrill seeking, pleasure hungry sensualist," heedless of the hangover (*Kitchen Confidential*, p. 18). Exemplifying the Cyrenaic, as a hungry, hungry hedonist, Anthony Bourdain explains in great detail the orgasmic delight that the dining experience can create. For example, in one famous anecdote, Bourdain remarks on how "unforgettably sweet" his first experience of consuming a raw oyster was and how it was a moment more memorable than losing his virginity (*Kitchen Confidential*, p. 16). According to fellow chef and friend of Bourdain, Scott Bryan, in *Bourdain: The Definitive Oral Biography*, "he had that junkie mentality. He was all in or nothing" (p. 354).

Like a Cyrenaic, Anthony Bourdain often exceeds his comfort zones. For example, thanks to the dangerous concoction of Bourdain's worldwide acclaim as a TV show host and his obsession with the movie *Apocalypse Now*, viewers are able to witness his journey to the most dangerous town on earth, Pailin, Cambodia, a place no westerner before him had ever dared to tread (*A Cook's Tour*, "Eating on the Edge of Nowhere"). Later, in Russia, just as a Cyrenaic would, taking no consideration for the consequences of current pleasures, such as hangovers from alcohol and bloating from high sodium consumption, Bourdain consumes gluttonous amounts of caviar and equal amounts of specialty Russian vodka, something that "unfortunately most Russians are unable to afford" (*A Cook's Tour*, "So Much Vodka, So Little Time"). In another episode, because of his notoriety amongst chefs, Bourdain is afforded the once-in-a-lifetime dining experience of a tailored, multi-course tasting menu at the French Laundry, courtesy of Chef Thomas Keller, complete with an innovation on his own vices—a coffee custard infused with Marlboro tobacco (*A Cook's Tour*, "The French Laundry Experience"). Bourdain's experience at the French Laundry is Cyrenaic because of its high pleasures and correspondingly high costs: expensiveness, gluttony, and general decadence.

Even several years and television shows later, Bourdain is still engaging in high-risk activities. For example, amongst the hustle and bustle of Vietnam's capital, Hanoi, viewers can see Bourdain partaking in one of the great pleasures of his life, the adrenaline rush of motorcycle riding through a "river of people rushing through the streets", where no stoplights or traffic guards maintain safety as commuters zoom all around and past you (*Parts Unknown*, "Hanoi"). Bourdain even goes so far as to suggest that there are pleasures in life that may be worth dying for. As he puts it:

> If next week I am hit by a truck, one of the things that will give me some comfort is: I saw the sunset over the Sahar, and I ate my whole roasted lamb. It's just perfect. It's just like the movies. Life finally lives up to its advertising. (*A Cook's Tour,* "Desert Feast")

Indeed, via Bourdain's various television series, like *No Reservations*, we viewers are able to partake in the extreme bodily pleasures of his gastro-travels—vicariously or otherwise—with, as the name implies, no reservations, which amounts to an apparent disregard for cost and risk. Whether in the pound of butter consumed at the French restaurant on Park Avenue or the unlikely pairing of TexMex tacos and pho at a bait-and-tackle shop in Palacios, Texas, through Bourdain's Cyrenaic experiences in various kitchens and various countries we learn which guilty pleasures are best. As Bourdain says in the first lines in the *New Yorker* article that made him famous:

> Good food, good eating, is all about . . . danger—risking the dark, bacterial forces of beef, chicken, cheese, and shellfish. Your first two hundred and seven Wellfleet oysters may transport you to a state of rapture, but your two hundred and eighth may send you to bed with the sweats, chills, and vomits. ("Don't Eat Before Reading This")

But, while the Cyrenaic lifestyle is certainly exciting—unlike the Epicurean lifestyle, which seems categorically opposed to excitement of all kinds—risk-taking does have its downsides. Eating can come with getting sick, feeling stuffed, or gaining weight. Traveling can come with lost luggage, financial burdens, physical exhaustion, and homesickness (amongst other forms of sickness). Although a Cyrenaic like Bourdain may experience the highest of highs, he also may experience the lowest of lows, because, by definition, he's willing to take the pains with the pleasures.

Bourdain embraces the hangover with the drink, accepting future pains for present pleasures, even to the point of trying

some of the riskier recreational drugs, one of the more controversial aspects of his life. Nonetheless, Bourdain is a heroic
hedonist who encourages us to get out of our comfort zone. The
upside of the Cyrenaic life is that you might make things better
for yourself, especially if the risk is simply not so bad as you
thought; the downside is that things will often be bad and might
be much worse than you thought. Such are the tradeoffs of a
Cyrenaic lifestyle. In the end, when you add up all the euphoria
and subtract all the misery, the Cyrenaic life might moment to
moment be a thrill, but the net good over bad may end up being
quite comparable to an Epicurean's life on average.

The Utilitarians (Low-Cost/High-Benefit)

According to Utilitarian philosophy of the kind advocated by
Jeremy Bentham, actions that result in greater benefits than
costs should be pursued; greater costs than benefits, avoided.
To Bentham, we should always minimize pain and maximize
pleasure: low-cost/high-benefit. In other words, although there
are situations where it would be irrational to take the high
risks for low rewards, there are also situations where it would
be irrational *not* to take a low risk for a high reward.

Seemingly Bentham and Bourdain would wholeheartedly
agree about this category, low-risk and high-reward; they would
eat together and toast the new experience. For example, when
Anthony Bourdain visits Houston, Texas, which some have
dubbed the food diversity capital of the US, he commends the
variety of low-cost good foods, a Utilitarian's dream (*Parts
Unknown,* "Houston"). Or, as Bourdain says of Poulet D'Orleans
on the island of Saint Martin, a vacation spot that he insists is
worth the while, "Let's put it this way. If you don't give this place
a try, you're too dumb to live" (*A Cook's Tour,* "Food Tastes Better
with Sand Between Your Toes"). As Bourdain puts it, like
Bentham, we want to avoid obvious pains:

> I have no wish to die, nor do I have some unhealthy fondness for
> dysentery. If I know you're storing your squid at room temperature
> next to a cat box, I'll get my squid down the street, thank you very
> much." (*Kitchen Confidential,* p. 74)

However, as he adds, we also don't want to deprive ourselves of
possible pleasures either:

> Do we really want to travel in hermetically sealed pope-mobiles . . .,
> eating only at Hard Rock Cafés and McDonalds? Or do we want to

eat without fear, tearing into the local stew, the humble taqueria's mystery meat, the sincerely offered gift of a lightly grilled fish head?

As the TV-dinner couch-potatoes that we are, the umph of Bourdain's oeuvre is to push us out of our comfort zone, to dare us to take those risks that are well worth taking: to try something new. Bentham would salute Bourdain for pushing us to discover and experience those pleasures we might not otherwise have had, to avoid obvious dangers, but to overcome mild discomforts and queasiness in the name of wild and wonderful flavors, and to generally open ourselves to the gamut of culinary experiences. According to Bentham, to act in any other way would simply not be rational, nor pleasurable, and Bourdain would surely agree.

Your Price, Your Prize

To most of us, aside from a few pain-seeking Ascetics, the good life is about calculating risks for the sake of rewards. For some of us, Bourdain's kind of risk-taking, flying close to the sun, may be to our taste; to others, it may be more comfortable to sit back and watch Bourdain partake, while we bask in the comfort of a tried-and-true leftover. Ironically, Bourdain's television shows have this dissonance between medium and message. The medium is Epicurean, because watching TV can be a low-risk, low-reward activity. The message is Cyrenaic because world travel can be a high-risk, high-reward activity. Furthermore, both of these options can be equally rational, as a philosopher like Jeremy Bentham might recognize, because both can have a similar net result. The low pleasures and low pains of the former may cancel out, as might the high pleasures and high pains of the latter. Ultimately, it's your pain, your pleasure; your cost, your benefit; your risk, your reward; your price, your prize.

Either way, as the Utilitarians will point out, whether you are more Epicurean or more Cyrenaic, there may indeed be risks not worth taking that even Bourdain might admit are foolhardy, since risk is not an end in itself, but there also are good risks, low-cost/high-benefit adventures absolutely worth a try. In other words, get off your couch, if only to visit that new restaurant down the street and give the chef's special a try, because there are things you are missing, risks worth taking, countries worth visiting, and foods worth trying, as should be clear from the word and life of Anthony Bourdain.

3
The Nasty Bits

Scott Calef

Whatever doesn't kill me only makes *my drink* stronger.

—Pseudo-Nietzsche

During an early but decidedly memorable adventure in India, Anthony Bourdain attended a palace banquet at the invitation of one of the local maharajas. The ensuing four-course meal consisted of eyeballs, brains, live snakes, and insects. Following the desert course, our hero politely emphasized that he would never intentionally give offense to his host, the prince.

Okay, that was Indiana Jones in the *Temple of Doom*, not Anthony Bourdain. But you must admit, the two figures bear some remarkable resemblances. Both would be pretty handy in a fight. (See Falcioni's chapter in this volume.) Both are daring, dashing, good-looking, globe-trotting, entertaining, historically, geographically and culturally well-informed on-screen adventurers with a conscience, much beloved by millions.

And though we don't actually witness Indiana eating the snake surprise, giant cockroaches, eyeball soup, or chilled monkey brains served at Pankot Palace, Bourdain very likely would have, especially if necessary to be a gracious guest. Anthony's philosophy was that, if someone went to the trouble of sharing some of their food or local 'cuisine'—often lovingly prepared and sometimes in regions where food is scarce—he would be loath to insult the offering. And, Bourdain *did* eat snake (including the so-fresh-as-to-still-be-beating heart of a cobra), insects (maggot fried rice, for example, and a South Korean "Soup of Death" replete with silkworm larvae), eyeball (seal, specifically, with the Inuit) and brains (though he admitted: "I'm not a big brain fan. It's just . . . that custardy sort of

25

texture coupled with a sort of nutty taste, frankly, I'd sooner grab a big handful of nutsack. So to speak.").

Steven Spielberg, the original director of the Indiana Jones franchise, pretty clearly included the *Temple of Doom* dinner scene—complete with gratuitous belch by one of the mustachioed, turban-clad attendees—largely for its gross-out appeal and shock value. It worked. The meal itself is, of course, disgusting, and would likely strike pretty much every Western viewer as such. Indiana's dinner companion, Willie Scott (Kate Capshaw) tries to throw up in Short Round's (Ke Huy Kwan) cap.

Early on in his television career, beginning with *A Cook's Tour*, Bourdain also became associated with eating "exotic" (i.e., revolting) foods, like the above-mentioned cobra heart, and he did so at least partly for entertainment value, publicity, and ratings. Tony gradually came to regret some of those initial on-camera decisions as he adopted a more mature conception of his real calling. The more evolved vision of his mission became, not simply to amuse or titillate, but to educate, to foster a wider, cross-cultural understanding and respect. One way to do that was to help his audience experience vicariously the truly wonderful and delightful diversity of food around the world. Tom Vitale, Tony's long-time producer, said:

> people would often ask him . . . "What's the weirdest thing you've ever eaten?" And that was very upsetting to him because . . . aside from a few missteps earlier on that were done for shock value perhaps, it was always very important to him that the food that he was eating was not weird food. It was what people . . . were eating and it was popular there. Even if it might've been weird to . . . an American audience . . . it wasn't weird to the people that he was spending time with. And so, the question, what's the weirdest thing he ever ate, really cut him because that . . . was not what the show was about. (Molly Harris, "Anthony Bourdain Producer")

And yet, with all due respect to Mr. Vitale, Bourdain *did* eat foods, even towards the end of his career, that would give most of us pause, and in at least some cases, gave them his chef's palate's seal of approval. For example, in addition to the cobra heart, seal eyeball, maggots, and pork brains already mentioned, he notoriously also ate:

- **raw, uncooked blood soup,**
- **unwashed warthog anus,**
- **fermented, rotting shark fin,**
- **bat,**

- fetal duck eggs, complete with embryos, bones and feathers,
- bull penis,
- ortolan,
- bird's nest soup (made from strands of a swiftlet's "gummy saliva"),
- sheep's testicles,
- beaver,
- live, still writhing octopus,
- stomach bile soup,
- deer tendon, and
- something called a "meat slushy" (apparently involving lots of bone marrow slurping).

In addition to foods that might strike many of us as unpalatable, if not outright repellant, Bourdain also sometimes ate foods that were, frankly, dangerous. Fugu, for example, is a Japanese Blowfish which contains powerful neuro-toxins. Every year people die from eating it if it hasn't been properly prepared by an expert. Bourdain ordered it enthusiastically, saying "I wanted the exhilaration of a near death experience. . . . a brain bending, lip numbing, look-the-devil-in-the-face dining adventure" (*A Cooks Tour*, pp. 153, 155). His only regret, besides finding it somewhat bland, was that he didn't, in fact, experience the lip-tingling associated with the onset of poisoning. In a northern Thailand episode of *Parts Unknown* (Season Three, Episode 7), Bourdain's on-show guest, Andy Ricker, informs him that, according to locals, if you eat too many brains "you'll go blind." "It has to do with parasites," Ricker explains, adding that a few years previously an entire family of seven died in Nan province eating them. And because live octopus is, well, still squirming, eating it is a choking hazard because "in a last-ditch attempt to escape your stomach acids, there's a chance the octopus could stick to your throat" (Samantha Maxwell); "the suckers on the octopus' tentacles can latch on and potentially suffocate the person eating it" (Ericka Blye). You know, kind of like in the *Alien* movie.

This all raises some interesting philosophical questions about what makes food disgusting, and how it might be possible, not just to *tolerate* gross "food" (in the way one might hold one's nose and eat a decomposing rat if literally starving), but even to enjoy it or find it delicious. How can food be both disgusting and delightful; dangerous yet desirable? Can food which arouses an apparently natural aversion nevertheless have aesthetic appeal? And if so, what is the source of that appeal? In the above-referenced Thailand episode, where Tony eats both uncooked blood soup and the pig brains he normally shuns, he conspicuously grimaces and clearly is peeved that Ricker ordered those particular items. When the blood soup arrived (thankfully, without the addition of *ki ang*, or "young shit"—the "partially digested juice from when a cow eats grass") Anthony grumbles that it looks "like a horror movie. Like CSI soup. I'm eating out of an open wound." After actually *tasting* the dishes, though, he exuberantly proclaimed, "Honestly, the best meal I've ever had in Thailand . . . so delicious that I'd eat it out of Chris Christie's jockstrap on a hot summer day" (thereby reminding us that some things are even more odious to imagine than downing a fresh bowl of pig blood). The disgusting, apparently, can be delicious. What's going on here?

What Makes Food Disgusting?

Carolyn Korsmeyer, a philosopher who has written extensively on aesthetics, food and the concept of disgust, has developed a provisional, six-fold classification of "disgusting things to eat." She admits that any such classification is bound to be controversial and somewhat culturally influenced. Also, what is initially considered disgusting can be aesthetically reassessed and our original taste opinion more favorably revised. (Bourdain's shifting stance on his aforementioned Thai meal is a case in point.) Still, as a point of departure, Korsmeyer's thoughtful categorization is worthy of consideration. Here it is:

1. Things with "initially repellant tastes." Korsmeyer instances gamy meat which tastes of decay or cod liver oil. In Sichuan province, China, Anthony gleefully tortures his good friend, Eric Ripert, with violently spicy-hot foods (*Parts Unknown*, Season Eight, Episode 3). ("He's the devil. Look at him," says Eric.)

2. Things which are good in small doses, but which are unpleasant and 'cloy' if eaten to excess. Korsmeyer's examples include sweet things like candies or rich desserts. (Though not cloying in excess, perhaps hot peppers like those with which a sadistic Anthony torments Ripert are also examples of "a little goes a long ways.")

These first two categories concern the actual taste properties of disgusting foods; the first class consists of things that are *immediately* disgusting and the second consists of things that *become so* in short order if over-consumed. The four categories which follow, by contrast, mostly concern *what* is eaten, not what it tastes like.

3. "Objects that are too alien from ourselves and that we recoil from when we encounter them in nature, such as spiders or snakes. Something repellant to touch is doubly repulsive to touch with the tongue." Pretty much everything served in the *Temple of Doom* scene would qualify, as would many (but not all) of the bullet-pointed items previously referenced.

4. The opposite of 3, those things that are "too close to us, not alien enough". Korsmeyer cites eating another human being as an example; perhaps because they are closer to most of us than the barnyard animals we routinely consume, dogs and cats might also fit here. (Dogs and cats are two things that Bourdain reportedly was *unwilling* to eat.)

5. Creatures that look to be—or are—still alive. The wriggling eels in the banquet scene from *Temple of Doom*, for example. Westerners prefer to purchase meat that has already been skinned, sliced, minced, or plucked. In other words, packaged protein that no longer looks much like a cow or chicken. In Chapter 1 of *Medium Raw* ("The Sit Down") Bourdain describes illegally eating Ortolan, "a tiny, still-sizzling roasted bird—head, beak, and feet still attached, guts intact inside its plump little belly." Because of the shame associated with eating such a (disgusting?) thing whole, diners cover their heads with a cloth, feigning anonymity.

6. Rotting or decomposing food. (This category overlaps the first.) Road kill, sour, curdled milk, very moldy bread.

Korsmeyer makes no pretense that the above categories exhaust the possibilities. Bourdain's writings and shows suggest that sometimes food-related disgust can also attend, not just the taste of the thing or the thing itself, but the manner of obtaining, preparing or serving it ("in Chris Christie's jockstrap on a hot summer day"). In Portugal and Borneo, for example, Tony participated in the slaughter, and subsequent preparation, of live pigs, and it clearly affected him. How could it not? The helpless struggle, writhing, thrashing and kicking, the ear-splitting shrieking and squealing, the cutting or stabbing, the exsanguination, the skinning. This is pretty gruesome stuff. But, one important aspect of Anthony's ethos around food is that "you should know where it comes from." The eventual meal was no doubt amazing. But the *process* of obtaining it had to be disgusting.

Another example of something Bourdain thought "disgusting to eat" that doesn't necessarily fit neatly into Korsmeyer's six-fold scheme is consumed by tens of millions of Americans almost every day: the ubiquitous fast-food hamburger. In *Medium Raw* (chapter nine, "Meat"), Bourdain writes: "I believe the great American hamburger is a thing of beauty, its simple charms noble, pristine." Unfortunately, much American hamburger is anything *but* pristine. We are not, Anthony continues, "designed to eat shit—or fecal *coli*-form bacteria." "Many of the larger slaughterhouses will sell their product only to grinders who agree to *not* test their product for *E. coli* contamination—until after it's run through the grinder with a bunch of meat from other sources" so as to provide plausible deniability to any particular purveyor (p. 98).

This all rightly makes Tony's blood boil—he has "more faith in the hardworking folks in their underwear and goggles who cut inner-city smack" than food giants like Cargill—but what really seems to annoy him is not infected beef that makes people sick. It's the industry's *acceptable* hamburger that *doesn't* make anyone sick. He quotes *New York Times* reporting that Cargill's ground beef consisted of "a mix of slaughterhouse trimmings and a mash-like produce derived from scraps . . . from slaughterhouses in Nebraska, Texas and Uruguay, and from a South Dakota company that *processes fatty trimmings and treats them with ammonia to kill bacteria*" (emphasis Bourdain's). Just getting warmed up, Anthony continues, "Call me crazy, call me idealistic, but . . . I believe that when you're making hamburger for human consumption, you should at no time deem it necessary or desirable to treat its ingredients in ammonia. Or any other cleaning product, for that matter" (pp. 96–97). "I believe I should be able to treat my hamburger like food, not like infectious fucking medical waste" (p. 99). And lest one think he's just being delicate, Bourdain reminds us: "Recall, please, that this is *me* talking. I've eaten the extremities of feculent Southern warthog, every variety of gut, ear, and snout of bush meat. I've eaten raw seal, guinea pig. I've eaten bat. In every case, they were at least identifiable as coming from an animal—closer (even at their worst) to 'tastes like chicken' than space-age polymer" (p. 97).

Some people find factory-farmed meat repulsive even though it looks innocuous enough in the grocery store and tastes good enough that they'll shop for tofu or tempeh that mimics the texture and flavor. It isn't primarily that fast food patties don't *taste* good; they are, after all, popular. Nor is it that they *look* alive or alien or all-too-human. In Bourdain's opinion, they're gross because of how they're produced, and it's disgusting that they contain "pink slime" just because it's convenient or a few pennies cheaper. This all suggests that disgust as it relates to food sometimes has a *cognitive* component—it's partly a product of what we *know* or believe, not just a matter of innate, spontaneous, visceral aversion. (In "Disgust and Aesthetics," Korsmeyer acknowledges the existence of what she calls "moral disgust" as opposed to "core or visceral disgust, whose elicitors indicate filth, contamination, mutilation, and decay.") This insight can help us to understand some of the possible sources of disgusting food's allure.

The Power of Horror

Korsmeyer introduces what she calls the "paradox of aversion": some experiences and artforms are beautiful or appealing, not *despite* being frightening or dangerous, but *because* they are. Think of how many people love horror films or shows like *The Walking Dead* or *The Last of Us*, for example. We can admire the artful nature of the editing, special effects, costuming and make-up, even as we recognize the gruesome and repulsive use to which they're being put. A zombie can exhibit a kind of well-crafted and meticulous beauty. We marvel at the skill required to realistically render someone half-decomposed.

When a young Anthony ate an infamous and life-changing mollusk in France, part of the *appeal* was clearly that it shocked and horrified his family. While on a working oyster boat one early morning, Anthony complained about being hungry and the boat's proprietor, Monsieur Saint-Jour, asked if anyone wanted to sample the catch. Tony writes:

> My parents hesitated. I doubt they'd realized they might actually have to *eat* one of the raw, slimy things we were currently floating over. My little brother recoiled in horror. But I, in the proudest moment of my young life, stood up smartly, grinning with defiance, and volunteered to be the first. . . . With a snubby, rust-covered oyster knife, he popped the thing open and handed it to me, everyone watching now, my little brother shrinking away from this glistening, vaguely sexual-looking object, still dripping and nearly alive. I took it in my hand . . . and with one bite and a slurp, wolfed it down. . . . I'd not only survived—I'd *enjoyed*. . . . I was hooked. My parents' shudders, my little brother's expression of unrestrained revulsion and amazement only reinforced the sense that I had, somehow, become a man. (*Kitchen Confidential*, pp. 16–17)

On that trip to France, Anthony said, "Things changed. *I* changed . . . I could gross out my still uninitiated little brother.

I'd show *them* who the gourmet was! Brains? Stinky, runny cheeses that smelled like dead men's feet? Horsemeat? Sweetbreads? Bring it on!! Whatever had the most shock value became my meal of choice" (*Kitchen Confidential*, p. 13). The fact that food could confound and repel meant that "Food had power." And *that* meant "It could inspire, astonish, shock, excite, delight and *impress*" (*Kitchen Confidential*, p.17). Food that made others recoil was, for that very reason, attractive and worth eating. Early in his TV career Tony continued to occasionally eat unfamiliar and intimidating foods for just these kinds of reasons. Like the fourth grader who's dared to stick his tongue to a frozen flagpole and does it to prove he's not afraid, the resulting spectacle is alarming but engrossing and guaranteed to gather a crowd.

Tragedy and Education

Greek tragedy provides another ready example of the paradox of aversion. When Oedipus "grabs a brooch from his wife/mother's hanging corpse and gouges his own eyes out" we're horrified and startled, to be sure. And yet, artistically, "Oedipus's suffering is awesome and breathtaking. And this is what it is to be human. Tragedy and horror at their best demonstrate how our capacity to suffer is the core of our nobility" (Owen Egerton). Aristotle argued that we enjoy depictions in art of things that we would recoil from in ordinary life in part because we're learning what it would be like to undergo those tragic experiences, but in relative safety. Since "all people by nature desire to know," our delight in learning new truths compensates for the harsh and unpleasant reality of the truths themselves. Disgust deliberately aroused by art "is not a signal of rejection or disapproval but rather is a feature of understanding and appreciation" ("Disgust and Aesthetics," p. 753).

Aristotle's account might help to explain why we, the audience, love watching shows like *A Cook's Tour*, *No Reservations*, and *Parts Unknown*. Even when Tony and his crew are in challenging or dangerous settings, like during their trips to the Congo, Libya, Beirut, South Africa, or Haiti, or when Tony is eating something outside our comfort zone that we wouldn't try ourselves, we're learning something about what it would be like to experience those sights, sounds, and tastes. It's a surrogate thrill by proxy. Our squeamishness is overcome by the gladness we feel at gaining new knowledge.

The Sublime and Psychical Distance

The aesthetic concept of the sublime also illustrates the paradox of aversion. Edmund Burke (1729–1797) distinguishes between two very different aesthetic categories, the sublime and the beautiful. (The following discussion is indebted to John Stone-Mediatore.) The beautiful is characterized by traits like softness, delicacy, smoothness, evenness, calm, gradual variation and subtlety. Burke thought such qualities are associated with emotions like love and sympathy. Examples of "the beautiful" might include female nudes, flowers, puffy clouds, an immaculate snowscape, rainbows or gently flowing streams. The sublime, on the other hand, connotes danger and is associated with fear, pain, or death. Its qualities include traits like vastness, roughness, sharp edges, power, darkness, loudness, hardness, harshness, bitterness, blinding light, obscurity, and suddenness. Examples include artillery fire, explosions, avalanches, thunderstorms, jagged outcroppings of rock, mountain ranges, the starry heavens, crashing waves and cliff edges. Such things evoke an aesthetic reaction, but unlike beauty, which seems 'safe', the sublime is apt to appear majestic, overwhelming, or awe-inspiring.

But how can we enjoy, aesthetically, something which threatens our self-preservation? Wouldn't sheer terror drive out the disinterested contemplation of an object for its own sake which lies at the heart of the aesthetic experience? Burke's answer is qualified. If we were actually to find ourselves in a small craft on a very rough sea, or at the base of a mountain when an avalanche dislodges, or on a high, exposed bluff with lightening flashing all around, we certainly would not enjoy it. We would be terrified. What enables the aesthetic appreciation of such things is safe distance: watching powerful waves or hearing the sound of thunder from the security of our homes, for example, or beholding an avalanche, volcanic eruption or tornado from afar. Cataclysmic events can be wonderous and enjoyable, *provided* they're sufficiently removed and we're out of harm's way. One way to achieve the required distance, of course, is to approach such subjects via artistic representations. A sea battle makes us quake and tremble; a *picture* of a sea battle, nicely framed and hanging over the fireplace, pleases.

Many of the foods we eat and enjoy are 'beautiful'. Nicer restaurants typically strive to ensure that their dishes are pleasantly presented, and people commonly say things like, 'It almost looks too good to eat!' Soufflés, bisques, salads garnished nasturtium petals, thinly-sliced and delicately-prepared filets, none of these are sublime. On the other hand, raw blood soup? Still-throbbing cobra heart? Live octopus? Fugu? Might not Bourdain's appreciation of live, dangerous or disgusting foods be rooted in an appreciation of the sublime? Perhaps 'disgusting' foods can be neutralized or elevated if subsumed under the right aesthetic category?

Korsmeyer notes at least two difficulties with this approach. First, Burke argues that the sublime object brings enjoyment *only from a safe distance*. Unlike sight or hearing, however, taste is a 'contact' sense. We literally put food into our mouths and bodies. So, absent the space or separation Burke thinks necessary to transform the dangerous and disgusting into delight, something else must be going on. Second, our sense of the sublime arises when we confront something majestic, overwhelming, powerful or threatening. By the time we eat our dinners, though—however imposing the animal might once have been—it has been conquered and thoroughly subdued. It poses no risk. It's dead. A mastodon would surely have impressed our ancestors. But a bit of rotisserie mastodon tail on a spit? Not so much. At that point, we're in control.

Another 'distance' theorist, Edward Bullough (1880–1934) argued that an aesthetic attitude is the result of *psychologically* dissociating the object of contemplation from practical concerns (including survival). What matters is 'psychical' distance, not kilometers or miles. Being lost at sea in dense fog is terrifying, but if you can 'distance' yourself from the sense of helplessness and despair and focus purely on the experience itself—the milky-whiteness of the swirling mist, the curious diffusion of the light—what was menacing and uncanny takes on new meaning and becomes sublimely beautiful. But, Bullough warns, when approaching art you must be careful to psychically distance to just the right degree. If we 'over-distance' a work will strike us as improbable, unrealistic, remote, irrelevant or dull. If there's too much psychical distance between a work and ourselves, we can't connect or relate to it. On the other hand, if we're too 'close', the work risks becoming little more than a mirror reflecting idiosyncratic and personal associations. For example, a jealous husband may find it difficult to enjoy *Othello* because he's distracted by suspicions of spousal infidelity. He's unable to "separate" the work from his preoccupation with his troubled marriage and "step back" from it. It "strikes too close to home." When I was in High School, I had homophobic friends (though we didn't have that expression then) who couldn't stand to listen to glam artists like

David Bowie, Queen, Lou Reed, Mott the Hoople, Iggy and the Stooges, or the New York Dolls. So much the worse for them. Because they couldn't achieve proper distance, they couldn't relate. (Musically, Anthony and I would have gotten along just great.) For Bullough, though, we aren't exactly aiming at middle ground; for most people, under-distancing is better than over-distancing. What is ideal is "the utmost decrease of distance without its disappearance." In the best case, we should be able to relate to an artwork and identify with it closely while still accepting it on its own terms and allowing it to speak for itself.

The distance Burke speaks of, then, need not be interpreted literally; perhaps 'psychical' distance is sufficient to do the trick. And if so, Korsmeyer's concern that disgusting food cannot be sublimely aesthetic because too close physically when consumed need not prove decisive. Maybe an adventurous eater like Bourdain is able to appreciate—even enjoy—something like blood soup because he's able to adopt an aesthetic attitude and the mental distance necessary to take it on its own terms, free from Western preconceptions or prejudices. Perhaps, à la Bullough, by focusing on the taste sensation itself rather than the danger it typically signifies or connotes, he is able to bracket his discomfort and actually enjoy the experience.

What about Korsmeyer's other objection that, by the time we come to eat, there's little risk? The sublime is associated with danger, but eating is relatively safe. Though not completely safe, as we have seen. Eating what, and where, Bourdain sometimes did can carry risk of parasitic infection, choking, allergic reaction, or outright poisoning: "Good food, good eating, is all about . . . danger . . . Your first two hundred and seven Wellfleet oysters may transport you to a state of rapture, but your two hundred and eighth may send you to bed with the sweats, chills, and vomits." ("Don't Eat before Reading This"). Or, as Tom Vitale casually notes, "The warthog anus in Namibia got him bad" (*In the Weeds*, p. 249). Well, it's useful to remember that the sublime need not be something *actually* dangerous; powerful or colossal artworks—a Wagner opera, for example, or monumental architecture—can be sublime. John Stone-Mediatore argues that much of rock music's appeal derives from its sublimity. To be sublime, it is sometimes enough that a thing *reminds* us of death, danger, or pain, or helps us to imagine them.

Korsmeyer seems to agree: "though our dinner poses no immediate danger" its "presence may nonetheless remind us of . . . mortality and loss . . ." ("Delightful, Dangerous, and Disgusting," p. 153). Eating things like snakes, which make us afraid, or things which can actually kill us, like snakes again, or fugu, or things with a hint of putrefaction, like gamy meat, puts us in physical contact with the reality of death, and so, with reminders of our own impermanence. And by not only surviving the meal, but enjoying it, we temporarily transcend death and disarm it. To quote Nietzsche (properly this time), "Whatever doesn't kill me only makes me stronger." In a London episode of *Parts Unknown* (Series Eight, Episode 4) Anthony is dining with food critic and author Jay Rayner and the following discussion ensues:

> BOURDAIN: I'm looking for a suspension of logic and reason. . . .There are some tripe dishes that are just uniquely wonderful. And it's a tricky ingredient. Once you're cooking it, it smells like wet dog.
>
> RAYNER: The way we smell things and taste them is very different. All the best foods stink.
>
> BOURDAIN: Yeah.
>
> RAYNER: And it's an extraordinary thing. These foods, there's a faint whiff of death about them, [they] are the ones that remind you that you're the most alive.
>
> BOURDAIN: The scent of your own mortality.
>
> RAYNER: Your own mortality.

Perhaps paradoxically, foods which remind us of death also remind us of life. (If so, this might also help to explain the preference some people, like Bourdain, seem to have for meat-eating over a more vegetarian diet. Although lettuce and beans were once living things, they weren't living things as we think of ourselves. Animals, on the other hand, are sentient, aware, somewhat intelligent, and capable of self-initiated motion. In sum, they're more like us. And so, their lives and deaths are more likely to provoke reflection on our own.) Because food is something 'other', we can distance ourselves from it, even as we absorb it. Eating involves a life and death exchange; life is taken from the prey and given to the predator. The eaten becomes the eater.

The Abject

So far, we've seen that dangerous and disgusting things can be enjoyed and appreciated, a. for the power they afford us to impress, shock, intimidate and the like; b. for the learning they occasion as we discover what something comes to as a possible form of lived experience; and c. aesthetically for their sublimity, provided we maintain the right kind of distance. One further possibility appeals to the relatively new aesthetic category of "the abject." (Some of the following discussion is indebted to Jere Surber's "New Shades" in *Radiohead and Philosophy* and Dino Felluga, "Modules on Kristeva.")

The abject has been invoked to explain our fascination with, and peculiar attraction to, things that at the same time repel and upset us. Why, for example, do so many of us feel compelled to gawk at accident victims or YouTube videos of "epic fails" where people injure themselves, sometimes seriously? Why do so many of us love horror films, true crime documentaries, pornography, depictions of bondage, sadism and violence, piercings, and tattoos? (Bourdain had at least twelve.) Why is so much *avant-garde* and modern art seemingly preoccupied with outcasts, with decay and deformity, with bodily fluids, functions and mutilation? Why is 'authentic' or 'realistic' art so often associated with what is unclean, gritty, dark, opaque, polluted, or slimy?

Philosopher Julia Kristeva identifies the abject as "the human reaction . . . to a threatened breakdown in meaning caused by the loss of the distinction between subject and object or between self and other" (Dino Felluga). Examples include corpses, open wounds, shit, and sewage. Such things are human, but also somehow not human at the same time. They defy the categories that we are accustomed to use to think about ourselves. A severed finger, for example, is recognizably a *human* finger, but it isn't attached to a human body. Some people faint witnessing childbirth (or have visceral reactions to the thought of abortion). The distinction between mother and child, self and other, fetus and baby, is blurred, and some find this unsettling. Human excreta, too, were once part of us, but a part that has now been 'eliminated'. Many people feel uneasy or uncomfortable visiting psychiatric institutions or being around people who suffer physical deformities or mental illness. Others, around Trans people. Bourdain notoriously had a phobia about clowns and mimes; their heavy makeup renders them only *somewhat* human in appearance. A lay person might be grossed out watching a surgery because the patient is a person and persons are normally associated with their visible exteriors; to glimpse inside someone's skin during an operation is to see the unconscious person, not as a self, as we are, but as an object, as something alien, frightening, and unfamiliar. When we encounter such things "our own eventual death is made palpably real" because our concrete existence as independent beings is called into question. Thus, the abject is associated with "the eruption of the Real into our lives" and our reaction to the abject (nausea, vomiting, horror, disgust) is a "rejection of death's insistent materiality". According to Kristeva, though, these reactions to the abject are *primal*, not intellectual. They result from a *breakdown* of order which *reveals* death without rendering it comprehensible. The lack of clear meaning is precisely what makes us anxious.

Although we react negatively to the abject, it clearly has become a bona fide aesthetic category, albeit an uncomfortable one. Abject aesthetics acknowledges that much of experience confronts uncertain, oft-ignored, and difficult to classify phenomena with fuzzy boundaries that break down our tidy symbol systems and conceptual schemes. (The concept of "the abject" itself strikes me as one with somewhat indistinct boundaries.) Art and religion, according to Kristeva, are "two ways of purifying the abject" by provoking catharsis. The strong and somewhat traumatic emotions aroused by the abject are released through art, and thereby purged. From personal experience, I can testify that many churches and cathedrals, especially in Europe, contain *extremely* graphic paintings and sculptures on a variety of religious themes: Christ, bloody and beaten, on the cross or in the arms of his mother post-mortem; Saint Sebastian pierced through with dozens of arrows; the Virgin, stabbed, with a large sword still protruding and dangling from her heart; the Baptist beheaded. The point of these, quite frankly, grisly depictions is presumably spiritual upliftment. Catharsis. Jesus suffered so that you don't have to. Contemplating the spiritual suffering, martyrdom or degradation of saints, paradoxically, is supposed to be enlivening.

With this in mind, we might ask whether some of Bourdain's more 'exotic' meals can be subsumed under the abject and whether eating or helping to prepare them might provide some kind of psychic release, satisfaction or fulfillment.

I don't necessarily have an answer here. But, it's certainly possible. Some of the things Anthony ate were undeniably abject in the sense that their boundaries and categories were fuzzy or blurred. Sometimes, Bourdain didn't know *what* he was eating, and not necessarily for lack of trying. "Mystery meat" consisting of "parts unknown" is only *possibly* something that a New Yorker would call food.

There may also be traces of the abject in Bourdain's insistence that we should "know where our food comes from." Killing food to eat it deconstructs our firm distinctions between living and dying. As unpleasant and even sickening as it may be to watch a pig slaughter—let alone wield the knife or drive in the spear—it couldn't be more clear in that moment that death is a part of, and gives rise to, life. And for that, a certain humility and gratitude seems appropriate. Before the resulting feast commences and we settle down to enjoy the comfort and pleasure of food with family and friends, many of us give thanks and ask blessing on the food we are about to receive, for the nourishment of our bodies made possible through the sacrifice of another living being. The horror of the kill is spiritually sublimated. Although Anthony was not religious, I do believe he was spiritual and he definitely was grateful. Whether dining in someone else's home or in a Mom and Pop restaurant, whether in Cambodia or California, Laos or Louisiana, no matter *what* he was served, he would eat it, appreciatively, and with humility and grace. To be disgusted by a dish offered in a spirit of generosity and love—even a vegetarian dish!—was contrary to Anthony Bourdain's core nature. And that, to my mind, dear reader, shows real class.

4
How Anthony Bourdain United the Local and the Universal

WALTER BARTA AND CANDACE MIRANDA

Anthony Bourdain was a tastemaker if there ever was one. He was the chef at an upscale French Restaurant, Les Halles, in New York; subsequently, he was a food writer and TV-show host on the Travel Channel and Food Network, including for shows such as *A Cook's Tour*, *No Reservations*, and *Parts Unknown*. His work covered the gamut of food and travel topics and set the standard of quality for a worldwide audience.

Thus, Anthony Bourdain's life and work might be better understood through aesthetics, the philosophy of beauty and taste. Specifically, we might approach Bourdain through the thinking of Pierre Bourdieu, a French philosopher of aesthetics, most famous for his book *Distinction: A Social Critique of the Judgement of Taste*. Far from being the stereotypical snooty French connoisseur though, Pierre Bourdieu was the ultimate critic of high society and upper-class values. Bourdieu believed that taste, while a subjective personal experience, was also a socially relative expectation that changes depending on where you are, what society you belong to, and who you are within that society. Furthermore, these distinctions in tastes themselves are then reinforced by social elites to maintain class differences and power structures between the more and less fortunate.

Bourdieu's main point was to reject the conception of taste developed by the influential eighteenth-century philosopher Immanuel Kant. In his *Critique of Judgement*, Kant outlined his philosophy of beauty and taste. In contrast to what Bourdieu later would believe, Kant thought that beauty and taste were "universally valid" and "universally communicable". To Kant, when we say something is beautiful or tasteful, we're implying that others ought to agree, even knowing they may not; in other words, baked into judgements of beauty and taste is the belief that at least in principle they may be appreciated by any audience, anywhere (*Critique of Judgement*, pp. 70–72). Bourdieu seems to reject Kant's conception categorically. To Bourdieu, taste is not a universal value but a socially constructed value that may not be universalizable.

We can think of social constructs as things that exist only because society has constructed them, in contrast to natural things which pre-exist our society's conceptions. Many things are social constructs. For example, Anthony Bourdain's restaurant, Les Halles French Cuisine, is a social construct, because restaurants do not exist in nature. Rather, the name "Les Halles" refers to a specific location in New York, a plot of land demarcated and established by the United States government, according to a specific system of laws regarding land allocation and property rights. "French" and "France" also refer, not to any natural place, for there would be no France without people to create it, but to a specific political, cultural, ethnic, and linguistic identity and geography in continental Europe. Even "cuisine" is a social construct, since a cuisine is a specific group of ingredients and techniques that originate from cultural and regional practices and have a social history and context.

But how is *taste* a social construct? Biologically speaking, there are five tastes that humans have five receptors for: sweet, salty, sour, bitter, and umami. But, as we all know, what we "have a taste for" is highly dependent upon our upbringing, our nationality, our ethnicity, and our experiences, all of which are environmentally formed and informed by the social factors around us. Anthony Bourdain, like the rest of us, was brought up in a society with ideas of what tastes good and bad. In other words, as Pierre Bourdieu puts it, "Taste classifies, and it classifies the classifier" (*Distinction,* p. 6).

Bourdieu groups these social factors into what he terms the field, habitus, and cultural capital, all of which affect and are affected by taste. This directly contrasts with Kant's more cosmopolitan view that the world can appreciate all tastes. But, are these categories of taste inevitably socially constrained, as Bourdieu seems to believe, or might there be a more cross-cultural exchange in the future, as Kant hoped for? Anthony Bourdain seems to embody a synthesis of these ideas, a combination of Bourdieu and Kant, acknowledging the social constraints of taste, while also showing us how to expand our horizons and develop a taste for foods that we are not initially inclined to enjoy.

Field

According to Pierre Bourdieu, all human interactions occur inside a social "field," which is the distribution of possibilities available to members within a grouping of people. Bourdieu thought of field as a physical constraint on human action (*Distinction*, p. 94). A person born near the ocean may have different access to foods than a person born on a ranch; a first-world country with means of transportation may have different access than a village in a rural underdeveloped nation; or even a child with a chef for a father may have different exposure to foods in the home than a child with parents reliant on fast-food chains. Various examples from Anthony Bourdain's work show the constraints of field as Bourdieu conceives it. In these, Bourdain both exposes and explores the social field.

When Bourdain visits a quaint fishing town in Nha Trang, Vietnam he encounters "a culture that revolves around the sea and seafood." Local women escort Bourdain to the seaside where he enters "this cool floating dock where you pick your lunch straight out of the water" via a small woven bowl-like boat covered in tar. Inasmuch as these villagers are only nourished by the sea beneath them, this instance emphasizes the physical constraints of availability on peoples' palates (*A Cook's Tour*, "Eating on the Mekong").

In other episodes, Bourdain is met with the resistance of the limitations of regional field. For example, in Risani, Morocco, Bourdain and his interpreter, Abdul, along for the ride to manage negotiations, attempt to procure a whole lamb in the back alleyways of the city, although the local butchers insist for one reason or another that it is not possible at the present moment. There's no Moroccan market they can find that has whole lambs ready-to-order off the shelf. The butchers offer to sell a leg of lamb or other parts, but Bourdain remains persistent, saying, "I want a whole lamb cooked in a clay oven like I saw in the movies—and the testicles!" Eventually, Bourdain obtains his lamb, but only after he utilizes his social status, financial resources, and persistence to transcend pressing constraints of the Moroccan social field (*A Cook's Tour*, "Desert Feast").

Sometimes the constraints of a region's field become custom. In one episode, Bourdain tours Oporto, Portugal, with friend and colleague, Jose de Meirelles, manager of Les Halles and native of Portugal, in order to "discover possibly the most important traditional staple of Portuguese cuisine, which is salt cod or *bacalao*." Bourdain asks why bacalao was and continues to be the backbone of Portuguese cuisine, and, as it turns out, bacalao is an example of Bourdieu's concept of field.

Firstly, this whitefish is common in the North Atlantic, near Portugal. Because Oporto is a port city, the locals consume "a lot of fish" and "one of the great things is that with any animal we eat just about everything. We don't let anything go to waste—nose to tail, all the innards, everything." Second, bacalao came to popularity as a shelf-stable protein that could be consumed without going bad, both during long sea voyages and back on shore. Although bacalao was created due to the necessity of shelf-stable food items whilst at sea, it slowly became a nationally beloved staple to the Portuguese: "as they say in France, there's a cheese for every day; in Portugal there's a bacalao recipe for every day." In other words, availability often dictates custom and taste (*A Cook's Tour*, "Cod Crazy").

Geographical constraint of field can even counteract culture. For example, Bhutan is a country that predominantly practices Buddhism, a religion with some vegan principles, but due to Bhutanese geography, they historically have consumed yak, sheep, and at one point even human. In a conversation between Bourdain and film director, Darren Aronofsky, Gara Durji, Bourdain's Bhutanese government representative, explains that

> The Bhutanese were considered cannibals. The only vegetable we had was potato and radish. That's it, nothing else. People don't kill, but they would, you know, eat one another if somebody dies. We are not supposed to eat each other . . . we are not supposed to eat meat . . . but culturally, because of terrain, we had no choice.

In other words, even religious vegans may be forced into meat-consumption by their geography (*Parts Unknown*, "Bhutan").

In these examples, the ingredients regionally available to people are constrained, and acquired tastes are limited by this availability. Thus, as Bourdieu philosophizes, taste is made by the field in which we find ourselves.

Bourdain himself overcomes social fields via his social status and renowned television shows, going everywhere in the world, flying around, transcending locality. And, even though we are not all world-renowned celebrity chefs, Bourdain's shows allow us to expand our fields by seeing the sights, hearing the sounds, and experiencing the world vicariously; perhaps we can even visit restaurants from Bourdain's televised adventures that we may have overlooked otherwise. Indeed, Bourdain has inspired other food critics and regular people to follow in his footsteps around the world, encouraging us to overcome the limitations of our own fields, as Kant dreamed of. At the same time though, Bourdain exposes the truth of Bourdieu's greater point, showing how the constraints of geography can create zones of decreased access, which, solidified into local "taste", create and reinforce social distinctions and hierarchies.

Habitus

According to Pierre Bourdieu, every human social system operates with a "habitus", a pattern of behavior that is normal for that group ("Cultural Reproduction and Social Reproduction," p. 57). For example, the average modern American may work forty hours per week, pick up take-out during their commute, and eat on the couch while watching reruns of *Parts Unknown*. In contrast, the average pre-Colombian American may have spent their day watching the herds of buffalo or tending corn. These activities would have been, respectively, the norms of either group of people, their way of life and means of interacting with the world, their habitus. Various examples from Anthony Bourdain's work feature the habitus of peoples. Through these, Bourdain examines and expands the human habitus, revealing other cultures while also breaking his own habits by immersing himself in new experiences—living out the adage, "When in Rome, do as the Romans do."

Bourdain's own habitus is laid bare in his shows. He admits that his own taste was influenced by childhood experiences, including trips to his ancestral France. Although we may now be able to find the standard French baguette at our local bakery, the Bourdain brothers upon visiting their paternal motherland prove that there are certain tastes that cannot be replicated. At the Arcachon neighborhood boulangerie he frequented as a child, Bourdain comments that the "Recipe is unchanged in twenty years . . . there's a slight, like, aftertaste that says, right here." This is the result of habitus; the French have been doing it the same way for a long time. Bourdain also describes another one of his most memorable and loved dishes, soup du pecheur, as murky, brown, and scary looking. These are not usually the types of adjectives one uses to describe the tastiest of foods, but it was a food he learned to like as part of his cultural upbringing. These habituated tastes are what divide what is unappealing to a foreigner and delicious to a local. His brother concurs—both nodding with approval as they savor the bread of their youth. These cultural habits and tastes influenced Bourdain's own palate and defined his future culinary choices (*Cook's Tour*, "Childhood Flavors").

Furthermore, Bourdain's habitus and taste is a function of his New Yorker lifestyle. There are few food items that are as quintessential to Bourdain's hometown as the New York hot dog, and Bourdain highlights Papaya King as one of the "temples of cuisine that he visits every time he comes to the Upper East Side." He regards it as a classic akin to "red wine and beef, white wine and fish, and ya' know papaya drink with a hot dog." Bourdain's habitus is to have hotdogs. Furthermore, Bourdain's adventures frequently contrast the customs of a place, the habitus, with the field, the availability. In other words, even though the hotdog meat itself is not necessarily produced locally, New Yorkers have the acquired taste for hotdogs, the right habitus to sustain many a hotdog stand (*Cook's Tour*, "My Hometown Favorites").

In most cases, social customs dictate what foods we eat, and acquired tastes are formed by frequently consuming said foods. We eat what we think tastes good, we repeat the experience, and we continue to think it tastes good. Thus, habit reinforces habit, until a habitus becomes entrenched in the customs and traditions of a society. Furthermore, as Bourdieu tells us, it's easy to see how the tastes of a given social class become habituated, themselves becoming markers of different classes, reinforcing class distinctions and existing power inequities.

Nonetheless, Bourdain tries to experience the habits of other cultures everywhere he goes, including the customs of all social classes. In an early episode of *A Cook's Tour*, visiting a floating community on Lake Tonlé Sap, Cambodia, restaurateur Philippe LaJaunie coaxes Bourdain into taste-testing a local woman's cooking—an experience not commonly provided on tour-guide-led family holidays—diving headfirst into the habitus. Bourdain then gives his take on this eat-local philosophy:

> It's simple, it's honest, and it tastes good. It's the people that make the difference, and if you're gonna travel, it's always wonderful to eat what the people are eating at your destination. This is the way they feed themselves. This is the way they live. This is what they're eating. This is not hotel food. (*A Cook's Tour*, "Wild Delicacies")

In other words, Bourdain revels in foreign cultures and customs, and especially in local flavors. While in Russia, Bourdain seeks to "steep himself deep in the Russian psyche," and he does so by doing as the Russians do—ice fishing and drinking copious amounts of vodka while doing so—partaking in the Russian habitus (*Cook's Tour*, "So Much Vodka, So Little Time").

Later, when in Glasgow, Bourdain and his friend Simon, a native Glaswegian, delve into Scotland's notorious fried treats. They start by dipping their toes in the oil per se with the normal, everyday, fried grub of fish and chips and fried Mars bars topped with a sprinkling of sugar. After this appetizer, Bourdain takes creativity into his own hands and requests a food never fried before—pickled eggs. Bourdain embraces the local flavors and methods and then even makes something new with them (*Cook's Tour*, "Highland Grub"). In this moment, Bourdain imaginatively expands the possibilities of cuisine, though while still working within the Glaswegian habitus of fried foods.

Furthermore, as viewers progress from episode to episode in *A Cook's Tour,* they see Bourdain develop a taste for the foods that are not common to his personal habitus, such as varied organ meats stewing in pots and crunchy insects from street vendors. In an early episode of *A Cook's Tour*, Bourdain is apprehensive about trying crickets in Cambodia; but, in a later episode in Mexico, he tries crickets without hesitation and even tries a meal of grubs. Thus, over time we see Bourdain's habitus, and with it his tastes, change as he grows accustomed to other cultures and their foods (*Cook's Tour*, "Tamales and Iguana, Oaxacan Style").

Although habituated by his own acquired tastes, Bourdain makes the greatest possible attempt to explore the customs of other cultures and change his own tastes to encompass the diversity of experiences. In this, Bourdain shows how tastes can change, perhaps even becoming "universal", in a Kantian sense. And yet, consistent with Bourdieu, Bourdain also shows how our tastes have the baggage of our personal experiences and habits, including our cultural contexts, and might only be changed by exposure to other cultures, changes which are also limited by the locations and cultures we experience through our own traveling habits.

Cultural Capital

According to Pierre Bourdieu, the artifacts of human culture have productive value and are a form of capital—cultural capital. To understand the concept of cultural capital, we might review the more well-known concept of economic capital. According to Karl Marx, the philosopher of politics and economics, most famous for his critique of capitalism and advocacy of communism, economic capital is the "means of production" by which more value is created in a society. As Bourdieu puts it, "Capital is accumulated labor" ("The Forms of Capital," p. 15). For example, a restaurant, like Bourdain's, is a form of economic capital that can be bought and then used to reproduce value in an economic system by making products and selling them for money. Similar but different, cultural capital is a form of cultural means of production that produces cultural value, instead of economic value ("Cultural Reproduction," p. 57). For example, Anthony Bourdain's knowledge of French cuisine, earned from his own French heritage and education at the Culinary Institute of America, was productive of economic value in the form of a job, but also accrued him great cultural value: he was able to receive the respect afforded to French chefs. Furthermore, he was able to then leverage that cultural capital to write a successful article published by *The New Yorker*, which itself had enough cultural capital to transform into a New York Times bestselling book, *Kitchen Confidential*, which subsequently afforded Bourdain offers from the Food Network and Travel Channel to host soon-to-be famous television shows, which itself afforded him worldwide cultural fame, so much fame that we are still writing books about him—like this one. Furthermore, because of the rich-get-richer and poor-get-poorer effect of capital, high class and popular tastes tend to separate and stratify, reinforcing class-distinctions. Notably, Bourdain's world travel project is only made possible by deploying his vast cultural and economic capital, the status and money earned as a celebrity chef, something the average viewer cannot emulate. Various examples from Bourdain's work reveal the influence of cultural capital and the separation of high-class and low-class tastes. In many relevant examples, Bourdain employs cultural capital but also turns it on its head by showing us the pleasures available to all of us, regardless of means—after all, as he says while in Salvador, Brazil, "Just as in many other countries, what was created by the very poor out of necessity is now a mainstay of the country's cuisine" (*A Cook's Tour*, "A Mystical World").

Bourdain often shows how money governs taste-choices. For example, regarding one of his New York haunts, Murray's Cheese Shop, Bourdain asks his viewers,

> Why doesn't every town or every major city in America have a cheese store like this? Why just New York? Traditionally New York is a melting pot of many, many cultures. In New York they can sell this.

In other words, a gourmet cheese shop simply would not be profitable outside of a major hub of cultural capital like New York (*A Cook's Tour*, "My Hometown Favorites").

Bourdain also showcases the delicacies of high-class fine dining. In one episode, Bourdain and fellow New York chefs treat themselves to California's French Laundry Restaurant. Just as Bourdain has created a mass following and popularity via his culinary critiques, Bourdain's idol, Thomas Keller, chief chef at the French Laundry, has done the same with his innovative cuisine. On the nervously excited car ride there, Bourdain's friend and fellow chef, Michael Ruhlman, describes his initial experience at the French Laundry as "the one meal of your life that changes how you forever see food and understand food." This experience is the ultimate in cultural capital: a bunch of famous chefs being served by another famous chef, defining fine dining. Not only did these chefs visit the French Laundry because it is a place of high culture, but their televised visit solidified the French Laundry nationally as a beacon of high culture. Thus, cultural capital reproduces itself: the cultured get more cultured, even through Bourdain's show (*A Cook's Tour*, "The French Laundry Experience").

In another example, flying to Cambodia from Japan and back, with a detour through Vietnam, Bourdain goes from a country with high cultural capital, Japan, to one with low cultural capital, Cambodia. He even observes how excited he is about Japan and how tepid he is about Cambodia, saying, "I knew nothing about Cambodia and it was the last place on Earth, I guess, I really wanted to go." The cultural capital of Japan is shown to be much higher than that of Cambodia, as expressed in his sentiment and subsequent adventures (*A Cook's Tour*, "Eating on the Edge of Nowhere").

And yet, throughout his work, Bourdain specifically attempted to undermine cultural capital everywhere he went. His first book, *Kitchen Confidential*, exposed the sometimes dirty secrets behind how high-class food like that at Les Halles is made, the so-called "culinary underbelly." By thus revealing the pretensions of French high-class culture, Bourdain follows Bourdieu, who was trying to similarly confront the French elite in his critique of taste. Even in Bourdain's TV-show titles, *No Reservations* and *Parts Unknown*, he expresses the desire to transcend high and low culture: breaking down his personal reservations and expanding what is known. *No Reservations* is itself a pun intended to convey, on the one hand, that Bourdain will "try anything" without reservation; but also, that Bourdain will be dining at establishments not fancy enough to require reservations. He will instead opt for places where "no reservations" will be required because he will be eating local or street foods. Although Bourdain has access to and is surrounded by luxury French cuisine at his restaurant, Les Halles, after work with his fellow comrades, just as anyone else after a long day, he enjoys the simple pleasures of hanging out, getting drunk, and eating "humble soul food type stuff" (*A Cook's Tour*, "My Life as a Cook").

In another episode, Bourdain visits Los Angeles and juxtaposes his evening in a fine restaurant with a day eating at hotdog stands. As he says, "I wanna eat everyday chow." This is the preface to Bourdain's quest for the humble hot dog of the west coast (*A Cook's Tour*, "Los Angeles, My Own Heart of Darkness"). We can also witness Bourdain doing this exact same thing in Russia as he has a nice working-class meal of hearty borscht and fish pie, before having a "really fancy high-end meal" in order to experience how the tsars ate. This is a meal that "unfortunately most Russians would not be able to afford." While in Russia Bourdain even demonstrates direct disdain for higher class values, remarking, "That's the problem with rich people—special requests . . ." Bourdain further goes on to valorize lower class cuisine and democratize taste. He says, "It's the simple food that's often the most satisfying . . ." (*A Cook's Tour*, "The Cook Who Came in From the Cold").

Although, as Pierre Bourdieu would have pointed out, Anthony Bourdain was himself a paragon of cultural capital, promoting high-class tastes and living a luxurious lifestyle, Bourdain also made a point to celebrate popular taste and unearth the delicacies hidden in the cultures of the lower classes and third world countries. Indeed, by making shows with international reach and appeal, Bourdain has provided us with the means to explore other cultures with no more capital investment than a television set and a cable subscription, rendering culture "communicable," to use Kant's terms. However, Bourdain thereby proves Bourdieu correct as well by showing that our tastes control our purchases but at the same time are controlled by the amount of cultural exchange we might afford.

Towards Universal Taste?

All this being said, far from being bound to his field, habitus, or capital, Anthony Bourdain studied and acknowledged but largely rejected social boundaries. Instead, Bourdain was more cosmopolitan. As he put it in his first book, *Kitchen Confidential,* "We are, after all, citizens of the world" (pp. 73–74). The concept "cosmopolitan" (or "world citizen") was coined by the ancient Greek philosopher Diogenes of Sinope. Diogenes lived while Alexander the Great was conquering the known world and making the possibility of world citizenship conceivable (*Lives and Opinions of the Eminent Philosophers*, pp. 240–41).

Although in ancient times transcending one's local social position, status, and role was a distant dream, in modern times it is a burgeoning reality. In 1795, in his famous essay *Perpetual Peace: A Philosophical Sketch*, Immanuel Kant laid the philosophical groundwork for modern cosmopolitanism. He believed that the world was gradually becoming more and more international, which would inevitably result in a world government and world culture, all in service of "the conditions of universal hospitality" (*Perpetual Peace*, p. 137). To Kant, cross-cultural communication could eventually undermine the more insular conceptions of culture that would be held by philosophers like Bourdieu; cosmopolitanism would overlap fields, blur habitus with habitus, redistribute cultural capital, and thus universalize taste.

However, not until the advent of modern technologies of globalization was crossing the boundaries of field, habitus, and capital made possible. Not until airplanes, television channels, and mass-market books—such as the *Pop Culture and Philosophy* series—have the popular and the high-brow tastes been able to be united. And not until figures like Anthony Bourdain has cosmopolitanism been embodied in actual people. Throughout his six books and five shows, Bourdain travels across the globe and finds hospitality in its many countries, showing the world to the world, in all of its grit and glamor, both the world-class restaurants in upper crust neighborhoods and the hole-in-the-wall mom-and-pop shops in third-world backwaters. He undermined and overcame many of the constraints that Bourdieu believed inevitable. He lived out what Diogenes and Kant could only imagine—the life of a man who is welcome in any country and considers the world his home. One might think, like Bourdieu, that Bourdain would be a part of the elite: his position of privilege as a restaurateur and media personality could have reinforced the brands and agendas of his class—the hospitality industry particularly. And yet, his greater project was to democratize taste. Whether drinking vodka with Russian ice-fishermen or dining on Cambodian houseboats, Bourdain seeks out the experiences that high culture has systematically left out. Furthermore, Bourdain shows us our commonalities even amidst our diversities. As he puts it, "You see certain constants when you travel around the world," the distinctiveness and yet communicability of taste (*A Cook's Tour*, "A Mystical World").

Beyond Our Tastes

Anthony Bourdain's culinary and cultural project was something like a synthesis of Pierre Bourdieu and Immanuel Kant:

Bourdain acknowledged the locality and economics of taste through explorations of field, habitus, and capital, but he also attempted to render provincial tastes palatable to the world. In as many ways, Bourdain puts into practice the project that Bourdieu merely theorizes and by doing so reinvents modern taste. By exposing the breadth of cultural differences, Bourdain asks us to think beyond our cultural horizon, beyond our tastes; he unmakes and remakes taste as a social construction and as a human experience and then shares it across borders, classes, and creeds.

II

Life

5

Friendship, Fun, Freedom, Food, and the Future

MICHEL LE GALL AND CHARLES TALIAFERRO

We want to mourn Anthony Bourdain in a productive way by following the example of Plato, whose remembrance of Socrates's death imparted insights about the spirit and power of philosophy. Bourdain was not an academic philosopher, developing abstract theories about the *meaning* of life; but his life's work does offer us a compelling philosophy as a *way* of life.

We wish to celebrate Tony in the spirit of new work in the history of philosophy that emphasizes philosophy's practical relevance for concrete ways of living. This new work shows how philosophy ('the love of wisdom') can model a flourishing life with integrity in a complex, sometimes unjust world.

Socrates taught that justice and truth are more important than bare, worldly power, and in his great work, *The Republic*, Plato extended this Socratic thinking to mean that political greatness and wisdom should meet as one. Famously, Plato wanted philosophers to be kings or, to reach the same end, for kings to become philosophers. While Plato has been rightly criticized for being anti-democratic, we need to bear in mind that his hero and teacher, Socrates, was executed in accord with Athenian democracy and that Plato developed his political vision with the aim of promoting virtue, unity, and peace while preventing evil.

Anthony Bourdain's wisdom lies in three areas:

- His valuing of how people respond when the quest to unite wisdom or virtue and power goes wrong,

- His depiction of how people experiment in resisting tyranny by engaging in activities that resemble what French philosopher Pierre Hadot calls "spiritual exercises," and

- Tony's bringing to light how personal choices invariably have political dimensions.

In *Parts Unknown*, Season One, Episode 6, Tony visited Libya, and in Season Four, Episode 6, he went to Iran. At the time of his visits, both countries were suffering the effects of authoritarian regimes. While these regimes now conjure up for us notions of tyranny, terrorism, and trampled populations, at the outset the rulers of Libya and Iran presented themselves to their people as Platonic "philosopher kings."

Bourdain helps us to see how the leaders of these two countries failed to live up to the Socratic heritage of uniting virtue with power. He also makes us sensitive to important differences between these states. These societies consist of real people, a fact belied by the "pariah state" or "states sponsoring terrorism" labels that dehumanize whole populations.   By bringing this to our notice, Tony helps to make the world a more understanding and tolerant place, and that is how we think he can best be remembered in death.

Philosophy as a Way of Life

Bourdain's achievement is in the spirit of philosophy as understood by the French philosophical historian Pierre Hadot. In *Philosophy as a Way of Life*, Hadot argues that much of philosophy, from ancient times until today, consists primarily in identifying fulfilling ways of living, and not in building great abstract theories. According to Hadot, the practice of philosophy can help us to live in the present, learn to be free from (or less trapped by) anxiety, know when to practice resignation or to resist what appears to be inevitable, know how to eat and drink, understand how to cultivate friendships, and further many other practical aims.

Hadot cites the Greek philosopher Epictetus to illustrate a way of life commended by philosophy: "A carpenter does not come up to you and say, 'Listen to me discourse about the art of carpentry', but he makes a contract for a house and builds it . . . Do the same yourself. Eat like a man, drink like a man . . . get married, have children, take part in civic life, learn how to put up with insults, and tolerate other people." Hadot offers the following portrait of one of the most important schools of philosophy in Ancient Greece: "The Stoics declared explicitly that philosophy, for them, was an 'exercise'. In their view, philosophy did not consist in teaching an abstract theory—much less in the exegesis of texts—but rather in the art of living."

While Anthony Bourdain sometimes appears in his writing and on television as a bon vivant, as a quasi-Bacchus spirit, he also appears in good philosophical company. In the great tradition celebrated by Hadot, he is steadfast in promoting the formation of life-affirming relationships, cultivating calm resistance to threats, renouncing the drive to personal wealth and power, and not allowing anxiety to overshadow the pleasure of present goods like food and drink.

We see Bourdain as celebrating and commending what Hadot refers to as *a way of living* that involves friendship, fun, freedom, food, and the future. Bourdain's way of living is both sustaining and in radical contrast to tyrannical regimes that impersonate Platonic philosophical regimes by presenting themselves as virtuous, peaceful, and unified when they are nothing of the sort.

The Libyan and Iranian Context

In Libya, a country of seven million Sunni Muslims, Muammar Gaddafi (who ruled from 1969 to 2011) presented himself as a revolutionary liberator, overturning corruption tied to the influence of western powers and oil companies and championing the interests of oppressed peoples everywhere.

In his three-part *Green Book* (published between 1975 and 1981) Gaddafi promoted democracy, rejecting both capitalism and communism. He appeared to strike a balanced, moderate socialism. He rejects capitalism, communism, and representative democracy in favor of a direct democracy, guided by the General People's Committee, that enables political participation for all adult citizens. In actuality, the book is more a collection of aphorisms and loosely associated ideas issued as part of the regime's effort to bolster Gaddafi's image in Libya and in the southern hemisphere as a revolutionary philosopher, the modern counterpart to the philosopher king. In the wave of political unrest that spread across North Africa and the Middle East in 2011, Gaddafi was deposed and killed, and Libya fell into a protracted civil war that lingers to this day.

Under the Shah (who ruled from 1941 to 1979), Iran's population of 85 million Shi'i Muslims experienced great oppression, the use of secret police, and torture until the 1979 Revolution. Guided by Ayatollah Khomeini, the '79 uprising threw off a western-backed, secular regime and established what promised to be a just and religiously observant state. For his part, Ayatollah Khomeini cast himself as the Supreme Leader and in his book, *Governance by an Islamic Jurist*, he justified the "absolute authority of the jurist." Unlike Gaddafi's *Green Book*, there is a clear rigor to Khomeini's work which is rooted in a keen understanding of the Shi'i Islamic legal tradition. Currently, the Islamic Republic is witnessing co-ordinated, massive popular demonstrations against the perceived tyranny and restrictions on individual rights imposed by the religious leaders in charge.

Friendship, Freedom, and Fun

The *Parts Unknown* Libya episode, that first aired on May 18th 2013, opens with scenes of destruction, and then cuts to children shooting off firecrackers in the central square of Tripoli outside the walls of the old city. They are "giddily happy" says Anthony Bourdain. But he quickly proceeds to the key issue: "How to build a whole society overnight and make it work in one of the most contentious and difficult areas in the world . . . is what people are trying to figure out."

Freedom from Gaddafi was hard fought in Libya. A regime that at the outset had promised meaningful change for the benefit of the masses of this small country eventually became, over the decades, an authoritarian tyranny. And so, with the Arab Spring of 2011, thousands of young men took up arms against the Gaddafi regime. Omar, a one-time travel agent and medical student, joined the ranks of those fighting the regime alongside other students, garage mechanics, engineers, teachers, and government workers.

As Bourdain described it, they went from "kids playing PlayStation to hardened fighters" in a matter of weeks. Freedom in the context of Libya is therefore something very hard to define since its priorities are unclear. Is freedom synonymous with democracy? Is it a matter of free speech or is it the freedom to consume? For sure, it is more than freedom from tyranny and political repression.

In one scene, Bourdain introduces us to Jawhar, a young man whose cousin was killed by the Gaddafi regime. As they sit in a restaurant that is a Kentucky Fried Chicken knock-off called "Uncle Kentucky," our host muses that for Jawhar "a few pieces of greasy fried chicken eaten in a brightly colored fast-food setting mean something more than a calorie bomb . . . It's the taste of freedom." Yet earlier, on an almost contradictory note of circular logic, Bourdain explains, that "young Libyans hunger for more than just freedom. They hunger for places like this . . . Uncle Kentucky." As is typical of young revolutions, freedom and fantasy blur. Being "free" to eat at brightly colored fast-food joints is at once a taste of freedom but also somehow illusory since Uncle Kentucky is hardly a real American fast-food joint, just an awkward local clone. Nevertheless, here the personal choice of eating fast food carries a powerful political statement about the rejection of Gaddafi's tyranny and state-sponsored "direct democracy" under which such simple consumer pleasures were unavailable and frowned upon. Whereas we may eat a burger on the fly and give no thought to the act's possible socio-economic or political implications, for Jawhar eating at Uncle Kentucky is at once an act of rebellion and an overt embrace of what he pictures as emblematic of an open, democratic society.

The revolution that overthrew Gaddafi did not seem, however, to have necessarily changed all deep-rooted social and religious values. Just as was the case under Gaddafi, women dressed modestly, did not mix with men, and never occupied any positions of power in the regime, other than perhaps in some school or university settings. In fact, as Anthony Bourdain explains, there is still a "tug of war" over what is acceptable in terms of social behavior and conduct in public. A case in point is the celebration of the birthday of the Prophet Mohammed in the streets of the old city of Tripoli. In those scenes, we see men leading a parade whereas the women peer out of windows above. This is still a society where certain conventions remain unchallenged and norms that favor men over women are still cherished and protected by men, young and old.

If freedom ranges from the right to indulge in irrational exuberance or unbridled fun by setting off firecrackers or eating fried chicken, it also comes at a very heavy price in Libya. As the *Parts Unknown* crew travels around the country, we are bombarded with images of destruction. In towns like Misrata we see row upon row of collapsed buildings, walls pockmarked by bullets, burnt out tanks, abandoned weapons, and a country that is an armed camp overrun by many factions and competing militias. Yet, absent in this quest for freedom seems to be any common notion of what Libya represents as a nation or what kind of social contract should be drawn up between a post-Gaddafi state and Libya's citizens.

Michel Cousins, founder and editor of *The Libya Herald*, offers an explanation for this seemingly unfocused sense of freedom. He says, "Gaddafi stole the identity of Libya. Gaddafi stole the freedom of Libya . . . we knew there was another Libya. But we talked about it as you do about a dead person. Suddenly there was a resurrection. The dead came back to life."

The dead may have come back to life, but the Libya that Anthony Bourdain shows us is a country in the grips of civil war and in a moment of almost uncontrollable self-destruction. Friendships are uncertain. Neighboring villages are aligned with rival military factions. Suspicions abound. And yet, despite all that, people seem happy and extend a warm and sincere welcome to the CNN crew. There is an undeniable happiness in the air.

Iran, by contrast, seems to be a country where people enjoy much less apparent freedom, but in other ways seems to have a more focused sense of purpose. And, yes, they are bound by strong friendships and fun. The episode on Iran opens with a brief review of American-Iranian relations, the overthrow of the Shah, and the Iranian hostage crisis of 1979. Bourdain pointedly asks, "How does one have fun in Iran these days?" Whereas Libya appears to be in the sudden grip of a "tug of war" between the Muslim cultural norms long embraced by Gaddafi and the possibility of real change, Iran is a country where "the line is constantly being tested." That uncertain line is one that ripples back and forth between a long-standing tradition of modernism which has empowered women and brought important societal change and the Islamic norms that the regime wants people to toe.

What follows in the Iran episode are a series of short vignettes of young men and women, most of whom wear modernized hijabs, playing foosball, pinball, and bowling. There's an easy mixing of the sexes and a sense that despite an oppressive regime there are still ways to find simple pleasures. So, as Anthony Bourdain explains, "you can listen to rock, sort of, but you yourself cannot be seen to rock or visibly rock." As the episode progresses, we meet a number of Iranians, young and old, in their homes. We also encounter *The Washington Post* journalist, Jason Rezaian, an American Iranian, and his wife and fellow journalist, Yeganeh Salehi. Whereas in Libya there was a sense of unbridled public exuberance, in Iran things are more measured, more guarded, and often confined to the indoors. (Rezaian's on-camera candor ultimately landed him in an Iranian jail for a spell.) Conversely, we see none of the wanton destruction that plagues Libya and instead are treated to panoramas and scenes of beauty and calm, from people visiting mosques to those having fun in the great square of Isfahan, Naqsh-e Jame plaza, as they ride their bikes, wade in the fountains, and picnic.

This display of life can create a site for philosophy as a way of life. Once tyranny recedes, people are free to engage in spiritual exercises. Hadot maintained that ancient Greek and Roman philosophers essentially embraced spiritual exercises intended to transform how we perceive our world, and therefore our being. He defined "spiritual exercises"—a nod to St Ignatius of Loyola's *Spiritual Exercises*—as "an effort in changing and transformation of the self."

In the case of Libya and Iran, we maintain that in the wake of a revolution or during periods of protest, the men and women of the street are engaging in "spiritual exercises" of sorts—trying out different ways of living and behaving, testing boundaries, and exploring ways of being that were formerly unknown or forbidden to them. With that in mind, we suggest that while ideology plays a vital role in political upheavals such as those in Libya and Iran, the real practical change comes about through what the French call "tâtonnement," feeling, groping one's way in the dark along poorly lit paths. And that "tâtonnement," that testing and trying, is tantamount to large-scale popular spiritual exercises—whether it's eating Uncle Kentucky chicken or placing women in the frontlines of dissent and protest as is the case currently in Iran.

One byproduct of such individual spiritual exercises is that the political and the personal are invariably intertwined. What you eat, how you dress, the pastimes you engage in, all reflect what you aspire to and serve as touchstones to what you hope for yourself, your country and its future. In western democracies, this is less the case since elections provide the vehicle for popular expression and private conduct tends to remain in the personal, not the political sphere.

Food

The ability to appreciate food in a family setting and see it as a mode of cultural expression is a middle-class value. Prior to the modern era, most people followed a simple subsistence diet. And that is true of cultures around the world. In premodern times only the very wealthy, those participating in imperial and court cultures, had access to any kind of sophisticated food because its preparation is so labor intensive. It's only within recent memory and thanks to modern appliances that elaborate food preparation and enjoyment have become central to the middle classes of many cultures.

"Iranians love guests and never get tired of guests who love their food," Bourdain tells us. Family and community are the experiences and the values that lie behind Iranian cooking. In fact, the great food of Iran is cooked in people's homes and secret recipes that are passed down in families are "treasured possessions."

In a series of different sequences, Bourdain visits several families and enjoys several outstanding and well-known Iranian dishes. These are dishes that are at once sweet and savory and mix meat and fruits along with spices such as cinnamon and saffron. There's the national dish, "Chelow Kebab," marinated lamb on a skewer served with buttery rice. Other standout dishes include "Fesenjan," a chicken stew with walnuts, pomegranate, tomato paste and dried apricots. Along with that goes "Tahdig," crispy rice which is cooked in a dome shape until the bottom is brown and then is flipped over. As Bourdain notes, "rice in this country is like nothing you've ever had." On another occasion, we are introduced to "Halim," a breakfast dish of wheat bulgur and meat porridge, in this instance made with turkey, sugar, and cinnamon.

Food provides Iranians with almost a protective cocoon and inner sanctum. That such a strong tradition exists has largely to do with Iranian's middle class, a class made up not just of art dealers and pistachio merchants but also accountants, lawyers, and professors, many of whom Bourdain introduces to us. Food in Libya is a different matter.

With no robust middle class, Libyan cuisine is less varied and elaborate than that of Iran and consequently it's perhaps no surprise that all the meals we witness in Libya take place in public spaces and not in family settings. There's the seafood lunch at Barracuda, a restaurant where you pick your fish from the rich Mediterranean catch, and it's grilled before your eyes. The highlight meal in the Libyan episode is the seaside barbecue that opens with the brief pursuit and slaughtering of a lamb and then the preparation of a stew made of kidneys, liver, and heart "served family style." As Bourdain notes, "Barbecue may not be the road to world peace, but it's a start."

The Future

What gives a country a better chance to make its way into the future and make good on those spiritual exercises and testing of boundaries? The answer may well lie with the importance of history—with knowing oneself and the past of one's country.

What is most striking is that Iranians apparently have a much stronger, deeper, and more personal sense of their history than Libyans and, consequently, a clearer and distinct sense of their culture and themselves. On several occasions, Bourdain's hosts share with him the origins of traditions and explain the unique blend of ancient Persian and later Islamic practices that in part account for Iran's uniqueness among Middle Eastern countries.

By comparison, Libya has little that is singularly and culturally distinct from its North African and Arab Muslim neighbors. And while Libya is endowed with Roman ruins of rare quality, notably those in Leptis Magna (which Bourdain visits), few Libyans seem to know much about their past other than the narrow national narrative shaped during the Gaddafi years. So, the long trajectory of Libya's history from past to present is for most Libyans foggy at best, while that of Iran is clearly appreciated by its people and rooted in ancient Persian culture, modernism, and Islam. Gaddafi bears a large responsibility for Libya's collective historical amnesia since he succeeded in severely distorting, if not destroying, Libyans' sense of their own history. Through Gaddafi, Libya's history was largely limited to the country's victimization and struggle against their Italians colonizers (1911–1945). That rather gray depiction of the past may in part account for the sense of despair or resignation that presides in much of contemporary Libya as the country remains divided and elections set for 2021 have been indefinitely deferred.

In line with Hadot's portrait of philosophy as being principally a way of life, an invitation to test and exercise (spiritually and materially), Bourdain sees the celebration of friendship, freedom, and fun, as well as hope for the future, as the key ingredients of life and the antidote to the seductive desire for worldly power and domination.

Live to Uncover Your Philosophy

Whether he intended it or not, Bourdain's episodes on Libya and Iran raise some basic philosophical questions about how to live your life. Each school of ancient philosophy, according to Hadot, was a response to a different experience of this world. Epicureanism was "the voice of the flesh: 'not to be hungry, not to be thirsty, not to be cold'." Stoicism said that people's unhappiness arises from their ill-fated pursuit of things that they cannot obtain, and it advises instead to pursue virtue. The ancients also disagreed about the role and function of intellectual contemplation in pursuing the good life. Aristotle, for example, advocated the "incredible pleasure" of investigating and contemplating all the works of nature as its own end. Contrast that with the Skeptics and Cynics who sought *eudaimonia* (happiness) by withholding judgment altogether or

flouting conventional authority. They were wary of how stri-
dent judgments often lead to warfare and costly, sometimes
futile action.

Diogenes of Sinope (often cast as a Cynic) was famous for his
being unimpressed by authority, military power, and wealth—
even in the person of Alexander the Great. The Cynics, like
Diogenes, were known to have advanced their philosophy
through dramatic, unconventional action rather than speeches.
Hadot remarks about the Cynics that "philosophical discourse
was reduced to a minimum—sometimes to mere gestures." In all
these contexts, philosophy was constructed by proper living more
than by discourse alone.

Just as Hadot maintains that the different schools of ancient philosophy were expressions of different approaches and
experiences of life, they nonetheless shared certain commonalities to the extent that each school advocated "a complete rever-
sal of received ideas: one must renounce the false values of
wealth, honors, and pleasures, and turn towards the true value
of virtue, contemplation, a simple lifestyle, and the simple happiness of existing."

In Plato's dialogue the *Symposium*, Socrates invites us to
the love of beauty which can lead to a life of lasting fecundity,
as distinct from pursuing worldly glory. Worldly glory is fickle
and often has recourse to violence as distinct from pursuing
true beauty that involves vibrant, life-affirming desire.

What Bourdain shows us is that life—even in Libya and
Iran—is about testing, trying on new ways of fun while also rel-
ishing old traditions that bring family and friends together.
And in that process, one learns more about oneself and how to
share happiness with others. In that sense, Bourdain's
approach is very much in keeping with Hadot's notion that the
choice of a way of life is not at the end of some philosophical
process but is instead a process of "reaction to other existential
attitudes" and, one might add, experiences.

It's worth emphasizing that Bourdain makes one point
absolutely clear and in so doing, goes beyond the confines of
Hadot and the ancients who emphasize personal happiness
and virtue. Bourdain clearly shows how the personal is political in these countries beset with political upheaval. Playing
ping-pong, eating greasy chicken, or organizing a sumptuous
family feast, each of these acts is also a political statement.
That is the case to the extent that such actions involve or imply
political attitudes about freedom, fun, the status of women, and
the relationship of the individual with, and their responsibilities to, the broader community.

The very notion that the political is personal is not necessarily foreign to Islamic political traditions since the faith of the individual Muslim, speaking in the broadest of terms, is above all enshrined in communal acts, such as public prayer, as well as in the broader activities of the community, including work and play in public spaces. (That said, in many Muslim countries men and women are often segregated and there are clearly defined private spaces for women and families.) Consequently, the line between the personal and political tends to be more difficult to draw. Contrast that with the United States where the political and personal have traditionally been quite separate. It was not until the 1970s that the expression "the personal is political" gained currency as feminists maintained that the personal experiences of women were circumscribed by their position in the reigning male hierarchy of power relationships. So, if a woman were to receive a smaller salary than her male counterpart who had identical responsibilities, then the broader social organization played a large role in accounting for this disparity.

Bourdain and Care of the Soul

It's just shy of a decade since the first of these two episodes aired on CNN. In both pieces Anthony Bourdain maintains a tone of cautious optimism. Above all, he underscores the theme that these two countries offer far more than just disturbing news of violence and repression. First and foremost, he celebrates the experimentation, the resilience, and the undeterred optimism of two very different peoples and societies. And above all their openness and welcoming spirit despite a political and historical legacy fraught with pain.

In the meantime, Libya, and Iran, like many other societies in the Middle East, will have to contend with what the US military has termed "VUCA"—volatility, uncertainty, complexity, and ambiguity. And those were forces that Anthony Bourdain also had to confront personally in his fascinating but troubled life.

There may or may not be one key element or message behind Bourdain's spirit of friendship, freedom, fun, food, and hope for the future, but there seems to be another connection between Bourdain's work and a question that was monumental in ancient Greece. From the seventh century B.C.E. Archilochus to Socrates two hundred years later, to Plato and Xenophon in the fourth century B.C.E., there was debate about whether the life of a tyrant was (or could be) a happy one. In the *Gorgias*, Socrates argues that the unjust life of a tyrant—with its apparent pleasures and power—is not true happiness; it is instead an ugly self-indulgence, an affront to the true flourishing of your soul and those around you.

The Socratic philosophical tradition is first and foremost one that seeks to expose fabrications and illusions, to move us away from mere shadows to what is truly good and fulfilling. In this spirit, Bourdain has promoted what Socrates would say is the care of the soul. Anthony Bourdain has pointed to where true happiness and joy can be nourished, delighting in the guest-host relationship, befriending a wide circle of people who were strangers moments earlier but who are united in their love of freedom, whether in Iran or Libya, or wherever you are when you've finished reading our chapter.

6

Authenticity in a World of Bullshido

RYAN FALCIONI

Anthony Bourdain was passionate about everything that he pursued. His drive to fearlessly and unapologetically advocate for the world's cultures, foods, and social justice, gained him many admirers. One of Bourdain's passions that seems to get the least attention is his obsession with Brazilian jiu-jitsu (BJJ).

Although rooted in traditional Japanese judo/jiu-jitsu, BJJ emerged in the early twentieth century in Brazil as a new art, focused on takedowns and submissions. It is known for its brutal effectiveness and the intensity of its rolling (sparring) sessions. For both of these reasons, and many others, most BJJ gyms seem to attract quite an eclectic mix of hobbyists and addicted devotees. I once heard BJJ described as "Murder Yoga," and this is about as apt a description as I could imagine.

Bourdain's naturally intense disposition, mixed with his borderline masochistic desire for ego-slaying reality checks, made BJJ a fitting choice for his forays into the world of martial arts. During the last few years of his life, he was known to train nearly every day—and often twice a day. During one summer-long vacation in the Hamptons, he would helicopter to Renzo Gracie's academy in Manhattan several times a week to train ("Renzo Gracie Calls Former BJJ student Anthony Bourdain 'a Great Soul'"). He was also a serious competitor, winning the gold medal in his division of the 2016 IBJJF New York Spring International Open Championship. This is no small feat! Under the handle, NooYawkCity, he was a regular contributor to the r/bjj subreddit. In these writings and in his interviews about BJJ, it is clear that he had found a new outlet and obsession. In his own words:

Why am I doing this? I don't know. I'm like a dope fiend at this point. If I can't train I start going into withdrawal. Wander around, twitching, restless and pissed off. At least with dope, you feel GOOD afterwards. After training, I feel like a rented and unloved mule . . . Yet I insist on getting squashed on the mats every day and feel bereft if I can't. This is not normal. When I talk about BJJ, old friends look at me like I have an arm growing out of my forehead. But I won't stop. Can't stop. (www.reddit.com/r/bjj/comments/2aaqb1/chicken_fried_steak)

Bourdain's writings and public statements about BJJ are illustrative of his broader personal struggles and also reflect philosophical and ethical tension within the various worlds of martial arts. Broadly speaking, this tension involves a struggle between virtues and vices. It's probably easiest to think of virtues and vices as character traits or dispositions. Virtues are the good ones (like courage, honesty, integrity, and wisdom). Vices are the bad ones (like cowardice, dishonesty, arrogance, and stubbornness).

Virtue theory runs deep within the veins of philosophical traditions in both the East and the West. One particularly helpful way of framing Bourdain's struggle between virtues and vices comes from Aristotle, whose "doctrine of the mean" provides a way of viewing the often-fraught relationships between many virtues and vices. Aristotle's doctrine of the mean holds that ethical virtues are states that are in between two extremes. Every virtue exists along a continuum between two vices: a deficiency on one end and an excess on the other.

The goal is to cultivate what is often called a "golden mean" between the two extreme states. By way of one example, a virtue like courage exists as the mean between the deficient state of cowardice and the excess state of foolhardiness. For Aristotle (and for Confucian and Daoist virtue ethics) it is essential that humans consistently endeavor to cultivate virtues. In many ways, this is what essentially defines us as humans. For most virtue ethicists, the human project is to develop these virtues through first understanding them, and then consistently striving to act in accordance with them while simultaneously avoiding the lure of vices on both sides. Bourdain's journey through BJJ is illustrative of his own struggles to cultivate virtues and avoid vices. This struggle played out in virtually all of his endeavors . . . often very publicly. But it is through his engagement with martial arts and the specific virtues and vices that they often trade in, that we get a particularly revealing look at Bourdain's personal ethical journey.

We often encounter the virtues of martial arts in advertising that targets parents of wayward children. They also frequently appear on "Virtues of Bushido" posters inside your local dojo. Furthermore, many books and articles have been written addressing (and often touting) the various virtues that can be cultivated through martial arts training. A brief Amazon search will reveal the near ubiquity of book titles with the following formula: The "Way," "Path," "Code," or "Journey," followed by "of the," and then some martial artsy practitioner like "Warrior," "Samurai," or "Ninja." As predictably pithy and apologetic as much of this content can be, I am an unabashed fan! Take a dive into these texts and we are treated to stories, sayings, and even secret techniques of the founders, grand masters, and emerging stars from many different traditions. There is often quite a lot to be learned and appreciated in these volumes.

As indicated in their titles, one of the primary foci of many of these tomes is indeed the ethical code or rules to be followed on the path to martial arts mastery. These sections offer a glimpse into the world of martial arts virtues. And although generally light on empirical research, I find these discussions to be frequently enlightening. At their best, martial arts traditions have the resources and methods to help cultivate many virtues and mitigate many vices. BJJ in particular, often prides itself on embodying the virtue of authenticity and in having a Bourdain-like, no nonsense approach to learning and applying compellingly effective methods of self-defense: What works, stays; what doesn't, goes.

We see a revealing iteration of this journey and struggle between virtues and vices in Anthony Bourdain's own engagement with Brazilian Jiu Jitsu during the final years of his life. His experience reveals the cultivation of many of the interrelated virtues of humility, perseverance, courage, and authenticity. In this 2014 exchange with journalist Charlie Rose, we observe these virtues on full display as Bourdain describes getting started on his BJJ journey:

> BOURDAIN: To recreate that feeling of being the lowest person on the totem pole in a kitchen back when I was seventeen, knowing nothing in a very hard world. The incremental tiny satisfactions of being a little less awful at something every day . . . It is a very steep, very painful learning incline . . . I just want to suck less tomorrow.

> CHARLIE ROSE: And what is satisfying is getting/being a little better each day?

BOURDAIN **interjects:** Or looking forward to the day where you might possibly be a little bit better . . . It is a never-ending journey and uh . . . it appeals to some part of my brain that . . . I haven't visited before ("Anthony Bourdain on Cooking and Jiu Jitsu").

His posts on the r/bjj subreddit continually echo his newfound humility, courage, and perseverance on the mats: "I love all of it. The soreness, the carrot fingers, mat burn, the ego-destroying ass kickings, just when you think you're getting somewhere. I'm hooked . . . I will probably never live to see black belt or win any competitions. But I'm pretty sure I will suck a little bit less every month" (www.reddit.com/r/bjj/comments/2k50b9/who_started_bjj_over_50).

His experiences and budding cultivation of some of the virtues associated with martial arts will sound familiar to most practitioners. For what could be more consequential than attempting to fend off an attacker with an ineffective technique, unquestionably believed to be effective due to the gullibility cultivated through the authoritarianism, traditionalism, and groupthink that exists in many martial arts communities?

Although cultivated in a wide variety of ways and to varying degrees, many traditions and individual schools make a unique contribution to the development of such vices. Thankfully, much of Bourdain's experiences with BJJ were not generally plagued by these. Bourdain was under no illusions about his martial arts prowess nor was he in the grips of an authoritarian "master" who promised him an unrealizable panacea for all that ailed him. As his journey in BJJ progressed, he spoke with a refreshing, self-deprecating honesty about just wanting to "suck a little bit less each month." His journey into BJJ reflected a broader, arguably lifelong, struggle to cultivate the virtues of authenticity, honesty, and humility in a career and lifestyle that incessantly pulled him towards the vices of inauthenticity, self-delusion, and pride.

Bullshido: A Feast of Vices

Bourdain's efforts to cultivate virtue in and through the world of martial arts reflect an internal ethical tension within many schools and traditions of martial arts themselves. Another insight of Aristotle's virtue ethics involves the interconnectedness of particular 'mean' virtues and their related vices of deficiency and excess. Many of the same activities and situations that provide profound opportunities for the cultivation of virtue are also the locus for the cultivation of vice.

Think here of the occasions for the development of courage that emerge during times of war. These same circumstances can also bring about great cowardice, or again the false bravado of rashness or foolhardiness. There is a great subjectivity involved in each person's journey to cultivate virtue. An experience that generates an opportunity to successfully exercise great courage for one, can bring about utter moral failure for another. And, in martial arts studios and dojos around the world, this drama plays out every day on the tatami.

Although I am a fan of many martial arts and a current practitioner and professor (black belt) of Brazilian Jiu Jitsu, I have become increasingly concerned at the abundance of 'fake' martial arts and fraudulent 'masters'. One of the more creative terms to capture the various species of nonsense that goes on in martial arts is bullshido. This is a mashup of the word for the samurai code of conduct, *bushido*, and the bullshit that goes on in fake (or often just bad) martial arts. This term captures quite a variety of communities, beliefs, and practices.

On one end of this bullshido continuum, we have the cheesy Americanized McDojos and their often cult-like hero worship of an uncoordinated, untested, and invariably lumpy 'master'. Think here of Rex Kwon Do from the *Napoleon Dynamite* movie: "After one week with me in my dojo you'll be prepared to defend yourself with the strength of a grizzly, the reflexes of a puma, the wisdom of a man."

As seen in such schools, bullshido's pervasiveness is definitely a matter of degree. There can be legitimate martial arts education in such places. Many virtues can still be cultivated. Yet, the authoritarianism, emphasis on conformity, lack of live sparring, and unchecked egos of such leaders can be fertile breeding ground for vices like gullibility, self-deception, pride, and closed-mindedness.

At the more morally abominable end of the bullshido spectrum, we have cases of severe physical abuse and sexual exploitation. Somewhere in the middle (but very much connected with both ends of the continuum) is the world of outright fraudulent martial arts systems. There are numerous traditions that promise, and often unintentionally humorously 'demonstrate', no-touch knockouts, ki/chi energy ball attacks (think here of Ryu's Hadoken attacks from the *Street Fighter* franchise), and other forms of martial-arts-themed quackery. Bourdain was both aware of such bullshido and reserved some of his snarkiest comments in personally excoriating some of its most prominent purveyors. In a reddit discussion about the legitimacy of Steven Seagal's alleged martial arts prowess, Bourdain stated:

> Seagal is a 'deadly mofo' if you get between him and the all you can eat pasta bar. The hair is definitely deadly though. A wad of that Dynell weave comes undone during a fight with Lightning Chunks of Death and you could choke (www.reddit.com/r/bjj/comments/3b0qhf/steven_seagal_sambo_cha mpion).

And as humorous as this is, it reveals Bourdain's commitment to authenticity in his newfound passion.

In recent years, there have been many exposés of such fakes. Chinese MMA fighter, Xu Xiaodong has made it his mission to combat fraudulent martial arts "masters" through challenging them to public fights. It should be no surprise that he has beaten every one of these masters . . . most of them quickly and brutally. But the price that he has paid both economically (Chinese courts have ordered him to pay large fines for insulting such masters) and personally (his social credit rating was lowered to such a degree that Xu's ability to travel freely and rent/buy property has been virtually eliminated) is extremely high ("Xu Xiaodong Ordered to Apologize and Pay Damages After Insulting Tai Chi Grandmaster"). Most striking, if you take the time to watch some of the videos of Xiaodong's challenges, is the genuine surprise and confusion seen in the reactions of both the masters and their students. Side note: If you have a free afternoon and think you might enjoy watching alleged 'masters' being pummeled senseless or submitted by practitioners of MMA, boxing, or jiu jitsu, there are many rabbit holes to follow on various YouTube channels and websites. A solid place to start for all things bullshido is the bullshido.net website. In virtually all of the videos that I have viewed, the masters clearly believe that they will be victorious.

To have gotten to the point of accepting the fight with Xiaodong (it's worth noting that some of these masters have initiated such challenges), they must have been feasting on a heavy diet of moral and intellectual vices for quite some time. The levels of self-deception, pride, closed-mindedness, and foolishness that they have cultivated, and no doubt cultivated in their academies, is staggering. And despite their being confronted in a most visceral way with the ineffectiveness of their systems, it is apparent that most of them (after engaging in some embarrassingly transparent delusional rationalizations) have simply returned to their schools and students. There are a lot of similarities between these communities of fake martial arts and those of charismatic faith healing. There are even a handful of YouTube videos that show footage of charismatic evangelists like Benny Hinn, slaying people in the spirit, infused with sounds effects and graphics from *Street Fighter II*. Humor aside, the way that these videos work seamlessly is revealing of the gullibility, self-delusion, groupthink, and other vices that thrive within both communities. The susceptibility of the faithful to the power of suggestion and the social pressure to be a 'good', 'obedient', or even an 'enlightened', member of the flock is profound.

Bourdain's engagement with BJJ consistently exemplified both his pursuit of authenticity and humility . . . and his low tolerance for bullshit. Unlike many celebrities (who will not be named but whose names could be revealed through a quick Google search) who engage with martial arts primarily through private lessons and other ego-coddling arrangements, Bourdain was known to roll with just about anyone. He craved the authenticity of both the art itself and also of his teammates and sparring partners.

> Bourdain was not the type of celebrity who stuck to private lessons designed to keep faces unblemished and egos unbruised. Just as he got down and dirty with real people and foods, Bourdain sought the unfiltered BJJ experience—'gen-pop' classes—wherever he went. He wanted to be strangled by a thick-fingered bricklayer in Dublin, arm-locked by a mangy-haired hipster in San Francisco, hip-tossed by a tree-trunk-thick judoka in Okinawa. And that's what he did, though it certainly wasn't easy. ("The Lost Diary of Anthony Bourdain")

Bourdain's push for authentic expressions of, and experiences with, BJJ reflect his broader commitment to doing justice to the lives of real people. His insistence on training with the general population 'gen pop' classes at the local schools he visited is but another example of his commitment to authenticity. He was even critical of the often pretentious way that food critics and others upheld a notion of 'authenticity' that itself ignored the deeper notions of authenticity that emerge when you actually engage with people across the world. "The word authentic has become a completely ridiculous, snobbish term. There are so many first- and second-generation immigrants making wonderful mashups of food they grew up eating. On the other hand, I'm pretty sure that every time Guy Fieri puts barbecue pork inside a nori roll, an angel dies" ("10 Questions with Anthony

Bourdain"). In all of his endeavors, Bourdain appeared to always find the people and traditions that were as unpretentious as possible.

A (Brief) Case Study in Bullshido

A few years ago, I partnered with a new(ish) white belt at our BJJ school. As we prepared for our first round of sparring, he asked if he could use techniques that he had learned from another martial art. I obliged. As the bell rang to start, I reached in to grab his collar. He immediately pounced on me, jamming his thumb somewhere in my shoulder, pressing furiously. Now I must admit that a more quick-witted me would have immediately flopped to my back, writhing in pain as if I had just been hit by a bolt of Force lightning from Emperor Palpatine. But, my surprise and mild discomfort overrode my sense of humor and good timing. I simply locked in my cross-collar grip and promptly scissor-swept him flat on his back. The look of crestfallen surprise on his face was tragic. I actually felt rather guilty for being the vessel of his disillusionment. He mumbled something about it "usually working" and that it had "been a while" since he had used this particular immobilizing technique. I later heard that he regaled many of our teammates with stories of his previous masters killing animals at a distance with some sort of energy fields. I opted to make this a teachable moment. I decided against saying that such techniques are bullshido. I merely said that in BJJ, such moves are not generally effective. We focus on joint locks and chokes that have a very high rate of success in combat and competition. By the look in his eyes I could tell that he did not really believe me. Or at least he wasn't quite ready to give up such magical beliefs.

Epistemic Viciousness

Philosopher Gillian Russell has written about the cultivation of intellectual vices that are endemic in many martial arts communities. Building upon the classical philosophical framework of vices and virtues going back to Aristotle, Russell labels the type of self-delusion in many martial arts as a type of mental vice, or "epistemic viciousness." Viciousness is used here to denote the *"possessing of vices"* and not an act of brutality or cruelty (Epistemic Viciousness in the Martial Arts", pp. 129–130). The emphasis on tradition, authority, and esoteric knowledge in many traditional martial arts is a perfect recipe for developing certain vices, with the potential for outright fraud.

That said, in most martial arts schools, such tendencies are generally kept in check through regular sparring against resisting opponents and real talk from instructors about the limits of the craft. However, if left unchecked, in a training environment where your skills are not live-tested against resisting opponents, mixed with the often cult-like hero worship of an authority figure, there is plenty of room for the vices of the mind to take over.

In accounting for the features of numerous martial arts subcultures that facilitate the descent into vice, Russell notes the ways in which many aspects of martial arts are treated as sacred. Masters are venerated and seen as infallible. The relatively arbitrary customs (uniforms, bowing, names of techniques) are baptized as holy and not to be violated or questioned. The ways that other martial arts and often neighboring schools are talked about can be eerily similar to interreligious rivalry. They are not just neighbors or even fellow travelers on this martial arts journey . . . they are infidels.

Russell addresses some of these (and a few more) features of martial arts cultures that make them susceptible to cult-like behavior and the epistemic viciousness that they engender. If you add in the reality of our existential search for meaning, it should not be surprising that gullibility, self-delusion, and predation can flourish. In Russell's own words:

> In religion, people seek something that will satisfy their desire for the special, mysterious, and meaningful in their lives, which is exactly what some of us hope to find in the martial arts . . . people who are hungry for something special-and that's all of us to some degree- are more likely to be suckers, because strong desires make people vulnerable. (p. 133)

As with the world of religious cults and faith healing, the cultivation of vices in martial arts can be quite costly. In self-defense situations, nothing could be more tragically consequential than being delusional about your abilities to defend yourself. Failing to stop a mugger with a no-touch knockout as they attack you is too high a price to pay to maintain loyalty to your sensei or your 'art'. Furthermore, there can be disastrous effects on other areas of your life. Overestimating the ability of a martial arts lifestyle to help both physical and psychological ailments is an all-too-common feature of martial arts mythologies. Many friends and colleagues of Bourdain have commented on this particular dimension of his engagement with BJJ. On one end, it was clear that Bourdain experienced significant mental and physical benefits from BJJ. Of his newfound commitment to a BJJ lifestyle, chef and longtime friend, Eric Ripert commented, "And, I know for him it was very good for his mental health, and it changed him—he lost a lot of weight, built a lot of muscles. It was good for his cardio. He stopped smoking, he stopped a lot of things. He started to eat better, and so on, and be more cautious" (*Bourdain: The Definitive Biography*, p. 326).

Bourdain made it clear in various interviews that his new-found hobby/addiction was an integral component on this path to a healthier life. However, many of his vices were still lurking in the shadows. It's not for me to speculate about the degree to which Bourdain put his faith in the modes and methods of BJJ to improve his life. But it is clear that at the end of his life, he had again returned to many of his bad habits. Director, friend, and longtime *Parts Unknown* collaborator, Morgan Fallon, offers the following account that references Bourdain's internal struggle with both health and authenticity more generally at the end of his life:

> He wanted to be a rock star again, and all of a sudden it was right back to smoking, and not just smoking, but smoking on camera, which was totally unheard of. That moment in the Puglia [episode of Parts Unknown] where he lights up in scene: that was pretty intense, and kind of a really depressing signifier of him, in some ways, being like, Fuck it" (p. 330).

I do not believe that any of Bourdain's BJJ professors made fantastical claims about the gentle art's ability to cure Bourdain of what ailed him. But there is a tendency in many martial arts communities (often after experiencing significant benefits from training) to believe that it is something of a panacea for life's problems. "Jiu Jitsu saved my life!" is as close to a mantra as anything in the testimonials touted by many BJJ academies and on many online forums.

This is a profound moral failure of the martial arts communities that are the purveyors of such viciousness! We can have respect for our teachers, founders, histories, and traditions without falling into the vices of gullibility and self-delusion that can emerge if such respect is not tethered to reality. Respect . . . but verify. Test the claims and techniques of your sensei or historical tradition in the proving ground that is your school/dojo! They are literally the arena (or petri dish) for the effectiveness of your martial art. I think here of the evidential-ist dictum of philosopher W.K. Clifford: "It is wrong always, everywhere, and for anyone to believe anything on insufficient evidence." I do not believe that this maxim is absolute. But, it provides a fitting counterbalance to the type of unchecked credulity that is at the core of many instances of bullshido.

In life and in martial arts, Bourdain continuously jumped into the messy business of doing justice to the complexities of people's lived experiences (including his own). He didn't look for simple explanations or solutions to the problems and issues that often plagued the people and communities with whom he engaged. At his best, he applied this approach to the issues in his own life. He reportedly said, "Life is complicated. It's filled with nuance. It's unsatisfying . . . If I believe in anything, it is doubt. The root cause of all life's problems is looking for a simple fucking answer" ("Anthony Bourdain's Most Memorable Quotes").

Cutting through the Bullshido

As is now abundantly clear, Bourdain became obsessed with BJJ during the last several years of his life. It seems pretty evident from his words and actions that he found something uniquely authentic about this martial art. Beyond the immediate encouragement of his wife, Ottavia, and their daughter, he was drawn to BJJ because of its difficulty, effectiveness, and authenticity. In typically candid Bourdain fashion, he describes his newfound obsession:

> 57 when I started. Had never been in a gym in my life. Lifetime heavy smoker. Overweight. Coming up on 59 now. I train every day, wherever I can. If I'm home, I'll do a private followed by GenPop class . [*sic*] Every day. . [*sic*] If away, I'll take what I can get: preferably classes with some hard rolling . . . Conventional wisdom is that I should allow myself recovery time [*sic*]. That training every day is not wise. I say fuck that. The clock is ticking. Im [*sic*] not getting any faster, more flexible or more durable. Gotta get in what training I can—learn as much as I can, get as good as I can before I leave this life like I began it: diapered and screaming.
> (www.reddit.com/r/bjj/comments/30z933/older_practitioners_how_old_were_you_when_you)

Bourdain clearly craved this daily dose of difficult and authentic martial arts. To hear most BJJ practitioners tell it, we are drawn to this art precisely because it is brutal, real, immediately effective, and constantly humbling. For many, BJJ is instrumental in their cultivation of many of these related virtues. These claims of BJJ's brutal effectiveness are at the very core of the 'origin story' of BJJ in America. If you happen to get stuck next to a BJJ practitioner on an airplane (or at the Thanksgiving table) you will invariably hear some version of the following: BJJ proved it was the most effective hand-to-hand combat discipline in the world during the first Ultimate Fighting Championship (UFC), in November of 1993. Expert practitioners of various martial arts (including boxing, kickboxing, Taekwondo, Karate, Savate, Sumo, Shootfighting, and BJJ) participated in a single-elimination, eight-man submission tournament. Although shrouded in both legend and controversy, the UFC settled the age-old debate about martial arts supremacy when a slight, unassuming member of the legendary Gracie family of BJJ, Royce Gracie, submitted all of his opponents skillfully and quickly (averaging less than two minutes per fight). For Bourdain (and me for that matter), the continued success of BJJ in all areas of mixed martial arts, makes it a compelling candidate for a martial arts path.

At its best, BJJ is a bullshido free zone. There are many features of BJJ (and numerous other martial arts) that actively work against the cultivation of certain vices like self-delusion and gullibility. One particularly (and often painfully) enlightening feature of BJJ is that there's little room for self-deception regarding one's martial arts prowess. In his essay, "The Pleasure of Drowning," neuroscientist and philosopher Sam Harris puts it nicely:

> There are few experiences as startling as being effortlessly controlled by someone your size or smaller and, despite your full resistance, placed in a choke hold, an arm lock, or some other 'submission'. A few minutes of this and, whatever your previous training, your incompetence will become so glaring and intolerable that you will want to learn whatever this person has to teach. ("The Pleasure of Drowning")

In virtually every training session, on the BJJ tatami across the globe, practitioners must roll (spar) for several rounds with partners of various belt/skill levels. Thus, for the first few months/years of training, you're daily confronted with how easily, while fully resisting, you can be murdered at the hands of another. Sticking with a BJJ school after the first few sessions (when most people apparently quit) is to enter a world of daily ego-slaying humbling in a most visceral and authentic proving ground.

You might be asking: why if BJJ can be so effective in training the body and mind and in helping to cultivate the various skills and virtues of humility, self-control, and authenticity, does Bourdain's journey not end happily or with higher levels of personal discipline and enlightenment? This is where paying closer attention to many of the schools of thought that engage with the virtues of combat can be illuminating. Lurking behind and within each of these philosophical schools of thought are cautionary remarks regarding the connections between martial arts training and other areas of your life. Intense martial arts training can indeed be very self-revelatory. It can show us our personal and moral strengths and weaknesses. It can provide one valuable component of a path forward to self-improvement. But . . . in an unbalanced life, it can wreak havoc. It can never become a surrogate for the cultivation of other virtues, and for the cessation of core vices.

Authenticity and Appreciation

Bourdain seemed invariably driven to live a life of authenticity and radical honesty. He often spoke with uncomfortably self-deprecating honesty about his limits (and even failures) as a chef, author, TV personality, martial artist and even friend, husband, and father. He brought a similarly refreshing authenticity and compelling curiosity to his engagements with the people, foods, and customs that he encountered. Beneath all of his work there appears to be a deep existential desire to live both fearlessly and authentically.

Authenticity is often conceived of as a personal or even existential virtue. Philosophers such as Martin Heidegger connect this virtue of authenticity with a host of other traits and other virtues (such as integrity, perseverance, and openness) that must be cultivated to live authentically ("Authenticity"). At his best, Bourdain exhibited a profound degree of authenticity in his work and in his life. This is arguably what is most compelling about him and why millions of fans enthusiastically tuned in to watch the many iterations of his travelogue shows. Many journalists, friends, and scholars have written about his traits, virtues, and vices as they are often on full display through his works.

He too was very candid about his struggles with addiction, relationships, self-doubt, and general recklessness. And again, many fans love him precisely because of his candor and the seeming fearlessness with which he articulated and explored his own existential mess. And although not a primary focus of Aristotle himself, our philosophical understanding of authenticity can be enhanced through seeing its relationship to the vices that are on both ends of the continuum. Contemporary philosopher Ernesto V. Garcia describes authenticity in a way that fittingly captures Bourdain's struggle:

it resembles traditional Aristotelian virtues insofar as it can involve steering a middle course between two extremes, viz., a 'deficiency' (i.e., various forms of inauthenticity) and an 'excess' (i.e., a type of narcissistic self-centeredness which critics of authenticity rightly disparage). ("The Virtue of Authenticity", p. 273)

In a very tragic and disturbing way, the *Roadrunner* film chronicles Bourdain's existential crisis near the end of his life. These themes of the virtues of loyalty, authenticity, and integrity run into his vices of egoistic excess and self-deception. I would like to think that his commitment to BJJ provided some solace, enlightenment, or at least a much-needed escape from the vicissitudes of life with which he struggled. Perhaps it's no coincidence that during the final months before his death, he had moved away from his daily BJJ routine and returned to many unhealthy habits. Longtime friend and collaborator, Michael Steed remarked:

> There was this peak period where he seemed happy. That addictive personality was just all focused on jiu-jitsu. He wasn't asking about my family or anything, but he looked great; he had all this energy. At one point, at the end of a scene, he almost hugged me and I was kind of like "What the hell?"
>
> And then fucking what's-her-name enters his life, and he starts smoking again, and it just sort of got back into that negative energy that fit this weird fantasy character that he felt he was, and needed a counterpart to. (*Bourdain: The Definitive Biography*, p. 330).

Many of those around him were aware of both the positive role that BJJ played in his physical and mental life, and also how deeply he still wrestled with living authentically. In the end, I only wish that BJJ (or anything else) could have better served him in his existential struggle for peace.

I am grateful for Anthony Bourdain's larger than life presence on this planet and his legacy of passion and curiosity for the people, food, and customs of the world. I am thankful to have shared in this brotherhood of the Gentle Art of Brazilian jiu-jitsu. I believe that it has the tools to make us better fighters, better peacemakers, and more virtuous members of the communities in which we find ourselves.

7

Anthony Bourdain's Extremely Objectionable Stories

ERIC HOLMES

Perhaps we need to hear stories like this. Perhaps we deserve it.

These words, spoken by an unnamed storyteller in Anthony Bourdain's *Hungry Ghosts*, speak to the love that Bourdain had for storytelling. While largely known for his work in nonfiction and documentary television, Bourdain also had an affinity for retribution-laced tales of terror and moral-of-the-story imparting fables. He was especially partial to EC Comics New Trend titles like *Tales from the Crypt, The Vault of Horror,* and *The Haunt of Fear.* Bourdain's love of EC Comics was so pronounced that he and co-author Joel Rose dedicated their graphic novel *Hungry Ghosts* to those much-reviled works of horror fiction.

Much like the fables of Aesop (except with a lot more corpses and histrionics), EC Comics' tales offered fitting and often hilarious examples of evil plots gone awry and antagonists suitably chastened. EC Comics did not invent the concept of *just desserts*; the folk tradition carries with it a wide array of similar tales, many of which have been published in a variety of media, including in *Hungry Ghosts.* As a volume, *Hungry Ghosts* offers tales of terror that include an underlying theme that is also reflected in many of the stories told by Aesop: be decent or be destroyed.

Aside from Bourdain's love of EC Comics, he was familiar with the works of Aesop, as the title of his 1995 novel *Bone in the Throat* is a direct reference to Aesop's notable tale of a wolf with a bone stuck in his throat employing the aid of a crane to remove it, much to the crane's dismay.

Hungry Ghosts is a collection of nine horror stories drawn from Japanese folklore with a distinctively EC Comics-like presentation in both form and content. Like much in the realm of folktales, each story is a cautionary tale that entertains while it conveys a lesson to the readers. Like EC Comics horror tales published in *Tales from the Crypt, The Vault of Horror,* and *The Haunt of Fear* in the 1950s, *Hungry Ghosts* offers satisfying and schadenfreude-filled stories of bad people being punished for doing bad things: a cold-hearted cook who refuses to feed a hungry vagrant and is summarily consumed himself as a result; a ravenous glutton of horsemeat trampled by the angry spirit of a horse that he devoured; a bully who is taught the error of his ways by a vengeful spirit who literally removes whatever is stuck up his ass that makes him so mean; and on it goes. As well, the stories often include particularly fitting methods of punishment being meted out upon the depraved antagonists and *Hungry Ghosts'* second tale, "The Pirates", is a prime example.

In "The Pirates," a ship happens upon a lone woman stranded at sea, clinging to life. As the men approach her in the water, one comments, "I believe there's a Latin phrase for this situation", which is greeted with a response of, "Yeah, I think it's called 'rape'," bringing about raucous laughter from the ship's crew. Upon boarding the ship, the woman is tormented with crass comments and the captain invites her to join him in his cabin, his lascivious intent plain to see. He then comments that once he finishes his ghastly task that, "my men will also be requiring . . . some attention." Once inside of the captain's chambers, the woman castrates the captain and summarily castrates all members of the crew, revealing herself to be a *Sazae Oni,* a shapeshifter whose true form mimics that of an enormous shellfish. *Sazae Oni* pretend to be drowning or lost at sea to lure in their victims and the crew in "The Pirates" literally felt the bite of their folly.

In these tales, acts of evil and even merely intended acts of evil are met with brutal rejoinders, albeit in the form of violence and terror instead of wit and humor. Bourdain, in his *Hungry Ghosts*, pays homage to the use of the narrative form to convey morality through the coercive use of cautionary tales.

Hungry Ghosts, despite being published as a limited series of comic books and later as a collected graphic novel, is a work of folklore. Each story is a re-imagining of a classic Japanese folktale focused on characters who commit sins and are thusly punished by the universe for their moral turpitude. Whether suffering the cardinal sins of greed, lust, gluttony, or other disreputable acts such as bullying and breaking a promise, the culprits are punished for their indiscretion.

Stories like the ones published in *Hungry Ghosts* fall under the category of *fables* or *legends,* as they include too much supernatural and fantastical content to be considered the more-believable *urban* legends. While urban legends abound with stories of hook-handed killers, babysitters tripping on LSD, and Kentucky fried rats, they do not abound with tales of hauntings, possessions, and horrific monsters. By and large, people are less inclined to believe fables with their fantastic notions than the more grounded urban legends but that does not take away from their use in narrative-based argumentation. Despite their on-the-surface absurdity, fables are culturally vital, as they represent societal aspirations for decorum and civility.

According to folklorist Jan Brunvand's work on urban legends, the inclusion of a "meaningful message or 'moral'" is a defining characteristic of fables. Aside from their value as entertainment, tales like those in *Hungry Ghosts* use a coercive strategy to convey basic morality.

In the chapter of *Hungry Ghosts* entitled "The Snow Woman," a young man and his father get lost during a snowstorm while on a hunting trip. The young man awakens to find a female specter killing his father, who then proceeds to seduce the young man, sparing his life if he promises never to tell anyone what happened. Upon returning home, the young man meets a young homeless woman who is new to the village. He offers her a job at his family's business and they soon after fall in love and marry. Years later after the death of his mother, he decides to share the story of his father's death with his wife, who is soon revealed to be the very same specter who seduced him years earlier. In a rage, she kills him and vanishes, leaving their children orphaned.

In "The Snow Woman," the young man broke a promise, albeit for the decent reason of being honest with his wife about his past and the death of his father. Despite his motive, he violated a covenant that he agreed to and was thereby punished. Fables like "The Snow Woman" offer an implied threat toward the audience in the form of a warning, using the fate of others as an example. Brunvand notes that such tales provide "good examples of 'poetic justice'" and stories like those in *Hungry Ghosts* are vital parts of the social fabric that fill an essential need. These stories work to instill in the audience the idea that actions have consequences and that there are behaviors that are categorically repellant and deserving of punishment. Brunvand explains that "to be retained in a culture, any form of folklore must fill some genuine need, whether this be the need for an entertaining escape from reality, or a desire to validate by anecdotal examples some of the culture's ideals and institutions" (p. 12).

Aside from a modern folklorist like Brunvand, there is another notable thinker who has expressed his fandom for the use of stories to convey moral teachings—Aristotle. In his work *Rhetoric,* Aristotle argues in favor of using yarns like those in *Hungry Ghosts* due to their accessibility and ease of use. He notes that, "Fables are suitable for addresses to popular assemblies; and they have one advantage—they are comparatively easy to invent, whereas it's hard to find parallels among actual past events." As a tool to connect to the masses, nothing beats entertainment and the continued use of stories to convey morality since the world of the ancients demonstrates that. Just as the ancient Greeks flocked to watch the tragedies of Sophocles and to hear the heroic epics of Homer, modern audiences flock to watch the movies of Marvel Studios and to read the *Harry Potter* novels of J.K. Rowling. Despite their utility, stories like those in *Hungry Ghosts* and their use as a moral dowsing rod has a notable detractor: Plato.

In *Republic,* Plato argues to his brother Adeimantus that there is a need for educating citizens on stories both true and false, noting that "we first tell stories to children" and that "these are false, on the whole, though they have some truth in them." The stories that Plato is referring to are fables, those charming tales shared by Aesop that offer a moral to the audience to inspire proper behavior. Plato, however, is not a fan of the type of tales told in *Hungry Ghosts.* In a dialogue with Adeimantus in *Republic*, Plato defends censorship of tales that have the potential to damage people's delicate sensibilities. In discussing the Greek myth of Cronus castrating his father and throwing his testicles into the ocean, Plato states that such tales of woe must, "certainly not be lightly told to young and thoughtless persons." Plato's reasoning is that "a young person cannot judge what is allegorical and what is literal; anything that he receives into his mind at that age is likely to become indelible and unalterable; and therefore, it is most important that the tales which the young first hear should be models of virtuous thoughts." While that's fine and dandy in theory, any readers of this book who happen to be parents know that scary stories are highly effective parenting tools.

Young children lack the cognitive development to fully understand nuanced argumentation of the sort offered by moral philosophers. With that in mind, coercive strategies may be necessary. Want your son to stop sucking his thumb? Tell him that the scissor-man will cut it off. Want your daughter not to play with matches? Tell her that she'll burn to death if she does and that her pet will be sad. Plato, however, disagrees, asking, "shall we just carelessly allow children to hear any casual tales which may be devised by casual persons, and to receive into their minds ideas for the most part the very opposite of those which we should wish them to have when they are grown up?" Clearly, Plato never had the misfortune of raising a child who insists on clogging the toilet because it's fun. The Boogeyman, El Coco, Magnus, and the Baba Yaga are all used to elicit children's compliance under the auspice of "Act poorly and you'll get eaten," while Santa Claus serves as the yin to that yang; behave and be rewarded. Plato's lack of fandom for coercive tales is notable in that it comes from Plato, but he generally stands alone in his assessment, as later generations felt differently, including his own pupil Aristotle.

Despite his insistence that terror tales should not be told to children, Plato frequently sang the praises of fear. In *Euthyphro*, Plato crafts a dialogue between his mentor Socrates and religious prophet Euthyphro wherein Socrates differentiates fear into two camps: fear without shame (such as fear of illness) and fear with shame. Fear with shame is brought about solely by your behavior and the inherent dread that derives from the threat of that behavior being discovered, thus earning you a "reputation for wickedness." In *Protagoras, Laches,* and *Laws,* Plato mimics this notion, arguing that fear is a result of the "anticipation of pain" and an "expectation of future evil." Aristotle shares this sentiment, arguing in *Rhetoric* that, "Fear may be defined as a pain or disturbance due to a mental picture of some destructive or painful evil in the future." While the tales told in *Hungry Ghosts* are works of fiction that are often set in the past, the dread that they provoke on the part of the readers concerns a future filled with doom if they themselves step out of line.

In *Republic,* Plato differentiates shame and fear with an example of an attack on an elderly person by a younger one: shame would prevent the action internally while the fear of external consequence ("the fear that the others would come to the aid of the victim," as Plato states) would equally prevent it. Finally, Plato expresses in Books I and III of *Laws* that fear is essential toward good citizenry, what he calls "modesty." In detailing the means for creating a nation in *Laws,* Plato states that, "Two things, then, contribute to victory: fearlessness in the face of the enemy, and fear of ill-repute among one's friends" and that "Every individual should therefore become both afraid and unafraid." Later, Plato offers a callback to the idea of modesty, noting that, "we have called this fear 'modesty' often enough, and we said that people who aspire to be good must be its slave." Despite his opposition to using terror tales as an argumentative tool, Plato clearly supports the use of fear to curb people's baser desires, a sentiment mirrored almost two thousand years later by Thomas Hobbes in *Leviathan.*

Regardless of his mentor's opposition to the use of terror tales upon impressionable audiences, his own praise for stories as a tool to connect to audiences, and his note on the occasional need to frighten an audience, it's clear that Aristotle would approve of *Hungry Ghosts,* and he would not be alone.

From the early-nineteenth-century publication of the tales collected by the Grimm brothers to Heinrich Hoffmann's *Struwwelpeter,* violent tales of moral impact have long been marketed to children. EC Comics used the same storytelling model in the 1950s with its New Trend line of horror comics, which served as an inspiration for Bourdain in his writing of *Hungry Ghosts.*

The use of stories to convey moral lessons and cultural truths is as old as language itself. It's fitting that Anthony Bourdain, a man who always maintained his humility despite significant fame as well as a man who was never too good for any food offered to him, would see the value of folktales to keep people's baser desires at bay.

Or at least keep them from encountering their baser desires. In Chapter 10 of his book *Medium Raw*, Bourdain details his efforts to keep his daughter away from fast food. In that work, he acknowledges that well-researched and reported works like Eric Schlosser's *Fast Food Nation* will fall silently on the ears of young children who want a Happy Meal and the branded toy that it includes. With this in mind, he relies upon that method that Aesop seemingly invented, EC Comics illustrated, and he himself re-envisioned: the cautionary tale.

He writes about a conversation with his then two-and- a-half-year-old daughter wherein he states that McDonald's mascot Ronald McDonald, "has cooties . . . and you know . . . he smells bad too. Kind of like . . . poo!" to which his daughter asks with concern, "If you hug Ronald you can get . . . cooties?" His reply? "Some say . . . yes . . . Some people talk about the smell, too . . . I'm not saying it rubs off on you or anything—if you get too close to him—but . . ." to which his daughter replies with a horrified "Ewwww!"

On his efforts to sway his daughter away from fast food, Bourdain writes, "The stakes are high. As I see it, nothing less than the heart, mind, soul, and physical health of my only child" and that "An early, traumatic, Ronald-related experience can only be good for her."

Clearly, Anthony Bourdain sees the value of the cautionary tale as more than just entertainment; he sees it as a tool for educating an audience on decorum and propriety. Bourdain's statement from *Hungry Ghosts* that started this chapter is true: we need cautionary tales to show us that actions have consequences and that at the end of the meal, the check is due. Whether we deserve cautionary tales like those told to us in *Hungry Ghosts* remains to be seen.

8
Why Do We Care Who Bourdain Really Was?

Margot Finn

Helen Rosner's 2018 eulogy of Anthony Bourdain in *The New Yorker* describes him as the "best-known celebrity in America," not meaning that he was the most famous person in the country, but that he was the famous person most truly known by his fans.

His fame was not, she said, "the distant, lacquered type of an actor or a musician." Instead, "Bourdain felt like your brother, your uncle, your impossibly cool dad—your *realest*, smartest friend. . . . Another way of putting it is that Anthony Bourdain built his career on telling the *truth*" (emphasis added). Bourdain is often celebrated for being authentic. From *Kitchen Confidential*'s "wild-but-*true*" glimpse at the hidden underbelly of New York City restaurants to his globe-trotting television shows, he had access to places his readers couldn't go and promised to bring them his genuine impressions, raw and unvarnished.

He also earned his fans' devotion by convincing them that he was offering them himself, raw and unvarnished: casually profane, open about his likes and dislikes, eating and drinking and smoking his way around the world on no one else's agenda. The introduction from the episode of *Parts Unknown* about Mexico periodically surfs through my social media feeds, usually anchored by a photograph of Bourdain flashing his middle finger at the camera with one hand, an open longneck beer bottle in the other. His diction was infamously peppered with especially enthusiastic use of the word *fuck*. Because he so clearly refused to cater to the norms of polite society, it is often assumed he was being true to himself.

For example, Patrick Radden Keefe's *New Yorker* interview "Anthony Bourdain's Moveable Feast" is summarized in their search results: "Bourdain speaks to Patrick Radden Keefe about how he makes television while staying *true to himself.*" However, in the article itself, Keefe concludes that Bourdain's "sensualist credo" was something of an elaborate façade: "if you spend any time with Bourdain, you realize he is controlled to the point of neurosis: clean, organized, disciplined, courteous, systematic. He is Apollo in drag as Dionysus."

In *The Birth of Tragedy*, Friedrich Nietzsche uses the Greek gods Apollo and Dionysus to represent two competing cultural forces: Apollo corresponds to the rational, analytical, and controlled while Dionysus, set in opposition, represents the wild, intoxicated, and insane.   Rosner also suggests Bourdain was something of a false satyr, and more truly like the calm sculptor god than some ecstatic reveler. She notes his insistence on being "twenty minutes early to every appointment, to the minute" and the obsessive care with which he crafted every episode of *No Reservations* (originally broadcast on the Travel Channel from 2005 to 2012) and *Parts Unknown* (2013–2018, CNN), "plotting every shot, musical cue, and visual flourish." While authenticity need not always be spontaneous, the meticulous intentionality in his self-presentation seems at odds with the idea that what Bourdain was delivering was really the unfiltered, unvarnished truth.

Rosner's claim about how well his fans knew him also seems strange in light of the many examples she gives of how cagey and protective he was about his personal life. She describes a time he grilled her about how she had intuited his romantic involvement with the Italian actress Asia Argento. "He took his phone out and scrolled through his recent tweets," Rosner reported, "asking me to point out specific evidence. 'We're trying to keep it under wraps', he said." Rosner herself notes that "particularly when he wasn't the one controlling the narrative, Bourdain could be slippery about personal matters."

Many of those close to Bourdain also refused to speak to Charles Leerhsen for the "unauthorized" biography published by Simon and Schuster in October 2022. According to Kim Severson, Leerhsen was given access to Bourdain's laptop and phone by his estate, which is controlled by Bourdain's wife. However, Bourdain's agent reportedly instructed people to keep mum, and many who were close to Bourdain including Argento, Bourdain's brother, and his close friend and fellow celebrity chef Eric Ripert have all distanced themselves from the book and disavowed its contents.

Who Was Bourdain Really, and Why Does It Matter?

Unlike most celebrities, whose personas seem designed to cater to the desires and expectations of the public, Bourdain seemed irrepressibly, even defiantly, unconstrained by social convention. The persona he crafted and convinced many was congruent with his true self seemed essentially, existentially free. And he appeared to be living the proverbial dream: traveling around the world in search of the most interesting and pleasurable food and enjoying it with fascinating locals, friends, lovers, and the occasional sitting US president.

The nature of his death raises inevitable questions. As Leerhsen describes the mystery he set out to solve in writing the unauthorized biography, "We never had that big story, that long piece that said what happened, how the guy with the best job in the world took his own life." But unlike Leerhsen, I don't feel entitled to an explanation for Bourdain's suicide nor expect to find one in his final texts and emails. Nor do I expect to get an answer to the question of who Bourdain really was. However, I think it's notable that the persona Bourdain created and seemed to inhabit was defined in some ways by its claim to authenticity.

Unlike restaurants where you only see the perfectly plated dish, tour guides that only recommend restaurants that cater to tourists, or travel shows whose itineraries and narratives are carefully sanitized to omit unpleasantries like colonialism and drug wars, Bourdain promised and convinced many of us that he was offering us something grittier and realer, less pretty perhaps but often more beautiful, always more interesting, and closer to something that feels true. Perhaps that makes us care about the veracity of the Bourdain we thought we knew. Or maybe it's the fear that his death is a kind of cautionary tale about what looked very much like an embodiment of individual freedom. Could Bourdain's last secret, hidden truth be that traveling around the world and eating whatever you like, beholden to no one, is actually miserable?

The kind of freedom Bourdain represented does not strike me as especially Dionysian, although it is easy to be misled by the sensual pleasures highlighted in his culinary adventuring and things like his openness about his use of heroin and smoking cigarettes. He styled himself very much like a hedonistic reveler, but that image never fit with his meticulous crafting of his shows or careful control of what personal information he allowed to become public. The freedom he represented was less the freedom from his own internal Apollonian restraint than a freedom from external social forces.

The difference is exemplified by a scene in *Parts Unknown*, Season Eleven, Episode 3, "Newfoundland," where Bourdain and two of the chefs he was eating his way around the Canadian province with were enjoying a multi-course meal at the kind of restaurant where the wine served with each course is announced as it is poured. Just after one of these announcements, the men clink glasses and say "Cheers," and then one of them adds, "To the Queen," almost as an afterthought. The other two men proceed to take a sip, but Bourdain stops short at the mention of her majesty's name. "No man, I hate the aristocracy," he says, moving to put his glass back on the table. If Bourdain represented freedom, it was not the freedom to enjoy Dionysian intoxication without any fear of the consequences, but freedom from the requirement to go along with obsequious gestures of fealty to an authority you don't believe in.

Freedom and Suffering

The notion that conforming to society's expectations is the cause of most modern unhappiness is central to the philosophy and fiction of Jean-Paul Sartre. In his plays and novels, the characters' suffering is almost always caused by their caving to external, social pressures. Again and again, his didactic fables insist that the cause of *mauvaise foi* or "bad faith" was prostituting one's true, personal desires and individual self-expression in the name of conformity. It's not clear whether Sartre thought this species of misery was particular to the stuffy bourgeoisie of his and Simone de Beauvoir's upbringing or more widespread, maybe even the characteristic psychological condition of modernity. However universal, his sketches of the tension between the self and society remain among our most indelible. The ending lines of *No Exit* distill his refrain to its purest essence: *Hell is other people.*

As if he'd conjured himself as some sort of existentialist superhero, Bourdain's personal brand was oriented around the refusal to conform to what society expected or wanted. Even being taciturn about his family and romantic life doesn't undermine his authenticity because it violates the nature of celebrity itself. In *Dead Famous*, Greg Jenner defines the *celebrity* as, in part, "a unique persona made widely known to the public via media coverage, and whose life is publicly consumed as dramatic entertainment." Bourdain's refusal to let his entire life become entertainment and insistence on keeping some matters private was just one more way he refused to capitulate to anyone else's expectations. No matter how meticulously crafted, his public persona felt congruent with his real persona, not designed to please anyone else. He seemed like the same person wherever he appeared.

His suicide is perhaps even more of an affront than suicide always is by its very nature, or more puzzling than most self-willed deaths for those who mostly want to live. He wasn't the first to create popular entertainment out of the culinary travelogue, but it's a peculiar genre in some ways. As with pornography, it titillates with pleasures that are, by definition, out of reach for the viewer. The pleasures of watching Bourdain eat his way around the world were less about the food itself or the gustatory experiences he was having than they were about the fantasy of moving through the world as he seemed to, free from the bad faith of stuffy bourgeois propriety and posturing.

Who's the Boss?

This was never more evident than in the infamous episode that kicked off Season Eight of *Parts Unknown,* "Hanoi," which ends with him eating bun cha and spring rolls and drinking a beer with President Barack Obama near the end of his eight years in office. A full thirty minutes of the episode go by before Obama's appearance, which is immediately preceded by Bourdain getting scanned with a metal detector as the presidential motorcade pulls up to the street market where the voiceover noted moments before, "the lady selling vegetables and gum and cigarettes taking a nap under a piece of corrugated tin has no idea what's about to happen." As Obama steps out of the car, the James Brown song "The Boss" plays and cheering crowds wave and take pictures.

It's a scene designed to emphasize in every possible way the magnitude of the sitting President's celebrity and how much it was due to Obama's own particular brand of coolness. In a lecture given at the New York Public Library on the eve of his first election, Zadie Smith compares the multivocal, multi-racial Obama to Cary Grant, who was born Archibald Leach in Bristol, England, and became an American film star with a suave, placeless accent: "'Everyone wants to be Cary Grant,' said Cary Grant. 'Even I want to be Cary Grant.' It's not hard to imagine Obama having that same thought, backstage at Grant Park, hearing his own name chanted by the hopeful multitude: Everyone wants to be Barack Obama. Even I want to be Barack Obama."

Standing at the street market under the watchful eye of a limited security detail, the president everyone wanted to be and the man with the best job in the world make small talk about the aromas, culinary and otherwise, that you smell everywhere outside the US. Then, they enter what Bourdain tells us in voiceover is "one of these classic, funky, family-run noodle shops you find all over Hanoi" where "dinner and a beer cost about six dollars." "How often do you get to sneak out for a beer?" Bourdain asks the president, and Obama replies, "First of all, I don't get to *sneak out* ever," before describing how even on the rare occasions he and Michelle go out on a date, they typically get shunted off into restaurants' private dining rooms.

The episode shows Obama asking for guidance on how to put together the bowl of bun cha as Bourdain's voiceover praises the president's skill at handling the sticky, cold noodles. Their conversation ranges from the fried fish and rice Obama enjoyed at a street stall in Indonesia, where he spent some time as a kid, to oblique references to then-candidate Donald Trump's promised border wall. The interview with Patrick Radden Keefe took place immediately on the heels of filming the episode. Bourdain blames his recent resumption of smoking on Obama and seems to be planning the soundtrack as he talks to Keefe:

> He sang the chorus to himself—"I paid the cost to be the boss"—and remarked that one price of leadership, for Obama, had been a severe constraint on the very wanderlust that Bourdain personifies. "Even drinking a beer for him is a big thing," he marveled. "He's got to clear it." Before he said goodbye to Obama, Bourdain told me, he had underlined this contrast. "I said, 'Right after this, Mr. President, I'm getting on a scooter and I'm going to disappear into the flow of thousands of people'. He got this look on his face and said, 'That must be nice'." (Keefe 2017)

If the cameras captured that exchange, Bourdain didn't include it in the episode, but the implication seems clear enough nonetheless: at least in that moment, *even Barack Obama wanted to be Anthony Bourdain*.

It's a pretty epic flex. What's better than being the so-called "leader of the free world"? Being Anthony Fucking Bourdain, that's what. What's something the President of the United States cannot do? Have a beer in public without security clearance getting involved, eat a six-dollar bowl of noodles, and disappear into the Hanoi night on a scooter.

According to a short retrospective on the *Parts Unknown* website called "Director's Cut: Why Obama Wanted to Sit Down with Bourdain" written by the White House staffer responsible for helping set up the meeting, Obama's people agreed that Bourdain could choose the locations and Secret Service would find a way to make them work: "Exceptions were made to allow Obama to go to a small noodle shop where the other diners hadn't gone through security screening. As someone who traveled inside the presidential bubble, I could only guess at how challenging this had been as we rode in a smaller-than-usual unmarked motorcade to meet Bourdain on a simple side street in Hanoi."

The reasons Bourdain chose such a motorcade-unfriendly location are made clear by the episode's opening, which is a paean not just to Hanoi and Vietnam, but specifically to the mode of independent transport most common to their crowded streets. "Listen to me. *Listen. To. Me.*" Bourdain begins, "There's no other way to see this city Hanoi than from a motorbike or scooter. To do otherwise would be to miss it *all*. It is one of the great pleasures of my life to join the river of people rushing through the streets." This also serves to explain the nearly two minutes at the beginning of the episode devoted to showing Bourdain and others riding these personal crotch rockets, often while glancing down at phones in the midst of weaving through traffic and each contributing their individual rumbling part to what subtitles will tell you in brackets is a *cacophony*. The whole story of the episode is about the freedom Bourdain enjoyed riding his scooter through the streets of Hanoi. Even the coolest president in memory of the most powerful country in the world couldn't simply disappear into the cacophony, apparently dependent on and beholden to no one, free to go wherever he will at potentially reckless speeds.

The Cost of Freedom

In the 2001 movie *Waking Life,* philosophy professor Robert Solomon notes that "Existentialism is often discussed as if it's a philosophy of despair." Thanks to the precision of social media's targeted advertising, I am the proud owner of a shirt that reads, *My unyielding melancholy brings all the existentialists to the yard*, which apparently makes enough sense to enough people to merit mass production. But as Solomon explains, that wasn't how existentialists themselves characterized their philosophy: "I think the truth is just the opposite. Sartre, once interviewed, said he never really felt a day of despair in his life. One thing that comes out from reading these guys is not a sense of anguish about life so much as, a real kind of exuberance, of feeling on top of it, it's like your life is yours to create." The notion that you could and should choose individual desire over suffocating social expectations was meant to be liberating.

Still, Sartre acknowledged that there were costs and displeasures associated with casting off social norms. Absolute freedom may have been desirable, or necessary even, to avoid the trap of *mauvaise foi*, but it was also vertiginous. As Søren Kierkegaard poignantly put it, "anxiety is the dizziness of freedom." Existentialists argued that our capacity to interact with the world according to our own individual choices was the only thing keeping us from leading useless, fleeting lives entirely subject to external forces. However, they acknowledged the difficulty involved in doing so. That's why so few people are willing to really rebel.

Bourdain's suicide, the self-willed death of a self-styled rebel, raises questions about the desirability of liberation. Perhaps Bourdain was seized by some species of romantic despair, as Leerhsen's account seems to suggest, or struggling with the long afterlife of his addictions, or depressed due to a neurochemical imbalance that could have been ameliorated with the right treatment, or maybe not. The possibility that haunts me is that the freedom he sought became its own kind of trap, that in the end the despair he could not escape was caused in some fundamental way by the terrible burden of being Anthony Bourdain.

A passage from Leerhsen's biography suggests that Bourdain was preoccupied with not being "a pretender," although he disliked the word *authentic*:

> He often said he hated the word "authentic,"—his nearly two decades of world traveling having taught him the futility of striving for the unalloyed version of anything—but on a personal level, authenticity, in the sense of being the real thing and not a pretender, was his lifelong preoccupation. He wanted to show the world not who he was at bottom but rather who he preferred to be . . . Hence the inability to disengage himself from the television juggernaut that had turned him into Anthony Bourdain. (*Down and Out in Paradise*, p. 143)

There seems to be a contradiction here between his theoretically wanting to be "the real thing and not a pretender," and yet "show the world *not* who he was at bottom but rather *who he preferred to be*." Perhaps this is the inevitable curse of celebrity, and how famous people are often expected to simultaneously be who they really are and also who we want them to be. However, far more than most celebrities, Bourdain's persona was based on the notion of genuineness and truth telling. The character he crafted with meticulous care in his writing and television shows was supposed to be perfectly coeval with his real self. Leerhsen describes the character he seemed to prefer to be as "a genuine battle-scarred badass," but maybe having to be a badass all the time so as to not be found out to be "a pretender" got exhausting.

Disappearing in Plain Sight

Despite the many restrictions on Obama's life, there is a sense in which he may have been more free than Bourdain. In her lecture, "Speaking in Tongues," Zadie Smith argues that what made Obama so unusual as a politician was his ability to adopt many voices, not performatively, but authentically. Calling him a "genuinely many-voiced man,'" Smith says that if his story "has a moral it is that each man must be true to his selves, plural." The many voices Obama adopts convincingly in his memoir *Dreams from My Father* include young Jewish male, black old lady from the South Side, white woman from Kansas, Kenyan elders, white Harvard nerds, black Columbia nerds, activist women, churchmen, security guards, bank tellers, and even a British man called Mr. Wilkerson. This ability of Obama's to speak other people was a "disorienting talent in a president," Smith says, and likely contributed to the questions that dogged Obama through his campaign, especially from older Black politicians like Jesse Jackson, about whether Obama was really Black or Black enough.

However disorienting his liminality, Obama's talent for code-switching was crucial to his political career. It may also have given him more latitude to evolve even while living under intense public scrutiny. Bourdain did not speak other people the way Obama did. Instead, Bourdain spoke the same way at white tablecloth restaurants and Atlantic City diners and in the streets of Hanoi. The punctuality and politeness that so impressed both Keefe and Rosen was evident in every episode of television he filmed. Aside from his liberal use of f-bombs, Bourdain was unfailingly courteous, practically self-effacing.

The Hanoi episode sets up an exaggerated contrast between Obama being treated like royalty no matter where in the world he goes and Bourdain as a nobody in comparison to the Rock Star in Chief. Episode-framing scooter rides notwithstanding, it's surely a flight of fancy to imagine the towering, 6′4″ celebrity chef with his shock of white hair genuinely disappearing into a crowd in Vietnam, or perhaps anywhere. Though not as instantly recognizable around the world as Obama,

Bourdain was familiar enough to be hailed on his death as the "best known celebrity in America" in the pages of *The New Yorker* magazine. How easy was it for him to ever disappear? What was the cost of being Anthony Bourdain?

Bourdain's noteworthy courtesy strikes me as consonant with his conversational humility. Even when he was in front of the camera, he was always trying to redirect attention away from himself and onto whomever he was talking to. What made his show most unusual, not just in the realm of culinary television but any media anywhere, is how carefully and ardently he listened. His conversations never emphasized his own culinary expertise or experience, but always put the focus on the knowledge and stories of the people he was eating with or those involved in the work of cooking the food. It is Bourdain's apparent affinity for the disappearing act he dramatized at the end of the Hanoi episode, but performed in a more figurative sense in almost every recorded conversation, that makes me wonder if inhabiting the public persona he'd created for himself might have become a kind of prison.

Straightjacket or Spine?

In a staged conversation with Zadie Smith at the Nashville Public Library just after Obama's time in office had ended, author Ann Patchett asked her about meeting Obama in person. Late in his second term, he invited Smith and roughly a dozen other writers to a luncheon at the White House. "It's an extraordinary thing to meet someone who's in such a position of power who's still recognizably human, that's not such a usual state of affairs," Smith begins, and when Patchett presses her on how many people she's met in "such a position of power," she considers for a moment before continuing: "He's the only person I've ever met like that who, when people ask me what it's like to meet him, I say *it's exactly as you'd expect* because there is no gap between the person you see on TV and the man. There's a kind of congruence which is unusual I think. So it was nothing surprising but mainly because he was that guy who you think you know, the same person." Then, just to punctuate how unusual this quality is in politicians, Patchett asks, "What are you going to do if the next president is the same?" eliciting an eruption of rueful laughs and guffaws from the audience.

Bourdain did not have Obama's capacious code-switching ability, but both men were remarkable and unusual in the consistency with which they seemed to show up in the world.

Unlike most celebrities and politicians, both Bourdain and Obama managed to convince many of us that they really were the guys we thought we knew, that they were the same men in person who we saw on TV. Instead of the pandering we expect from those performing for votes and accolades, they seemed not to be constantly contorting themselves for other people. If being *authentic* is a meaningless or futile standard to strive for, then perhaps the word for it is *integrity*.

Maybe the desire to find the same kind of consistency in Bourdain is less about solving the mystery of his misery than an unquenchable hope in the possibilities he seemed to represent: to clearly enjoy Dionysian intoxication and pleasure, but also harness Apollonian rationality and control; to be famous enough to do what he did for a living, but be unconstrained by fame in the ways Obama was; to have the attention and love of a mass audience, but the privacy of someone with no celebrity; to be beholden to no higher authority or stuffy moralizing, but nonetheless live with integrity.

What we wish for Bourdain, and perhaps also for ourselves, is social recognition that feels less like a set of constraints than a form of structural support, an identity that functions less as straightjacket whose constraints are designed to cause suffering than the vertebrae of a spine that may support the changing shapes of our endlessly malleable, unpredictable, and utterly unreplicable selves.

9
Anthony Bourdain's Inquiring Mind

DOUG ANDERSON AND SAMANTHA MAURO

Over the course of his career, Anthony Bourdain came to embody a life of inquiry—of ongoing learning. He was neither a professional scientist nor a professional philosopher. He was a chef, a writer, a traveler, and a television personality. But in a pragmatic sense, he was a natural inquirer.

As a young chef, he was brash and self-assured with a willingness to expose the workings of kitchen life and to criticize and exclude others and their beliefs based on his prejudices, hearsay, and the thinnest of evidence. His love of food, however, entailed travel and ongoing encounters with different beliefs; people in other cultures eat differently, cook differently, and believe differently than a young, white American from New Jersey. As Bourdain matured and traveled more extensively, these differences he encountered became a source of inspiration instead of derision.

In places like Cambodia, Peru, and Saudi Arabia he encountered otherness that challenged his beliefs. Instead of excluding this otherness, Bourdain overcame his dogmatic stances and chose instead to inquire. In response to his friend Eric Ripert's claim that Bourdain's thinking had evolved in good ways over the course of his show *No Reservations*, Bourdain responded: "If you see change over time, it's because you learn a few things along the way . . . . Hopefully you learn" (http://www.aveceric.com/on-the-table).

Bourdain came to exemplify a method of inquiry extolled by American philosopher Charles Peirce. In his well-known essay "The Fixation of Belief," Peirce described what he called the "social impulse"—the recognition that others do not believe as we do. In the face of this otherness, Peirce suggested, there are three options which reject the possibility of learning. First, we may dogmatically and tenaciously cling to our current beliefs and exclude all other outlooks. Second, we can ask some communal "authority" such as a church, a political party, or a media entity to arbitrarily decide our beliefs for us. Or, third, we may adopt a priori, "intuitive" beliefs that "seem" reasonable but have no actual evidence to support them. These three ways of avoiding inquiry can respectively be dubbed the way of tenacity, the way of authority and the way of a priori belief. Peirce offers us a fourth method for establishing our beliefs, one that leads to learning and self-correction. This is the method of inquiry. It requires that we expose our beliefs to public criticism and demands that we be willing to admit that our beliefs may be wrong, in whole or in part. Peirce's method of inquiry involves a movement from moments of surprise and doubt, to hypothesizing better beliefs, to testing those new beliefs in experience. Bourdain's growth as a Peircean inquirer, from *Kitchen Confidential* to *Parts Unknown,* provides a good model for all human lives.

I'm All about Doubt

The pragmatic defense of inquiry advocated by Peirce begins with the belief that, over time, inquiry has demonstrably shown that it can arrive at better "truths" that improve human lives. Embracing a "scientific" method of inquiry is an existential commitment to the belief that we can live better by learning more about ourselves and our environment, leading to self-reflection and moral development as well. History reveals that even when people are allowed to believe as they wish, beliefs can be manipulated by social media, television and radio, and political entities. Only a person who desires to inquire has the tools to address and to fend off such manipulation and protect the cultural health of our communities. This is a lesson that Anthony Bourdain attempted to bring home to his audiences. Bourdain had tattooed on his arm a Latin phrase roughly translated, "I am certain of nothing." His life involved "an endless learning curve" and he embraced "the joy of being wrong, of being confused" (*Parts Unknown,* Season Twelve, Episode 4).

Bourdain overcame the dogmatic stances of his privileged upbringing and chose not to exclude and dismiss others' beliefs. For example, in *The Nasty Bits*, he "recognized the dogma in" his "own relentless sneering about the evils of fusion" and came "to believe that any overriding philosophy or worldview is the enemy of good eating" (p. 274). He became a learner and, in doing so, his "world" of cooking and culture expanded tremendously. In *Parts Unknown,* Andrew Friedman says Bourdain would go to difficult places and "would evidence, I think, an incredible humility. He was genuinely curious. He wasn't trying to teach them" (*Parts Unknown*, Season Twelve, Episode 4). Bourdain was trying to learn from rather than teach his various hosts. At the same time, he was hoping to edify and to educate his audience concerning the things *he* was learning; in this he was, like Hunter S. Thompson whom he admired, a good Gonzo journalist. In his television shows he taught his audience how to learn and inquire in a down-to-earth way that seemed achievable by everyone.

Inquiry, according to Peirce, begins with a problematic situation and a genuine experience of doubt. "Certainty," Bourdain claimed, "is my enemy. I'm all about doubt" (*Parts Unknown*, Season Twelve, Episode 4). Facing problems and doubting are uncomfortable and can catalyze a desire to learn and to overcome, change, or modify your habits of thought.

Genuine doubt often feels like surprise or shock. The fact that others believe differently is one catalyst of surprise. We might be surprised to learn that other cultures eat dog meat or worship different gods or believe different stories of human origin. Learning that others believe differently than ourselves is the linchpin; we must embrace the surprise that leads to learning. Surprise may also be initiated by simple factual resistance. For example, you thought you left your passport on the kitchen table but when you go to look, no passport is found. The fact of the matter, the missing passport, causes us to doubt our prior belief about where we put it. Anthony Bourdain described a variety of such moments in his life—surprises and differences in belief that eventually led him to adopt the life of an inquirer. As he mentioned, "taking your belief system on the road—or to other people's houses—makes me angry" (*Medium Raw,* p. 259). He chose awakening to remaining asleep in his dogmatic habits of belief.

The World Is Bigger than That

Bourdain recognized at an early age that food is powerful. It started with a family trip to France when he was nine years old. His parents left him and his brother in the car to go enjoy a meal without the interruption of their rambunctious kids. When they didn't hurry back, Bourdain realized there was something of importance in that restaurant and he was missing out.

Then there was the oyster—something that only people sophisticated enough were supposed to eat and to understand. To kids it just looks gross. Even most adults scoff at this jiggling flesh in a half shell. Bourdain was very observant at his tender age and perhaps a tad precocious. Wanting to grow up and to be grown up, he swallowed the oyster and credits it for kick-starting his curiosity into the world of gastronomy. Bourdain's inquiring mind and stomach eventually led him around the world. As he stated in the introduction to *No Reservations*: "I write. I travel. I eat. And I'm hungry for more."

He knew it was important enough to try to understand why someone believed a dish was good. This became a habit for his life: try to understand the importance of, the meaning of, and the goodness in food. Dishes can carry history, heritage, and the legacy of a culture and he wanted to find out as much as he could, from as many places as he could.

Bourdain was forty-four years old when his best-selling book *Kitchen Confidential* was published. The book, a personal exposé of restaurant cooking life in the US, was filled with romantic accounts of the dark sides of kitchen culture and it was rife with cynicism toward those who did not fit Bourdain's vision of "real life" in American restaurant kitchens. These views were one dimensional and often dogmatically maintained. The cynicism was aimed at vegans, vegetarians, nice or kind people in general, and the new and growing class of "celebrity chefs." The central irony is that the fame of the book took Bourdain very quickly into the role of celebrity chef. This role led to more popular books and his television shows having to do with food and travel, beginning with *A Cook's Tour* in 2002. In these initial stages of his public career, Bourdain continued to evidence traits of the tenacious, authoritative, and a priori beliefs that filled *Kitchen Confidential*. He snidely asked, for example, whether vegans and vegetarians don't wake up in the night craving bacon. Later, Bourdain openly resisted his own cynicism:

> The best times are when it's impossible to be cynical about anything. When you find yourself letting go of the past and your preconceptions and feel yourself in your basic nature, the snarkiness and suspicion, the irony and doubt disappear at least for a time. When for a few moments or a few hours, you change. (*No Reservations*, Season Two, Episode 11)

In the two years of *A Cook's Tour*, we see not only the lingering traits of dogmatic beliefs but also the elemental beginnings of Bourdain's existential shift to living a full life of inquiry. On the one hand, many of the early shows focused on outlandish and attention-getting feats such as eating the heart of a cobra. Though Bourdain was in fact seeking different and extreme experiences, he later regretted some of *A Cook's Tour's* extreme moments because they focused simply on entertainment value at the expense of learning more about those in other cultures and foods of the world. However, there are glimpses in the back half of the first season of *A Cook's Tour* where we see the inquiring side of Bourdain's travels begin to emerge. For example, when he traveled to Portugal, he was surprised by the fact that the community he was visiting lived so close to the animals they ate, unlike in the urban areas where he grew up and worked. He was awakened to the fact that eating meat actually entailed killing animals, that meat didn't just arrive in a ready-to-cook state: "I'm causing this to happen, I kept thinking. This pig has been hand-fed for six months, fattened up, these murderous goons hired—for me" (*Cook's Tour*, p. 21).

Another example is from his forays into Cambodia. Bourdain chose to visit, he said, because he "knew nothing about it." Though he found it "a little depressing" at first, he gradually and experientially came to learn the beauties of Cambodia, its people, and its food. There he began his quest to "eat how everyday people eat," a quest that informed most of the rest of his career (*Cook's Tour*, Season One, Episode 5). His tour of Cambodia involved both the otherness of belief and the surprise that are the bases of doubt and inquiry. Bourdain began to awaken to the possibility of altering his own long-standing and deeply ingrained beliefs about life and food.

By the time of *No Reservations*, Bourdain's show with the Travel Channel from 2005 to 2012, the inquiring side of Bourdain's character began to develop as the central feature of his work. In Season One of this show, Bourdain was continuing to make the transition from dogmatic provocateur to inquirer. By Season Two, that transition was in full gear. In Episode 3 of the second season, he explicitly sought "enlightenment." He realized that his hosts were "giving till it hurts to show me hospitality." He acknowledged the privilege of his own American life as a celebrity chef and the danger of trying to understand everything he encountered from the pretentious position of his own US upper middle-class life that included stops at Vassar and the Culinary Institute of America. After experiencing life in the Amazon basin, he had the following to say:

> A writer friend of mine wrote that the older he gets, the more he travels, the less he knows. I understand what he meant now. It seems that the more places I see and experience, the bigger I realize the

world to be. The more of it I become aware of, the more I realize how relatively little I know of it . . . how many places I still have to go. How much more there is to learn. Maybe that's enlightenment enough. To know that there is no final resting place of the mind. No moment of smug clarity. Perhaps wisdom, such as it is for me, means realizing how small I am and unwise. And how far I have yet to go." (*No Reservations*, Season Two, Episode 3)

We cannot think of a better expression of intellectual humility and an inquiring mind. We would note his mention of *experiencing*, not just *seeing*. Tourists "see"; inquirers "experience" and learn.

Bourdain's humility is reflected in the thought of Peirce who wrote that "in order to learn you must desire to learn and in so desiring not be satisfied with what you already incline to think" (*Essential Peirce II*, p. 48). There are many ways in which we humans block the way of inquiry, from simply ignoring evidence before us to overtly disallowing inquiry as, for example, when Republican members of the U.S. Congress banned the keeping of certain statistics related to gun violence, and presently are attempting to ban the teaching of Critical Race Theory. Moreover, the realization that inquiry is an ongoing journey and leads only to more inquiry and not "a final resting place of the mind," squares perfectly with the pragmatic theory of truth. Little 't' truth is constantly changing as we learn more; big 'T' Truth is not something we attain so much as an ideal goal at which we aim.

Genuine inquirers don't assert that inquiry has all the final "truths" at any given time. The beliefs of inquiry and science evolve over time as more learning occurs—that is the strength of the method. It is the only method of believing that is self-correcting, that can overcome its previous beliefs in the wake of finding better beliefs. This evolution of "truth" and belief is guided by experience, evidence, and honest and open inquiry. Bourdain understood that our beliefs are not fixed, and that inquiring is an ongoing quest: "The journey is part of the experience—or was for me—an expression of the seriousness of one's intent" (*Cook's Tour*, p. 251). By Season Seven of *No Reservations*, Bourdain returned to Cambodia, to the place he ventured in the first season of his first show, but this time he traveled with more experience, more wisdom, and more thoughtfulness. In reflecting on that first trip, he said: "It was my first shoot in Asia, and I was doing this trip in particular for all the wrong reasons. Looking back at that grainy video, I see someone glib, green, and generally clueless. A guy who had a lot to learn" (*No Reservations*, Season Seven, Episode 2).

From his travels, Bourdain developed a deeper desire to learn and to experience, and the otherness of belief gradually brought about the evolution in his thought that Eric Ripert noticed. In Jamaica and India, he learned to appreciate some vegetarian foods and lifestyles. In Vietnam he learned the simplicity of eating a hot bowl of noodles while seated on a low plastic chair on the sidewalk. In his role as celebrity chef, he realized that others such as Emeril Lagasse were not the "sellouts" he had thought them to be. Perhaps the most significant change in Bourdain's approach to food, travel, and inquiry occurred in 2006 on a trip to Beirut. He and his team went to enjoy and understand the foods and culture of this particular place and ended up in the midst of an armed conflict. In retrospect Bourdain noted:

> That experience changed everything for me. One day I was making television about eating and drinking, the next, I was watching the airport I'd just landed in a few days earlier, being blown up across the water from my hotel window. . . . I came away from that experience deeply embittered, confused—and determined to make television differently than I'd done before.

His shows were no longer simply aimed at enjoying food and drink. "The world," he stated, "is bigger than that. The stories more confusing, more complex, less satisfying in their resolutions." At this juncture, Bourdain became an even more intentional inquirer aiming to show to the audience through his own experiences the more down-to-earth realities of the cultures he visited. As he put it: "I just saw that these were realities beyond what was on my plate—and these realities almost inevitably informed what was—or was not—for dinner. To ignore them now seemed monstrous" (https://anthonybourdain.tumblr.com/tagged/Beirut).

This new, more intentional approach was particularly evident in his 2008 visit to Saudi Arabia. *No Reservations* held a contest for viewers to help Bourdain choose where he should travel next. Hundreds of places were tossed into the ring, but ultimately trailblazing female filmmaker Danya Alhamrani, clad in her traditional abaya covering, persuaded Bourdain to venture to her home in Jeddah, Saudi Arabia, promising a good time despite it being a dry (in two ways) country. Bourdain appeared cynical and skeptical, wondering how he could possibly enjoy his time in the hot desert without his favorite alcoholic beverages to soothe his mood. One might argue that Bourdain made this particular journey not only to challenge his own beliefs but to challenge his viewers' as well. He admitted "there were a lot of preconceptions to overcome." With news headlines focusing on words like 'terrorist,' Bourdain said, "is there a country in the world about which Americans are more ignorant or less sympathetic than Saudi Arabia?" Through casual conversations over shared plates of food, Bourdain and Alhamrani were able to bridge the gap by asking questions instead of making assumptions, finding connections instead of differences, and swapping stories instead of insults. "Danya challenged me to see how ordinary Saudis lived their lives, feed themselves and entertain guests. And it would have been, I knew, utterly hypocritical of me and a betrayal of everything I've ever said, had I not, at least, given it a shot." We wonder if the Bourdain of Season One of *A Cook's Tour* would have been able to have such a meaningful and valuable experience?

In this episode, Bourdain opened himself to the possibility of learning. He was receptive and challenged his own preconceptions. In short, he experimented and inquired. He learned that "There's a cheerful, whimsical, good-humored and sophisticated atmosphere very much at odds with a kind of humorless fanaticism I was led to expect" (*No Reservations*, Season Four, Episode 13). The Saudi Arabia episode became an example for Bourdain's method of inquiry over the rest of his career.

Occasionally, Bourdain revealed a more fully developed method of inquiry as, for example, on a trip he made to Haiti in 2011. Haiti had been devastated by an earthquake a year earlier and was, at the time of his visit, awaiting the arrival of a tropical storm. Poverty, homelessness, and hunger were pervasive features of the culture. In filming his program, he sampled the food of a Haitian street vendor, and as he ate, he noted a group of young people surrounding him eyeing his food enviously; he faced a problematic situation and surprise and awakening ensued. Bourdain's privilege was brought home to him quickly and forcefully—he had a problem to be addressed. Bourdain hypothesized that if he were to buy all of the vendor's food and distribute it to the hungry young folks, he might "solve" or at least address the problem of his privilege, the vendor's income, and the hunger of the local Haitians. He noted in hindsight: "Easy to make the situation better, right?" He tested his hypothesis by buying her out and distributing the food to the hungry bystanders. What he learned was that the "fix it" mentality of the privileged is never as useful and easy as it might seem. He learned that genuine poverty and hunger can and do lead to dark competition and violence very easily. As he watched people fighting to get in line for the food and being bullied out of line, he learned that however much his buying of food made a few people less hungry, the overall problem was much larger than such a simple and well-intended act might ameliorate. Through the failure of his hypothesis, he learned some hard truths about poverty and hunger, and thus about the very meaning of food itself as simple fuel for surviving. Bourdain noted to himself and his audience: "We didn't think it through. We thought short-term—feel good, obvious-seeming solutions." But, in the end, "It all turned to shit" (*No Reservations*, Season Seven, Episode 1).

The importance of Bourdain's show from Haiti is that he willingly revealed his failure to his audience, indicating his openness to being corrected. He was an exemplary inquirer, even though it was a painful lesson, and he was inviting his audience to share his awakening moment. Learning to accept the difficulty and pain of failure is part and parcel of leading an inquiring life; and it is integral to leading a life of growth and improvement.

By the time Bourdain transitioned to CNN with his show *Parts Unknown* in 2013, the food was no longer the focus of his travels; it was merely the tool with which he could start a conversation and inquire about a bigger topic at large. Breaking bread, Bourdain found over the years, was an excellent and often disarming way to break the ice. Bourdain took his audience of *Parts Unknown* to places about which most Americans were ignorant or misinformed. Often, they were the hard-to-get-to or conflict-ridden areas, or places that simply had little-to-no coverage in our daily news cycle. Bourdain was intentional with his selection of locations—some of which he and his crew had yet to travel to, such as Iran and the Congo, and others he merely wanted to shine a light on. He knew the importance of telling these stories, to teach his audience that it wasn't so scary to talk with someone who had different beliefs or ways of life. "I just wish that more Americans had passports. The extent to which you can see how other people live seems useful at worst and incredibly pleasurable and interesting at best" (*Parts Unknown*, Season Eight, Episode 1). Bourdain asked more questions in *Parts Unknown* and let his guests do most of the talking, a stark difference from his early days on *A Cook's Tour*. To listen is to learn.

Bringing It All Back Home

One of the interesting things that Bourdain learned over the course of his international travels was that he should perhaps reconsider his beliefs about American food and culture, particularly in the places that he just assumed to be uninteresting, namely everything between New York and California. As he mentioned in *The Nasty Bits*, "I think all the international travel began to make it easier for me to see and appreciate my own country, and I stopped sneering and started looking at the flyover and the red states not as the enemy but as strange and potentially wonderful foreign lands" (p. 277). By the time *Parts Unknown* rolled around, he was more willing to travel within his home country, seeing parts of the United States that he might have once rolled his eyes at. As a native northerner he carried assumptions about the South, for example, seeing it as if it were a completely alien country:

> What do I—a pig ignorant Yankee—know about Mississippi?. . . . (Answer: Next to nothing) . . . As a New Yorker, with the drearily predictable worldview of my tribe, I took a dim view of Mississippi. Mississippi was the deep South . . . But I have long since learned to find myself comfortable in as 'foreign' an environment as Saudi Arabia, Liberia, or Cambodia. Why can't I get to know and love this part of my own country?
> (https://anthonybourdain.tumblr.com/tagged/mississippi)

Bourdain's legacy is, in part, his teaching us how to live the life of an inquirer. His disarming approach took away some of the fear of the unknown, showing his audience how to venture outside one's front doorstep and interact with cultures different from one's own, and to let go of one's prejudices long enough to see what is truly there. Bourdain chose food as the common denominator, because although we may eat differently than someone halfway across the world or even in our own country —we all eat. As Danya from the Saudi Arabia episode put it:

> "People from different countries and backgrounds—some of whom have been fundamentally at odds for centuries—shared a mutual respect for his honest portrayals of the cultures they loved. He was able to toggle between reverence and irreverence in a single sentence; he was an expert at identifying what was important, and what was not. He knew food was about telling a story, and he let the food, and the people who made it, speak for themselves." (Alhamrani 2018)

Bourdain's legacy of learning and experimenting also lives on through the work he started before his suicide in 2018. He found American fast foods to be atrocious, a problem to be addressed. But he did not reject the idea of fast food; he simply believed it could be done better: "There is delicious, even nutritious, fast food to be had in the world – often faster and cheaper

than the clown and the colonel and the king and their ilk produce" (*The Nasty Bits*, p. 14). He hypothesized, and hoped, that
the notion of fast food in America could be vastly improved by
taking a nod from the hawker stall model of Singapore.

> Imagine if there were a food court near you, at the mall, for instance,
> where instead of the soul-destroying mediocrity and sameness of
> American fast food, a wide spectrum of ethnically diverse lone propri-
> etors—all of whom had been perfecting their craft for decades—
> offered up their very best. (*The Nasty Bits*, p. 234)

Bourdain sought to impress upon New York and its myriad of
visitors a different way of approaching quick service meals and
laid the groundwork for such a hawker center to open, but the
plans fell through shortly before he ended his life. As of 2021,
the project was reinvigorated by Urbanspace and KF Seetoh,
two of the original participants in Bourdain's initial plan, and
as of September 2022, Urban Hawker, the Singaporean market
is now open. KF Seetoh says "We're not just selling food, we're
telling stories" (Werner 2022). What better way to carry on
Bourdain's legacy than through a true celebration of food?

These examples of Bourdain's influence highlight what is
perhaps his most significant contribution to our culture:
through his travels he not only presented the evidence of his
inquiries but also came to be a teacher of learning. He inspired
those of us in his audience to also become inquirers, to willingly
leave our beliefs open to public inspection. He taught us, by
example, to be willing to change our habits of belief. In the wake
of the #MeToo movement, public self-examination brought forth
a more mature version of Bourdain when he stepped forward as
an ally in the defense of victimized women such as his girlfriend
at the time, Asia Argento. While the "meathead culture" was a
theme in *Kitchen Confidential*, we find him speaking out in
2017 admitting to being part of the problem by not doing
enough to stop it back in the day. He learned along the way,
unlike some of his other chef comrades who were at the forefront of public allegations, that perhaps there were people in the
kitchen having a different experience than him. He acknowledged his privilege in a male-dominated culture and industry
and was "man" enough to speak out against it. In an article he
wrote for *Medium*, Bourdain confessed:

> To the extent which my work in *Kitchen Confidential* celebrated or
> prolonged a culture that allowed the kind of grotesque behaviors
> we're hearing about all too frequently is something I think about daily,
> with real remorse. (Bourdain, "Bad News," Medium 2017)

Bourdain's world expanded tremendously over the course of his travels. This growth is evident when comparing the flippant writer of *Kitchen Confidential* to the more refined, humbled host of *Parts Unknown*. He learned a lot along the way about what makes food good, why asking questions instead of making assumptions is important, and how expanding one's belief system is ultimately for the betterment of ourselves and society. Anthony Bourdain learned to learn over the course of his career—he became a pragmatic inquirer and urged his audience to take up a similar approach to life.

III

Death

10
Some Dark Genie

Scott Calef

You can't fully appreciate the sweet without a taste of the bitter.

—Tom Vitale (Tony's long-time producer)

I's easy to say that Anthony Bourdain had an addictive personality, but the more interesting question, if you don't mind a little speculation, is 'Why?'

People sometimes assume that if someone's an addict, they must've had troubled home lives or neglectful parents. That would be comforting in a way because it means that if I had a decent home and upbringing that I'm probably not at risk. Also, it means we shouldn't be too hard on or blame the addict but, perhaps, pity them. But Bourdain has always admitted that "I did not want for love or attention. My parents loved me. Neither of them drank to excess. Nobody beat me. . . . In school, I was not bullied . . . My counselor at camp did not molest me" (*Medium Raw*, Chapter 2). After his dad became an executive at Columbia records, he took young Anthony to concerts at the Fillmore East and got him free albums. Sounds pretty sweet to me. Besides, Tony's brother Chris didn't have the same sorts of issues with substance abuse, and presumably his upbringing was much the same as Anthony's. People from stable, middle-class families in nice neighborhoods use drugs too.

One might surmise that so-called addictive personalities are born that way, that having a greater-than-usual disposition to take drugs or get high is somehow a matter of being unlucky and inheriting maladaptive genes. This, too, might provide some reassurance: as long as my genes aren't messed up, I'm unlikely to become a degenerate and develop problems with alcohol or drugs. But again, Anthony's parents and brother weren't alcoholics or addicts, and so it certainly isn't obvious that heredity was a major culprit in Tony's case.

No, if one takes Anthony at his word (can you take recovering addicts at their word?), he *chose* to take smack and sought it out because he *wanted* to try it. Charles Leerhsen called him "an aspiring addict" for whom "getting hooked on heroin was the fulfillment of an almost lifelong dream" (p. 142). Tony confesses that "I'd wanted to become a junkie . . . since I was twelve years old" (*Medium Raw*, p. 20). By his own admission, he was not a victim of his family background or ancestry; he was responsible.

But there's an air of paradox to this: how can a person be responsible while doing something—becoming a heroin addict—that seems so very irresponsible?

Well, maybe it wasn't irresponsible, or at least, as irresponsible as we're probably inclined to think. There are two ways of approaching this possibility that interest me. One examines whether or not a decision to become an addict can be a rational decision. I think it can be, but with some pretty hefty qualifications, qualifications that I'm in no position to say applied in Anthony's case. But if, hypothetically, becoming an addict can be rational, then perhaps it isn't irresponsible (or at any rate, *wholly* irresponsible). Indeed, if something is rational, perhaps *by definition* it's responsible, for to act responsibly is to act reasonably. This conclusion, if applicable to Anthony, would at least partially be exonerating and inoculate him from the harsh judgment and condemnation many reserve for users. Whether or not Bourdain's decision to take drugs was rationally defensible, that it can be is a view voiced by one of his most profound cultural influences, and so I think it's worth a look.

The other approach to the question about abuse, responsibility, and rationality takes a psychological (or psychanalytical) angle. Maybe Anthony was responsible for engaging in self-destructive behavior because he didn't shy away from a self-destructive impulse that lies within us all. If so, the problem is not a matter of specific family heredity or parental abuse or the like, but something shared and common to the human condition. If it's a manifestation of what it is to be human, then it's hard to blame someone like Anthony with a drug problem; it may be, as it were, inborn, but by virtue of our psychology, not our genetics. On this interpretation, we all have a demon, it's just that Anthony was more conscious of his, or less inclined to repress it.

"I Have Made A Very Big Decision"
(Lou Reed)

Anthony Bourdain absolutely loved the New York underground music scene; about the time when, as a working chef, he and the kitchen crew were just getting off late at night, the clubs would be switching into high gear, and it was only natural for Tony to gravitate to where the action was. He dedicated *The Nasty Bits* to the Ramones, had a sit down with Iggy Pop in an episode of *Parts Unknown,* and adored bands like the New York Dolls, the Modern Lovers, the Velvet Underground, and Television. Bourdain biographer Charles Leerhsen notes that becoming a heroin addict meant that Tony "had at last summoned the courage to join the fraternity" of strung-out idols like "Burroughs, Lou Reed, Iggy Pop, Chet Baker, and Hunter Thompson . . . that he'd been emulating one way or another since grade school" (p. 142). Leerhsen continues, "His overriding emotion when he arrived at a state of junkie-ness . . . was not fear or excitement but pride" (p. 142). In a Massachusetts episode of *Parts Unknown,* Bourdain confesses that the first time he felt ill from withdrawal, "I looked in the mirror and I smiled."

It seems clear that, like so many impressionable young men, Tony wanted to be like his heroes, and his heroes weren't athletes or entrepreneurs but writers and musicians. But since cooks "were never rock stars" and "if any one of us could play guitar, we sure as shit wouldn't have cooked" (Leerhsen, p. 149), how to emulate these idols? Well, the primary routes open to lads lacking musical talent are fashion and debauchery.

On the fashion front, in a Hong Kong episode of *The Layover*, Anthony tells his tailor to "make me a suit my mother would hate" (Leerhsen, p. 143). But given that he was a pretty good-looking guy, prior to achieving international fame and fortune (and thus, the ability to have Hong Kong tailors make outfits to specification) sex and drugs—debauchery—may have proved the path of least resistance.

In the storied and seedy annals of New York underground and avant-garde music (and debauchery), *no one* casts as long and dark a shadow as Lou Reed. That influence was largely manifested through Reed's willingness to foreground realities of urban life sniffed at or conspicuously avoided by 'polite society'. These marginalized and usually overlooked street characters include homosexuals, transvestites, pimps, two-bit hustlers, and stoned-out drug addicts. Critics alleged that Reed and the Velvet Underground (the most crucial—and best—New York band ever, for which Reed was lead vocalist and chief songwriter), emphasize the *use* of drugs, but deceptively, because there's nary a mention of their soul-destroying consequences. By dedicating compelling art to topics like addiction, Reed was often maligned for glamorizing a tragic and often-deadly human failing. Based on some of the Leerhsen quotations above, this seems to describe the effect of music like Reed's on the young Anthony Bourdain, anyway.

Montreal chef Fred Morin noted that "Tony had this *thing* where he liked to pretend he was living scenes out of movies. . . . He was obsessed with movies and inserted a million movie references in his TV shows . . . but what a lot of people don't know is that he also designed them into his actual life. He'd imagine he was the main actor, but at the same time he was, in his mind, a kind of set director . . ." (Leerhsen, p. 144). On-and-off kitchen colleague Robert Vuolo similarly remarked that Tony's "addiction was always odd to me. I'm gonna be somewhat frank here: it felt often part of the persona that he wanted to portray of himself. He sort of constructed this image of himself that he wanted to perpetuate, and it involved this street, kind of on the edge of the law—I wouldn't say *gangster*, but he romanticized that kind of lifestyle. Tony was always playing with how he looked to other people; he was very conscious of it" (Woolever, p. 27). Vuolo also claims that, while working together, "We had a tape of the soundtrack of *Apocalypse Now* going on in the kitchen for months" (Woolever, p. 36). "When Jim Morrison started singing, 'This is the end, my brand-new friend . . . the end,' someone would toss a match on the brandy-soaked range top, 'causing a huge, napalm-like fireball to rush up into the hoods'" (Leerhsen, p. 140). It seems to me that what Morin claimed about Tony's life paying homage to favored filmic touchstones is no less true of Bourdain's musical inspirations: his life imitated the art he loved.

Consider, in this light, the following stanzas from the Velvet Underground's "I'm Waiting for the Man":

I'm waiting for my man
Twenty-six dollars in my hand
Up to Lexington, one, two, five
Feel sick and dirty, more dead than alive
I'm waiting for my man . . .
He's never early, he's always late
First thing you learn is that you always gotta wait . . .
Up to a brownstone, up three flights of stairs . . .
He's got the works, gives you sweet taste
Ah then you gotta split because you got no time to waste

I'm waiting for my man . . .
I'm feeling good, you know I'm gonna work it on out
I'm feeling good, I feel oh so fine
Until tomorrow, but that's just some other time . . .

This seems to me exactly the kind of scene that Tony would have cast himself in. "Ultimately, Tony would take his first snort of the drug [heroin] on his own, in a bombed-out tenement" (Leerhsen, p. 144). But we began by asking whether choosing to become an addict can be rational, which was a way of asking why someone might deliberately embrace it. Apart from the fact that it allows you to mimic Johnny Thunders or star in your own Scorsese movie, how could that be a choice anyone with a lick of sense would want to make?

Well, in the Velvet's song just quoted, the white boy in Harlem looking to score makes a connection, and after a "sweet taste" he's "got no time to waste." He needs to shoot up. But after he does he's "feeling good" and "feeling so fine" . . . until tomorrow. But for the junkie who gets high, tomorrow doesn't matter until tomorrow.

I'm not a drug addict, and never have been; nor have I ever done hard drugs. But I think people who don't have a drug problem often think those who do are short sighted. They're viewed as people whose perspective is clouded or confined to a very limited horizon. According to the stereotype, the craving for immediate gratification overwhelms ambition, incapacitates the user and prevents them from making necessary and life-improving changes. And so, whatever promise the future might hold is sacrificed for a transitory high; in the long run, the resort to a quick fix leaves major life problems unaddressed, and the addict languishes (or dies of an overdose). Nothing gets better until they get help.

This is a kind of utilitarian argument against drug use. Utilitarians aver that we should do what will produce the greatest happiness overall, and in the long run, addiction doesn't produce the greatest happiness. What is sacrificed is just too great, and the loss of a bright future is incommensurate with the very momentarily reward of "feeling good" and "feeling fine." Utilitarians judge the rationality, as well as the morality, of actions by subjecting them to a kind of cost-benefit analysis. Looked at this way, it's easy to assume that the costs of drug dependency outweigh the benefits. As Reed honestly admits in the song, tomorrow, when the drugs are gone and so is your money and you've got chills and cold sweat and the pain and cramps start to grip and squeeze. . . well, that's another time.

And for many people, perhaps most, the utilitarian calculation is almost certainly correct. But that argument is more easily made by someone who has, or can see in others, a bright future without drugs. In Episode Seven, Season 4, of *Parts Unknown*, Tony visits a Massachusetts support group for recovering casualties of the opioid epidemic. One participant shares, "What are the odds you're going to own a house? What's the odds that you're going to own a nice car? Any car? A place to live, all that stuff? Seems less and less likely all the time. Contrast that with what happens when you stick a spike in your arm, and why wouldn't I?" Professor Doll's chapter in this volume suggests that, for Aristotle and the Stoics, anyway, suicide can be a rational choice to end unbearable suffering. But if the choice to end life altogether can be justified when you see no end to hardship and heartache, why could addiction not be justifiable on similar grounds? Indeed, mightn't it be more rational to numb or eliminate your pain, for as long as you can, than to end your life entirely in an effort to achieve the same result?

In the most haunting and poignant drug song ever recorded, Lou Reed's "Heroin" (I recommend the live version from his solo release, *Rock'n'Roll Animal*), he writes, in the first person, "I have made a very big decision / I'm going to try to nullify my life." He's in despair and alone and beyond reach: "You can't help me, not you guys / Or all you sweet girls with all your sweet talk." He doesn't know where he's going, but "when I put a spike into my vein . . . things aren't quite the same." He's oblivious: "I guess I just don't know." But once that "heroin is in my blood / And that blood is in my head" and I "feel just like Jesus' son" then I'm "better off than dead." For a time, at least, he's able to escape and is transported "away from the big city / Where a man cannot be free / Of all of the evils in this town / And of himself, and those around." "When the smack begins to flow / Then I really don't care anymore." The closing lines tell the whole story: "Thank God I'm good as dead / Thank God that I'm not aware / And thank God that I just don't care / And I guess I just don't know / And I guess I just don't know."

Obviously, I love this song (as, I'm sure, did Anthony). But the point I wish to make is that the user in the song (whether or not autobiographically Reed himself) "made a very big decision" to nullify his life and thanks God that he was able to do so because the only escape from the reality he confronts in the "big city" and in himself and others is a narcotic stupor which renders him "not aware" and "good as dead." But—importantly—not *actually* dead. At least not yet.

The nineteenth-century British philosopher John Stuart Mill was one of history's most ardent defenders of personal autonomy. In his very influential book *On Liberty* (1859) he argues that the only just cause for interfering with the liberty of another person is to prevent harm to others. This has come to be known as "the Harm Principle." Paternalistically coercing someone to change "for their own good" is, for Mill, practically never permissible. But even Mill identified one interesting exception to this general rule. He considers whether or not you should be permitted to sell yourself into slavery and answers: "an engagement by which a person should sell himself, or allow himself to be sold, as a slave, would be null and void; neither enforced by law nor by opinion". But why not?

On the one hand, if it doesn't hurt anyone else, it seems it should be allowed by the Harm Principle. It's his choice to make, right? (We'd have to concoct a scenario where this makes rational sense I suppose. Perhaps I need money to pay for my daughter's life-saving surgery, and the only way to obtain it is to sell myself into bondage.) That's not Mill's take though. Mill thinks the very respect for autonomy which might seem to justify the decision forces us to condemn it. If the decision to allow me to indenture myself is rooted in a respect for my autonomy and a reverence for my personal choice, how can one, in the name of freedom, allow someone to forever surrender their freedom? How could it be defensible to, by a one-time decision, irreversibly surrender all future capacity to make decisions?

It's a fair question. But it isn't really applicable to Bourdain's situation, which we're presently considering. One might think the willing addict (that sounds like an oxymoron, but as Bourdain shows, it isn't) is choosing to deprive him or herself of choice in a way analogous to Mill's voluntary servitude example. Isn't the addict, in a sense, a slave to their drug habit? But, as Bourdain also showed by getting off drugs, this supposed "slavery" wasn't total or irreversible. Recovery is possible, and help is available. Also, when "ensnared" by narcotics, the addict isn't surrendering his autonomy to an oppressive human master who assumes absolute control. The "master," if the phrase can be used here, isn't a person, but a substance. It's not literally controlling you any more than gravity is. Less, in fact, because you can't break free of gravity.

Mill is also a utilitarian, and one might wonder whether embracing permanent subordination and degradation is consistent with maximizing happiness or the general welfare. But again, addicts can recover, and so the original decision to become a user *can be* reversed (even if, tragically, it all too often is not). Given, then, that the long-term outlook is at least somewhat open, the relevant question might be, "Does drug use result in less suffering than reality does unmedicated?" Depends on the circumstances.

Doctors prescribe drugs to post-operative patients and others to minimize their discomfort all the time. People take antidepressants for similar help with anguish of a different kind. The former medications are presumably not meant to be taken forever; the latter, in practice, are more likely to be. (As the opioid crisis shows, however, the preceding sentences are not really so true; painkillers prescribed for things like chronic backache often are taken indefinitely.) But is there anything *inherently* different about taking heroin, especially if you don't continue to take it once you no longer 'need' it? Lots of people take prescription drugs legally to numb themselves; as the opioid epidemic and the Oxycontin scandal shows, many of them became addicted in the process. But they often are only in a position to become addicted *because they had good reason to start taking the drugs in the first place*! It helped with their pain. Morally or rationally, how is the person who had a good reason to start taking Oxycontin different from Reed's narrator who "made a very big decision" to escape what, the song empathetically helps us to feel, is a bleak and unbearable situation?

So far as maximizing happiness (or, more to the point, minimizing suffering) goes, whether or not one can rationally choose to become an addict depends upon what one can reasonably expect by way of alternatives, or so it seems to me (and, presumably, the above-quoted fellow in the Massachusetts support group). It's facile to presume that there's always a better way out, that help is there, waiting in the wings, if only one has the courage and self-respect to seek it out. Whether one *has* courage and self-respect may not be entirely within one's control, after all.

Bourdain claims that, at a certain point, "I looked in the mirror . . . and I saw someone worth saving, or that I wanted to at least try real hard to save." Soon thereafter he sought help through a Methadone clinic. Thank God that he did. But why did he only *then* recognize his worth or believe that redemption was possible? Who knows? At one point, he chose to become an addict. At another point—but not sooner—he decided he could do better. The second decision doesn't prove that the first one was wrong or ill-considered (even if we think that it was). Reporter Patrick Radden Keefe, noting that Anthony's father died suddenly of a stroke at age fifty-seven, claims that Bourdain "more than once . . . told me that, if he got 'a bad chest X-ray,' he would happily renew his acquaintance with heroin." Food for thought to those who suppose that, post recovery, he must have come to regard that whole period of his life as a stupid mistake, never to be repeated. "When I'm honest with myself, I can look back and say that, on balance, I'd probably make exactly the same moves all over again." (*Medium Raw*, p. 20).

The fact is, Bourdain attributed the life-changing and career-making success of *Kitchen Confidential* to some of his more shady, prior misadventures. ("Had I not known what it was like to fuck up . . . that obnoxious but wildly successful memoir I wrote wouldn't have been half as interesting.") Because Bourdain had a fairly stable home life, grew up in an upper-middle class neighborhood, and went to fairly prestigious schools, we assume his life couldn't possibly have been so bad as the anti-hero's that Reed depicts in "Heroin." But *lots* of rich and famous celebrities are depressed and despondent (both before and after becoming rich and famous), and Bourdain insisted during an NPR interview that "when I became an adolescent, I was disappointed, very disappointed, bitterly disappointed . . . I seemed to have missed the good times . . . For whatever reason I was definitely a very angry, bitter, nihilistic, destructive and self-destructive kid" (quoted in Leerhsen, p. 26). In *Medium Raw* (Chapter 2, "The Happy Ending") he writes, "I was miserable. And angry. I bridled bitterly at the smothering chokehold of love and normalcy in my house . . . drugs were simply a manifestation, a petulant 'fuck you' to my bourgeois parents, who'd committed the unpardonable sin of loving me."

So, without diminishing obvious factors like the boyish urge to cultivate an image of rebellion or the desire to appear cool, drugs sometimes can also be an effective coping mechanism—even if one with an extremely short sell-by date. Not just Bourdain, but *all* people who gravitate to drugs do so for a reason, after all.

"Come Along on My Death Trip" (Iggy Pop)

Sigmund Freud is well-known for his writings on eroticism and what he called "the pleasure principle," "the psychic force that motivates people to seek immediate gratification of instinctual, or libidinal, impulses, such as sex, hunger, thirst, and elimination" (*Dictionary of the American Psychological Association*). But clearly, that's not the only fundamental drive in beings as psychologically complex and interesting as we are. Freud also noticed in some of his patients a resistance to therapy and attempts to sabotage or undermine its effectiveness. Others, such as soldiers with PTSD, may compulsively relive past trauma even though it's frightening and painful; the more "pleasant" thing to do would be to repress or ignore such disturbing experiences, or at least to recognize that they're mere memories of a past over and gone.

The pleasure principle is life affirming and promotes survival and creativity, but, Freud surmised, we also have an inclination toward annihilation. Bourdain exemplifies this chillingly in chapter three of *Medium Raw* ("The Rich Eat Differently than You and Me"). While in the Caribbean following the dissolution of his first marriage and "midway through a really bad time" he would "invariably find myself staggeringly drunk—the kind of drunk where you've got to put a hand over one eye to see straight." After smoking a joint he would "peel out onto the road with a squeal of tires. . . . Driving drunk. Every night."

He then describes how he would speed faster and faster along the cliff edges and make the split-second decision whether or not to jerk the car to avoid a deadly nose dive into the sea far below based on whether the radio DJ, who had rather eclectic tastes, happened to play at just the opportune moment a song that Bourdain loved or hated. Loggins and Messina? He launches airborne to a watery grave. The Chambers Brothers? He gets to play again mañana.

Freud dubbed this the death drive (*Thanatos*). *Thanatos* is initially aimed at "the reduction of psychical tension to the lowest possible point, that is, death" (APA Dictionary). Outwardly, the death impulse can manifest as aggression, but it also surfaces inwardly as self-destructiveness and the above-noted repetition compulsion. Freud was cautious in theorizing about the ultimate cause of the death drive, but proposed as a plausible conjecture that it was an attempt by the organism psychically to "restore an earlier state of things"—that is, to return to pre-organic being (*Beyond the Pleasure Principle*). Clinically, he thought the existence of masochism offered support for the idea.

Although it might appear that the death drive is unnatural and contrary to the requirements of evolution and natural selection, the German philosopher Arthur Schopenhauer argued exactly the opposite: Because life on balance contains more suffering and unhappiness than love and joy, the impulse to survive and carry on is actually counter-productive and harmful to the organism and its offspring. Freud was familiar with Schopenhauer's rather negative assessment according to which death is not just the *cessation* of life, but its end (as in, its *goal*). As Socrates also mused (much to Nietzsche's consternation), if death is nothingness, well, at least it's an end to our trials and tribulations; even the Great King of Persia could count on one hand the number of days and nights that are better and more pleasant than a night of dreamless sleep (Plato's *Apology* 40c–d). Or, as Lou Reed has it, "Thank God I'm good as dead / Thank God that I'm not aware."

Bourdain wasn't just a former heroin addict. He also appears to have been addicted to crack, tobacco, alcohol, his last relationship and (according to Porot and Simon's chapter for this volume) his phone. None of these seem particularly life-affirming, and if addiction isn't the model of a self-destructive and masochistic repetition compulsion, of *Thanatos* in action, I'm not sure what qualifies.

In the Massachusetts episode of *Parts Unknown* (Season Four, Episode 7), Tony says "There was some dark genie inside me that I hesitate to call a disease that led me to dope." "Some dark genie" sounds to me like *Thanatos*. I think Tony hesitates to call it a sickness because he accepts responsibility for his choices; people aren't responsible for having cancer or arthritis or Lyme disease. But it's also true, as he describes it, anyway, that there was something "inside me" that led him to do what he did. Because the urge to get high came from within—not from the usual suspects like abusive parents or extreme poverty or falling in with a bad crowd—he owns his actions. But this chapter began with a question about responsibility, rationality, and addiction. If Freud is right and we have within us "some dark genie," some psychic push towards self-negation, self-destructive behavior is at least *somewhat* like a disease. It's like an illness in the sense that someone doesn't choose to have a death drive any more than someone chooses to have AIDS. And if the impulse that leads to addiction is, in that sense, akin to a disease, we're neither responsible, nor not responsible for it, or at any rate, not completely. *Thanatos* is the counterpart to *Eros*. Perhaps, like catching Covid or falling in love, *it* happens to *us*. (People don't usually *choose* to fall in love; they just do). Some people are exposed to Covid, and get it (even if vaccinated); others are exposed, but don't (even if unvaccinated). Those who don't get it aren't better than their neighbors; they're just more fortunate or more advantageously constituted.

Anthony was able to recognize the good and the bad in his rather colorful background and he was able honestly to accept both. He marveled at his incredible luck—he frequently reminded himself and others that he had "the best job in the world"—and he also, as he puts it in the Massachusetts episode of *Parts Unknown*, struggled to "live in hope." Don't misunderstand me. I'm not saying that addiction is a good thing; only that, for some people and in some circumstances, it isn't the worst thing, either.

11

The One Truly Serious Philosophical Problem

DARCI DOLL

The wise man will live as long as he ought, not as long as he can.

— SENECA, "Letter 70"

In the opening scene of *Roadrunner: A Film about Anthony Bourdain*, Bourdain says, "It is considered useful and enlightening and therapeutic to think about death for a few minutes a day."

Anthony asserts that he doesn't want people seeing his body, and he doesn't want a party. Rather, he just wants to be "reported dead" unless more details could provide entertainment in a perverse or subversive way. Though spoken long before his death by suicide, these words become even more poignant given Tony's choice to end his life. Shortly after this quote is played, we hear Bourdain say "And I'm not gonna tell you how to live your life. I'm just saying, I guess, that I got very lucky." The narrator of this posthumous documentary then says, "Spoilers, it's not a happy ending; he committed suicide for fuck's sake."

Bourdain was charismatic and a source of inspiration for many, encouraging folks to live life to its fullest, experience things out of their comfort zone, and make their own way. A trailblazer in so many ways, Bourdain's death even under normal circumstances would have rocked the world. His choice to die by suicide deepened the sense of loss. It raises disturbing questions about how a person successful by most metrics could choose to end his life.

Suicide is something most people struggle to comprehend. But the hole left by Anthony's death was magnified due to his popularity, his sincerity, and his willingness to admit to imperfection. His agent, Kim Witherspoon, said he wasn't afraid of failure, that was hard-wired in him. So how do we come to terms with a person who found success through a series of fuck ups (his phrasing), who wasn't afraid of failure, who had faced and beaten demons (including heroin addiction), and yet made the decision to end his life?

Understanding what philosophers have said about suicide won't remove the pain felt by Anthony's absence. It might help us appreciate the way that he lived and died if we understand that ultimately, Anthony was, above all other things, a person who embraced autonomous choices. Bourdain's choices were consistently and unapologetically his own. As he said in the voice-over introduction to *A Cook's Tour*, he was looking for extremes of emotion, would try anything, risk anything, and had nothing to lose. He lived and died on his terms. While Bourdain eventually grew out of the television persona and "just became Tony," there were times when he was frustrated with the cameras and crews. At times he remarked that he felt like he wasn't living a normal life and had become a freak. And he declared that, when his fifteen minutes of fame were over, he'd be comfortable, if not relieved (*Roadrunner*).

The Only Serious Philosophical Problem

Death is the one great unknown and the uncertainty that surrounds it has made it both a cause of human anxiety and a source of philosophical exploration for millennia. While death, in general, can cause existential discomfort, the effects seem to be especially magnified when the death is untimely and the expression of an autonomous decision.

An autonomous decision to end your life can take many forms: Some choose euthanasia or assisted suicide due to an excruciating terminal illness. Others choose death through heroic and self-sacrificial acts in war and elsewhere, saving the lives of others at the expense of their own. In some societies or historical epochs, you might embrace self-immolation or avoidable martyrdom based on cultural or religious norms. These, while still unfathomable to many, carry with them a different weight than other types of self-killing. There's a justification for these that makes people *slightly* more comfortable with them.

But in Bourdain's case, death, so far as we know, was unprompted by any justified cause, and in the absence of a rationale it seems all the more senseless. To honor his memory and try to find some sense in his decision, it bears looking at a select philosophical history of self-killing. After all, as Albert Camus says in the *The Myth of Sisyphus*, "There is only one really serious philosophical problem, and that is suicide. Deciding whether or not life is worth living is to answer the fundamental question in philosophy. All other questions follow from that."

If Camus is right, and the question of suicide is the only serious philosophical question, we should follow Tony's sage advice to think about death, if not for a few minutes every day, at least for a few moments now.

Plato on Death

Plato describes the death of his philosophical mentor, Socrates. Having received a guilty verdict at the conclusion of his trial for corrupting the youth and irreligion, Socrates's sentence is death by hemlock poisoning. Prior to draining the cup calmly some time later (in one of Plato's most stirring tributes to his departed friend), Socrates argues that death is not to be feared because either it is like a dreamless sleep, which is the best of known sleeps, or it is an opportunity to spend time with the great people who have passed before you.

Given that the hemlock was to be self-administered, and given Plato's elevation of Socrates as a paragon of virtue, we might think that Plato was tolerant of self-killing. This doesn't seem to be his stance in general, however, and mandatory self-execution by decree of the State is hardly the same as a willing suicide. In the *Phaedo,* Plato writes, "Then he, or any man who has the spirit of philosophy, will be willing to die, but he will not take his own life, for that is held to be unlawful." Plato seems to be condemning suicide despite seeming to praise Socrates for his willingness to die as ordered by the state.

Plato's Socrates admits that this appears to be an inconsistency, but he clarifies things in the *Phaedo*, where he argues that gods are the guardians of people and people the possessions of gods. "Then, if we look at the matter thus, there may be reason in saying that a man should wait, and not take his own life until God summons him, as he is now summoning me." To take your own life would be to destroy the property of the gods without their permission, which surely would incur divine disfavor. For Plato, the time of death ought to be subject to the will of the gods, not mere mortals. As such, suicide is an irredeemable act. Even if death is not to be feared, to choose death against the wishes of the gods is an affront.

This may be unconvincing to some. What, if anything, creates a verified summons by the gods? If Socrates is allowed to take hemlock in accordance with the gods' wishes, what stops any other person from choosing to die in a way that they feel is in accordance with the gods' wishes? This goes largely unaddressed by Plato, but is a cause of consideration for those of us contemplating the nature and moral permissibility of suicide. Additionally, for an atheist like Bourdain such an appeal to divine rule will be uncompelling. And if Tony felt strongly that his death was the right thing for him, Plato's speculations about the will of the gods is not likely to have changed his mind.

Rather than explain how we can verify what the will of the gods is, Plato focuses on the nature of death itself, which he construes as a separation of the soul from the body. In Plato's metaphysics, the soul is pure and immaterial while the body is flawed and material. To die, then, is not something to be feared. Plato believed that once the soul is freed from the body in which it is imprisoned we can attain knowledge of true being; death is an opportunity to escape the pollutions, evils, and distractions of the body, all of which hinder the pursuit of true wisdom (*Phaedo*).

Still, while death is not to be feared and may even be a blessing, Plato is reluctant to condone suicide and says in *The Laws* that people who kill themselves because of sloth or "want of manliness" should be denied the rights of burial associated with an honorable or righteous death.

Bourdain said that it's good to think about death a little every day. In the *Phaedo*, Socrates describes philosophy as "practice for death and dying." Just as Bourdain says we should regularly contemplate death, Socrates thought true philosophy was just that. If, as Socrates suggests in the *Phaedo*, the true philosopher withdraws from bodily things as much as possible and strives instead to nurture the soul, apart from bodily lusts and distractions, perhaps Camus is right that the problem of suicide is the most important philosophical question.

When the general public thinks about the topic of suicide, they often assume that the decision indicates a weakness of character or something contemptible. Plato, however, thought an exception should be made when suicide is a response to extreme personal misfortune or the only alternative to participation in severely unjust actions. One reason Tony's suicide is so painful is because we don't know whether or not it falls within Plato's class of permissible self-killings; in Bourdain's case, we don't know of any extreme misfortune that might have prompted it. Nor does it appear to have been necessary to avoid committing severely unjust actions. Even so, when looking at Bourdain, perhaps we can find comfort in the Platonic view that his perfect soul will be joined with truth and knowledge. We may also take comfort in speculating that either Bourdain is in a dreamless sleep, or he's continuing his journey of conversing with others. Moreover, while we don't *know* the ultimate reasons for Bourdain's choice, it *may* have been a response to personal misfortune. Certainly his love life seemed fraught and anxiety-provoking towards the end. Plato suggests that if the future looks bleak (as often it does, for example, when euthanasia is contemplated) suicide might be interpreted as a rational decision to limit your life in such a way as to avoid future unhappiness. Suicide might be conceived of as a rational decision to will for oneself a smaller set of experiences than those entailed by living out one's natural lifespan—a smaller set which does not contain future experiences that are unpleasant or that one does not want. If so, Plato may grant Bourdain an exemption and conclude that his was not a dishonorable death.

Aristotle and Suicide

Aristotle, a student of Plato and the tutor of Alexander the Great, also discusses suicide, but is fairly vague about it. In the *Nicomachean Ethics,* Aristotle holds that suicide is a consensual act with oneself which could be considered an exercise of autonomy. This exercise of autonomy, though, often comes at the expense of the community. In his *Ethics,* Aristotle argues that we have both an obligation to develop intellectual and moral virtues in ourselves and also that we have a moral responsibility to help *others* become virtuous. By choosing to die, Aristotle concludes, you're violating your obligation to become the best version of yourself *and* foregoing your responsibility to help the community become more virtuous. This seems to speak to why those who loved Tony were hurt and even angered by his decision.

In *Roadrunner*, his friend and artist David Choe says, "I don't know where he is right now, but he let me down." In a similar vein, his longtime friend Alison Mosshart says, "I don't think he was cruel; you know, and there's a cruelty to that act. What the hell's everyone supposed to do?" In *Roadrunner*, Choe expresses his anger at Anthony's leaving behind his daughter. He laments that Tony would have loved to see her and would be so proud of her. The absence felt by Bourdain's loss is linked to the contribution he made to their moral and cultural development. By choosing to die, Bourdain stopped improving himself and others. Under this understanding of Aristotle, suicide can be a violation of your commitment to the community and others, so it's not to be condoned. If that's true, Tony's choice wasn't just an autonomous decision to curtail future suffering; it contributed to the suffering of those who loved and were affected by him. In Mosshart's words, it was cruel.

It's this connection to the community that truly resonates with those mourning Bourdain. Bourdain's cultural impact was felt in the way he helped open the world to his followers. He brought largely unknown, inaccessible areas of the world to the homes of millions. Whether he'd admit this or not, using food as a vehicle Bourdain became an ambassador to the world. He gave a voice to the oppressed, to the ignored and forgotten. According to those who knew him best, he thought his shows should have a level of controversy in order to provoke conversation. Anthony took issue with an episode if *everyone* liked it (*Roadrunner*). His long-time television producer, Tom Vitale, spoke of Tony's "shockingly countercultural voice" and the way he worked with countries that were dealing with the "fall out of what America had done to them." In this sense, Bourdain was a catalyst for enlightenment, awareness, and a shift in cultural perspective that made some people uncomfortable. It seems that the discomfort was part of the lesson. When asked if he was afraid of seeing the reality in Laos, he said no, "It hurts. You know, it should. I think Americans—every American should see the results of war. I think the least I can do is see the world with open eyes." Much like Plato's Socrates, it seems that Tony was a type of gadfly, enlightening the masses even if that made them uncomfortable. In life, Tony fulfilled the Aristotelian moral obligation to help others become better; in death, only his memory and body of work survive to do so.

Vitale said that Bourdain used his status to bring about positive change, albeit in a nonconforming way. In *Roadrunner*, Bourdain is quoted as saying, "People are not statistics. Surely there's value in—in showing the little things." "Travel isn't always pretty. You go away. You learn. You get scarred, marked, changed in the process. It even breaks your heart." In highlighting the change that comes through travel and giving light to the "little things" in people's lives, Bourdain used his fame to open the eyes of the world. In doing so, he probably performed a greater service than he realized. In *Roadrunner*, Mosshart said, "A lot of people loved him a lot. I don't know if he believed it."

According to the Aristotelian view, we can clearly see how Bourdain helped improve the global community. In the absence of Bourdain, there is an absence of that enlightening service. In mourning Bourdain, this absence is also mourned. When reflecting on Bourdain and his death, many struggle to articulate the loss and it's likely in part because it's hard to articulate the full extent of what Bourdain contributed to the global community. We can agree with Aristotle, though, that the community is worse off in his absence.

Stoicism and Suicide

Seneca, a Roman Stoic who died in the seventh century A.D., redirected the conversation about suicide from death to living well. For Seneca, the quality of a life is more important than the length of a life; what matters is living a virtuous life. For the Stoics, a virtuous life is lived in a way that is consistent with human nature and divine nature. They thought the highest means of accomplishing this was through rational achievement; the virtues were equated with forms of knowledge.

Stoicism teaches that our happiness is within our power because it is within our power to choose to be virtuous, and act rationally. This happiness is achieved through the rational choice to see and attain happiness in any given situation rather than to focus on perceived negatives. As the adage goes: you have no control over the things that happen to you, but total control over how you respond. In the *Moral letters to Lucilius,* Seneca claims that, with regard to suicide, we shouldn't focus on the idea of a life cut short. While it's true that such a life is ending earlier than it needed to, it's not always proper to think of this as an *inappropriately* shortened life. A life that's cut short through suicide can still be a complete and fulfilling life. That a life was complete, fulfilling and well-lived is not reversed or undone by decisions about how to conclude it. That is, if a person has acted in a way consistent with the rational virtues and attained flourishing, the value of that life is not negated by the way in which it has been ended.

In this sense, Tony lived a good life for the majority of his sixty-one years. Those good years that have been completed are not altered, affected or changed by anything that might happen subsequently, including the fact that there were no additional years. When we die, the sum total of our lives consists in what we *have* been, and if what we *have* been is good, death renders that fact permanent. I suppose, too, that if a life like Anthony's is supposed incomplete somehow because it was not longer, then *all* lives are incomplete, because none of them last forever (Plato's *Phaedo* notwithstanding). For the Stoics, a happy life is one of rational virtues, so it should not be a surprise that Seneca's primary focus would be on whether the person is acting rationally in a way consistent with freedom and self-determination.

For the Stoics, then, suicide can be a way to retain control of your life and exercise freedom and, if done with rational virtue, may be the act of a wise man. In *Letter 70,* Seneca writes that "the wise man will live as long as he ought, not as long as he can." Anthony had a barometer for bullshit and said that the greatest sin was mediocrity (*Roadrunner*). Tony extended that barometer and standard to his own life. In an email that haunts Choe, Bourdain asked, "David, this is a crazy thing to ask . . . but I'm curious and my life is sort of shit now. You are successful and I am successful. And I'm wondering: are you happy?" In retrospect, this appears to be one of the signs that Bourdain was questioning the quality of the life he had built for himself.

For those of us trying to come to terms with Bourdain's death, Seneca may produce conflicting emotions. On the one hand, it seems counter-intuitive to say that an autonomous decision to end one's life is consistent with the virtue of a wise man. After all, we're taught that the pursuit of life is one of our most fundamental, and valuable, biological (and perhaps moral) imperatives. And for many of Anthony's friends, family, and fans, his decision reflects the tragic ending to an admirable life. For the average person, it's hard to understand why one would want to stop living, so when confronted with suicide, the mind naturally rejects the idea and seeks to rationalize why it's wrong.

On the other hand, for some, discussing the many facets of suicide can help in coming to terms with Anthony's decision. It can help those mourning him but it can also help those considering suicide. While there might be a fear on the part of some that discussing suicide could cause impulsive suicides, I think it's more likely that having an open discussion can help people examine suicidal thoughts rationally and perhaps come to terms with mental anguish, whether one's own or that of another.

Frank discussion helps to dispel the stigma associated with suicide, a stigma that prevents too many people from addressing trauma and the feeling that life is no longer worth living. My hope is that by discussing Anthony and the impact of his choices, those affected by his death or by suicide in general can be benefited. A Stoic view like Seneca's can help us understand that the value of a person's life is not eliminated by their death, even if it's self-inflicted. In the case of Anthony, we can mourn his loss and lost potential; however, his decision does not negate the beauty of the contributions he made to the world while alive.

In *Roadrunner*, Anthony was described as a control freak, one who was passionate about his causes, and a nemesis to mediocrity. It was also mentioned that he was stubborn as fuck. If he set his mind that he wanted to leave, you'd have to physically stop him. In this sense, once Anthony decided he was ready to leave this world, there was no stopping him. As Seneca would say, his decision was an autonomous choice to decide that his life had been completed.

When discussing life with his friend Eric Ripert, a Buddhist, Anthony asks Eric whether he's concerned about how sweet their life is, and whether he wonders how the next life could possibly be better. He then says, "Enjoy every minute of this now, Eric. And pray. Pray, pray that this is it, because if you're right and there is a next life, we're fucked, my friend" (*Roadrunner*). And in that, we see the ultimate Anthony Bourdain: Enjoy the life you have, do the best you can with what you have, and pray because ultimately, we're fucked.

Lydia Tenaglia, Bourdain's executive producer, said that she doesn't want Anthony's legacy to be that he succumbed to his darkness, because that wasn't him. He created something that was so important, and that really needs to be—that is the legacy of his life, not the stupid bullshit act he did at the end (*Roadrunner*).

12
Bourdain's Taste for Freedom

CHRISTOPHE POROT AND ALLEN SIMON

Anthony Bourdain is celebrated for many things: traveling the world, eating with the poor, and bringing attention to our common humanity through the dinner table, just to name a few. He's celebrated for being so suave and cool and friendly, he's celebrated for being artistically gifted through his rhetoric and writing, and he's celebrated for being honest.

Behind all of this, perhaps because of it, it seems he should be celebrated for being a good person too. What made Bourdain so easy to like? How did he become a human that people across cultures all grew to love? As Bourdain fans ourselves, we'd like to think he was more than just conveniently charming, exploiting his brilliance to deceive us into believing that he had a heart. I suppose we could never know for sure what was within Bourdain's character or inner being, but we're willing to bet he brings meaning to the concept of being a good person.

Bourdain's Higher Mission

But what does it mean to be a good person? What's the meaning of goodness?

In philosophy today, there are three very popular ethical traditions: Deontology, Consequentialism, and Virtue Ethics. Deontological systems of ethics are based on obligation, or duty. According to Deontology, some things are just wrong, regardless of the consequences. We have obligations to obey a rule, or set of rules, without necessarily worrying about the outcomes of doing so. A nice benefit of Deontology is that it avoids having to engage in futurology, the unsuccessful science of predicting the future. As a Deontologist, you can know whether you're doing the right thing by virtue of whether or not you're following the right rule, and that's something knowable at the time you make your decision.

Deontology is unlikely to account for Bourdain's ethics because he was such a rebel. His willingness to break rules and live a life undefined is well-documented and would make painting Bourdain as a Deontologist seem very inaccurate. He certainly didn't care to adhere to traditional societal rules; he dabbled in drugs, embraced the counter-culture, and revealed the unpalatable truth behind the restaurant business. These and similar decisions suggest that society's rules didn't govern him. And though he had certain core internal rules, these too were constantly shifting and being played with.

As Bourdain once stated, "If I'm an advocate for anything, it's to move. As far as you can, as much as you can. Across the ocean, or simply across the river. Walk in someone else's shoes or at least eat their food. It's a plus for everybody." Bourdain was more interested in constantly adopting and experimenting with new rules than adhering to a fixed set of old rules.

Another popular option for ethicists is Consequentialism, the idea that we measure right and wrong by the consequences of our actions. For instance, Bourdain once tried to give leftover food from a shoot to desperately poor people in Haiti; unfortunately, competition for it led to an outbreak of violence. According to Consequentialism, Bourdain's gesture would've been deemed bad because the overall consequences were not good. From the Consequentialist perspective, the *intent* to do good is morally irrelevant; all that matters is the results. Now, which exact consequences we should be striving for is up for some debate, but according to Utilitarianism—the most common Consequentialist philosophy—we should seek to maximize pleasure and minimize pain. Utilitarianism seems like a closer fit for Bourdain than Deontology, but it's still hard to see how Bourdain could be perceived as a pure Consequentialist, calculating the pleasure and pain ratio of each and every morally significant decision.

That leaves us with Virtue Ethics, an understanding of ethics more concerned with the cultivation of character and what kind of person you are than with individual actions, duties, or results. A virtue, like honesty, is expected to go all the way down, insofar as it affects every part of your being. To be an honest person, then, would mean loving the truth for its own sake, having a distaste for dishonest behavior, and so on.

If one of these ethical theories accounts for Bourdain's goodness, it would most likely be Virtue Ethics because Bourdain, if nothing else, seems to have let honesty, humility, and empathy run *all the way down* his being. Moreover, it seems to us that Bourdain views freedom as central to his ethic of love and empathy. He encourages us to use our freedom to experience the world and see it through the eyes of those near and far from us. This lies at the heart of his 'goodness'.

Born Free

There are many philosophical options when it comes to explaining freedom, but the concept of 'positive liberty' is particularly relevant to discussions of Bourdain's life and ethics. Positive liberty is contrasted with negative liberty. Negative liberty is freedom *from* something whereas positive liberty is freedom *to become* something. When cooped up in a hotel in war-torn Lebanon, Bourdain's negative liberty was limited because it was too dangerous to move around the city of Beirut; there were external constraints on his freedom. When he was addicted to heroin, his positive freedom was undermined because his ability to become his best self was compromised; the addiction functioned as an internal constraint on his freedom. However, philosophical debates are never quite so clear and simple as this. There are tensions within the theory of positive liberty, tensions that I believe mirror ambiguities in Bourdain's own life. We could view his life simply as that of a drug addict, a suicide case, an adventurer perpetually seeking a new form of high, effectively denying Bourdain positive liberty.

After all, addiction is the paramount example of a situation where a person *lacks* positive freedom because, enslaved from within, they're prevented from achieving their higher goals. However, I believe that Anthony Bourdain did have a very clear idea of his higher goals, and that he was able to actualize them. A convincing case can be made that his life reflects positive liberty in its best form and that he was free despite his addictions in a sense that nevertheless complexly involved them. Before turning to that, though, let's dive a little deeper into the differences between positive and negative liberty.

What Is Freedom?

The philosopher Gerald MacCallum argued that positive and negative liberty share the same structure insofar as freedom is the ability to move from point A to point B without constraint. For instance, if you are hungry, or in fear, or poor, then moving from point A to point B is harder than it otherwise would be; your freedom is limited. What distinguishes the two liberties is their understanding of what constitutes a 'legitimate' constraint. In negative liberty, only external constraints (like being physically stopped) count as "legitimate" whereas in positive liberty internal constraints (like being addicted to a substance) also qualify. To illustrate: imagine Bourdain is driving, turning left and right as he pleases, but en route to his heroin dealer to buy drugs. According to the negative concept of liberty, he'd be free so long as no one was preventing him from continuing. According to positive liberty, he might be unfree because he is, in a sense, controlled from within by addiction.

There are two further distinctions between negative and positive liberty. First, what counts as a legitimate point B, or destination, is not the same in each theory. Positive liberty theorists measure freedom, not by the ability to satisfy immediate desires, but by the ability to achieve higher-order goals. For example, if Bourdain really were on a mission to bring peace through the dinner table, eating might be considered a higher-order goal. Eating has an ulterior purpose. If, on the other hand, he ate simply because he was a glutton for good food seeking immediate gustatory pleasure, eating would fulfill a lower-order goal. Both goals may be compatible, but emphasis should be placed on higher goals for the sake of understanding positive liberty. If Bourdain were to act in accordance with virtue ethics, whenever a conflict arises between the higher self (the virtuous self) and the lower self, he should tilt in the direction of choosing the higher self.

Negative liberty presupposes only one self, the self that acts. Positive liberty, however, divides the self between a higher and lower self. The philosopher Ian Carter describes the clash between these two theories of liberty as follows: "while on the first view [negative] liberty is simply about how many doors are open to the agent, on the second [positive] view it is more about going through the right doors for the right reasons." So, if we think of positive liberty as walking through the right doors for the right reasons, we might as well say that negative liberty is indifferent to what doors you walk through. To be enjoying your negative liberty does not require that you indulge your lower self, but you're permitted to still be considered free while doing so because there is no attention paid to the distinction between higher and lower self.

Positive liberty thus assumes a divided self within each human where a battle between the higher and lower selves is routinely at stake. The lower self tends to seek more immediate forms of gratification, which may be incompatible in the long run with future goals of the higher self. However, this isn't always the case; sometimes the two parts of the self harmonize to achieve positive liberty. We believe Bourdain's life is a good illustration of how positive liberty can be achieved without conflict. He actually seems to have lived up to his higher goals, embodying the virtues of love and empathy, by giving in to his lower self.

Why Is This a Problem for Bourdain's Liberty?

How can the lower self become a vehicle toward actualizing the goals of the higher self? Let's start with an example that many of us will find relatable. Apparently, one of Bourdain's 'addictions' was an addiction to his phone. He not only set up alerts on his phone for every time he was mentioned online, but is rumored to have obsessively checked his phone towards the end of his life for text messages from Asia Argento. Addictions to phones, screens, technological devices, and the internet have become commonplace.

If you look at the internet, the primary goal of many platforms is to increase user engagement. Digital platforms don't care *why* you're going there or *what you get* from going to the website so long as you *go* there. Website developers have learned that it's easier to pull people in and encourage predictable behavior if they appeal to people's instincts and addictions; if the lower self takes over, like through online gambling or obsessively rechecking social media, the behavior of the user becomes reliable. In exceptional cases, however, it's possible that the higher self is actualized through the internet. Imagine someone, drawn in through YouTube, who compulsively or habitually watches enlightening lectures about how to live a moral and meaningful life. In this case, it would seem, someone's higher self is encouraged by the algorithms adjusting to their online behavior. This possibility was recently featured in a funny *Onion* article ("Man Becomes Better Thanks to Algorithm") in which algorithms promote our higher selves, even though they're designed to appeal to our lower selves.

The main question that arises from such scenarios is whether or not positive liberty should be prioritizing *how* decisions are made (for example, whether in a rational state of mind) or simply *the end result* of those decisions (for example, whether they help you become a better person)? In other words, does it matter more whether the lower self made the decision or that the higher self grew because of the decision? Bourdain's ambiguous path exemplifies that tension within positive liberty. In a sense, when he's addicted he's acting through his lower self. In another sense, this was the very process that made possible his becoming the higher self that he became, an ultimately edifying process he voluntarily participated in. We therefore like to view Anthony Bourdain as a 'noble rebel', a person who rebels against society, indulging in his lower, and sometimes illegal, impulses while in the process doing society a great service.

Feeling It All, a Curious Path to Understanding

In Bourdain's book *Kitchen Confidential* he notes that one of the most inspirational moments in his early cooking career was watching a chef have sex with someone else's newlywed bride, while high on cocaine, behind a dumpster near the restaurant where he was working. According to Bourdain, it was at this moment that he knew he wanted to be a chef. The rest of the book unabashedly continues this love of primal, uninhibited pleasures. Bourdain walks us through a tapestry of the joys and oddities of the world that he dedicated much of his life to, and does so without any sugar coating or false humility. In *Kitchen Confidential*, Bourdain was transparently sincere and never downplayed raw truth for the sake of lifting up humble virtues, demonstrating that he believes sincerely in the virtues he did embrace.

But there was a deeper intention behind all of this. Bourdain was not simply seeking out carnal pleasures and risky behavior for pure thrill-seeking. Rather, he understood that he could not fully embody the virtue of empathy unless he understood the full spectrum of humanity on a deep, first-hand level. Outwardly, this meant traveling around the world, meeting people of different cultures, and sharing food with them. But inwardly, this meant developing an understanding of human turmoil and suffering by enduring those states himself. In other words, it seems possible that Bourdain's indulgence of what is typically considered his lower self was actually a reflection of his higher-order goal of becoming more empathetic, not only through participating in dinners but also through experiencing those states of consciousness that so much of humanity refuses to shine a light on.

This notion of overcoming vanities or developing empathy through experiencing the human condition directly is attested to in various works of literature. Marcel Proust famously thought that pain was a kind of telescope through which we could see the world more clearly. Proust argued that the way over vanities was through them. A biography of Bourdain cites the following William Blake quote which speaks to this phenomenon: "The road of excess leads to the palace of wisdom." Proust's 'argument' for this was not made in a direct philosophical sense but rather through a story written by Proust in which the protagonist suffers the vanity of desiring to be in a high-class social circle. Once he enters that social circle, he finally sees how empty it is.

Maybe something similar can be said of Bourdain and success; Bourdain experienced powerful doses of success only to realize, in the end, that it's not the most important thing in the world. We don't intend to trivialize the pain or suffering associated with addiction and despair. But how could Bourdain truly know what was to be valued in life without having gone through those turbulent times? Bourdain himself was clear that we ought to experiment with life: "Without experimentation, a willingness to ask questions and try new things, we shall surely become static, repetitive, and moribund."

Another compelling literary example of this comes from the work of Hermann Hesse. In the novel *Siddhartha*, the main character (Siddhartha Gautama, who was to become known to history and legend as the Buddha) is seeking some kind of enlightenment. Along the way, he becomes a rich merchant who lives a life full of sex and vanities. All of this leads to a point where Siddhartha eventually asks, "How could I truly know these were empty pursuits if I did not experience them?" The Siddhartha that Hesse brings to life is not meant to be a purely accurate description of the historical Buddha, but this literary character does capture some of the essence of the Buddha, who is famous for advocating the Middle Way of religious and spiritual devotion. This principle has become a core part of Buddhism: fully giving oneself over to worldly pleasures and pursuits is not the way toward enlightenment, but neither is pure asceticism or withdrawal from worldly life. The Buddha was against extremism. This also lies at the heart of Aristotle's version of Virtue Ethics; for Aristotle, virtue lies in the mean between the extremes. Bourdain similarly stood against anything that divided people across artificial lines and therefore inhibited love and empathy. Bourdain advocates for a kind of intellectual humility which warns of the harms of extremism as a product of exaggerated self-confidence. For instance, he says, "If I have a side, it's AGAINST extremism—of any kind: religious, political, other. There's no conversation when everybody is absolutely certain of the righteousness of their argument."

Bourdain's stance against stagnating along any one particular ideological set of ideas about the world is also reminiscent
of Socrates, the ultimate and foundational paragon of wisdom
in Western civilization. Socrates's own definition of wisdom
was knowing what you do not know, and this is reflected in the
literary works by Plato that chronicle Socrates's conversations
with others. He would invite others to constantly question their
own firmly held preconceptions about life to show them directly
that nothing is known for certain. Similarly, Bourdain once
reflected, "Maybe that's enlightenment enough: to know that
there is no final resting place of the mind, no moment of smug
clarity. Perhaps wisdom . . . is realizing how small I am, and
unwise, and how far I have yet to go."

How could Bourdain, who became a chef and addict for the
sake of being like his idols, understand the beauty of life without
understanding its pain first? How could he have connected with
people across the world, apparently effortlessly, if his own story
wasn't one that was drenched in a sense that humanity is more
than appearances; that to be human is not as simple as being
born happy, living happily, and dying happy? So, we'd like to say
that Bourdain's open adventures across the world, his pain and
addiction, enabled him to become the globally empathetic man
who offered us all a sense of hope for peace through the dinner
table, for mutual understanding, for a code to enlightenment in
the face of a deep despair. Had he lived a perpetually easy life,
then the Bourdain we know may never have been.

Bourdain's awareness of what people might be going through
was born out of connecting to his lower self first, through various
passions and addictions, before growing into his higher self as a
consequence. Few people, especially in modern media, have
increased love, empathy, and compassion in the way that
Bourdain has. His purpose, his higher order goal, was achieved
in a self-directed and compelling way. David Klion wrote in *The
Nation* that Bourdain's shows "made it possible to believe that
social justice and earthly delights weren't mutually exclusive.
He pursued both with the same earnest reverence." He did not
merely understand people, he walked through the door and
showed people how to understand each other. He did all this
before his untimely death, which is a subject that cannot be
avoided in any serious account of the ethics of Bourdain's life.

A Mystical Death

Bourdain died by his own hand, as we all know. This act, the
act of suicide, is often treated as immoral and somehow in vio-

lation of some arbitrary obligation to keep living. We suggest instead that Bourdain's passing is better approached in mystical rather than cynical terms.

Not wanting to live is a risk that we must be willing to accept if we're to truly feel the world deeply and sensitively, in the way that many world-shaping artists have. Vincent Van Gogh ended his own life after producing some of the most compelling art the world has ever seen; Sylvia Plath committed suicide after stirring souls with her brilliant poetry; and, it may be argued, Christ allowed himself to be killed when he could have otherwise prevented it. This doesn't mean that in all three cases, the motivation to die was a product of feeling the world deeply but rather just that the death was voluntary, and that all three were highly sensitive beings.

Compassion, etymologically, means to 'feel with' and to feel with someone involves feeling their pain. The contemporary philosopher of religion, Charles Taliaferro calls this the paradox of compassion: in a world that is sincerely more compassionate there might be more suffering rather than less because when one person is suffering another suffers with them, doubling the grief. If you become as compassionate as Bourdain was, or as we believe he was, if you sacrifice the joys of life in pursuit of a higher goal, you may end up with a pain too burdensome to bear. Surely, we don't want to paint a picture of Bourdain that denies the hedonism involved in choosing the life he chose, but rather acknowledge that the path of pursuing joy led to great sorrow and compassion for him. So even if someone were to say that Bourdain chose the traveling life for pleasure, this doesn't undermine his life being a path to a certain kind of compassion; to play off the quote from *Siddhartha*, "How could Bourdain know that vanities are empty if he didn't pursue them?"

When Bourdain took his life, he had ascended through the upper echelons of empathy, he had already lost much of the pleasure and profound joy of family life for the sake of fulfilling his mission, and, in an undeniable way, he fulfilled that mission to the best of his abilities. Also, as the creator of shows like *Parts Unknown* he had taken on responsibility for the well-being and livelihood of many people, including his production team. Perhaps for a while he felt a commitment to them, an obligation not to let the whole thing burn. While he was going through it, though, he had moments of suffering that were enough to make him want to cry out, quit, and ask why the world had done this to him.

In certain mystical traditions, like Jainism, practitioners may starve themselves to the point of death when they feel their purpose in this world has been served. Maybe, despite his distaste for religion, there was truly something mystical about Bourdain's passing. Maybe he felt he had given the world all he could give, and it was simply time to let go. There are many speculations around Bourdain's suicide, including accounts that source the blame in his affair with Asia Argento, but this mystical interpretation has rarely been considered. If he bore the maximal suffering he could bear, if he strove to learn through feeling the world and its pains, a condition expressed by the fact that he chose to be an addict, then perhaps the suffering simply became too much, was too dizzying, and he chose to opt out of the equation after taking himself to the breaking point.

Bourdain said he didn't care what people did with his body after he died, but I think it matters what we do with his memory. If we fail to see Bourdain as a self-determining agent, as a free individual who gave the world a new sense of hope and empathy through a rare view into what it is like to be truly honest and compassionate, in a world otherwise driven by dishonest social media posts, then we have done a disservice to Bourdain. His body may no longer be with us, but his message remains clear: Bourdain taught us to live truthfully, to be empathetic, and to love, love, love until we can't love anymore. The philosopher Cornel West says that "truth is the condition of allowing suffering to speak," and Bourdain spoke the truth.

III

The Good,
the Bad, and
the Ugly

13
Anthony Bourdain's Antisocial Ethics

JILL M. KITCHEN AND FRANK SCALAMBRINO

If you've watched any of Anthony Bourdain's early shows, you may have immediately got the impression that he was a bit of an abrasive, opinionated asshole—and you may be right. Never one to keep his opinions to himself, he zealously displayed irreverent disapproval of popular culinary trends. The pumpkin spice everything craze, Americans' love affair with Starbucks, their taste for unsophisticated ranch dressing, celebrity chefs like Rachel Ray and Guy Fieri—all were targets for his not-so-thinly veiled vitriol. Always hungry for more than the socially-acceptable "Top Ten Things to Do" at (insert any location here), Bourdain's ethics advocates for an authentic connection to the people and the places we visit. Food is the conduit of that connection.

From everything that Anthony Bourdain said and did, we can get glimpses of his 'ethics for travelers', his view of the way people should behave when visiting foreign parts. There are three main ideas in Bourdain's ethics. The first recalls the original tagline to Bourdain's show *No Reservations*: "Be a traveler, not a tourist." The second recognizes that Bourdain gradually evolved a preference for community over society. This is perhaps surprising, given his early reputation as a foul-mouthed culinary bad boy with myriad pet peeves about food, travel, and pop culture. Finally, food is at the center of Bourdain's ethics.

'Community' brings to mind ideas of togetherness, cultural folklore, a common perspective, and communal dwelling. Community members develop shared practices because they cope with the same local circumstances. Groups of people who live near the ocean, for example, cultivate food practices involving seafood. Over time, these practices develop into traditional and local cuisine. 'Society', on the other hand, brings to mind more global concerns and social engineering. Society's concerns are not as immediate as community concerns. The desire for social justice and the desire not to die as your city is hit by a hurricane are different kinds of desires.

These desires differ in how they motivate us and in how they influence our thinking. Social concerns and desires tend to congeal into political thinking and questions about what kind of social engineering should be employed to change things. We're not suggesting that Bourdain was unconcerned about social justice. In fact, he spent much of the later part of his life as an ally and advocate for women and other marginalized groups. The point, rather, is that Bourdain cared more about authentic food experiences that helped him connect to communities and their concerns than about larger social issues which are often more abstract and conceptual. If you're starving to death, whether someone liked your recent social media post seems less important than finding your next meal. Philosophically, Bourdain's humanism is centered in communal concerns related to mortality, not the kind of social engineering wrought by Capitalism or political lobbying.

The humanistic aspects of Bourdain's ethics ultimately stem from the fact that we have to eat to live. This fundamental requirement naturally gives rise to shared cultural practices regarding food. Originally, a community's culture and shared practices are intimately tied to whatever environments and foods are local.

At the heart of Bourdain's prescription for authentic travel, then, we find food associated with the travel location. He believed food was the best way to understand a community and culture. In a 2010 interview with *Slate* Magazine, Bourdain states "food is everything we are. It's an extension of nationalist feeling, ethnic feeling, your personal history, your province, your region, your tribe, your grandma. It's inseparable from those from the get-go."

Bourdain illustrated this with what we would like to call an "antisocial" humanity. How can someone be both "antisocial" and concerned with humanity and community? How does someone who openly expressed disdain for fame and interviews, who demonstrated reckless disregard for his own physical well-being through drug and alcohol abuse, who once described himself (on NPR in 2017) as an "angry, bitter, nihilistic, destructive and self-destructive kid," become concerned with ethical travel and communal practices?

Bourdain Highlights His Dark and Anti-Social Tendencies

Bourdain was very open about identifying as someone with antisocial tendencies from a young age. In *Roadrunner: A Film about Anthony Bourdain*, he discusses having trouble reading in kindergarten and states "I was already exhibiting antisocial tendencies" and reports stealing a book and teaching himself to read. At the 5:45 mark he says, "My early heroes were musicians and writers. The idea that you could have adventures, no matter how antisocial, and make them somehow legitimate by writing something beautiful about them—the concept took an early hold on me." Bourdain was always drawn to movies, music, and literature and had a gift with words. Like many talented and articulate writers and artists, he appeared to have a deeply personal relationship with his darkness, a darkness that manifested itself in addiction and depression which, ironically, contributed both to his rise to fame, and ultimately, his demise.

Bourdain professed his love for the New York Dolls, Iggy and the Stooges, and many others from the New York punk scene, identifying with the genre's moody aggressive vibes that encapsulated the frenetic energy and antiauthoritarianism of rebellious youth. He often expressed reverence for dark and gritty criminal or war stories and movies, using many for creative inspiration while shooting television episodes. While filming the Congo episode of "Parts Unknown", for example, he repeatedly references Joseph Conrad's novel, *Heart of Darkness* and the 1979 film *Apocalypse Now*. While engaging in the local practice of killing chickens on a boat in the dark with a dull knife and collecting the blood in a bucket he quips, "It was written that I should be loyal to the nightmare of my choice."

In *Kitchen Confidential*, Bourdain relates his first memorable connection with culture and food, telling how he fell in love with vichyssoise on a transatlantic family voyage to vacation in France. He recalls a time from that same trip when, fed up dealing with typical child complaints about French cuisine, his parents left him and his brother in the car when visiting a restaurant. He writes "It was a wake-up call that food could be important, a challenge to my natural belligerence." Perhaps this was also a wake-up call to be more discerning with the use of his belligerence. In *Kitchen Confidential*, Bourdain extols the virtues of a proper *mise-en-place* and the importance of a flexible boning knife one minute, but the next he's quickly paying respects to the female and immigrant line cooks in the trenches. While the appeal of the memoir is that it is a fast-paced, irreverent, and honest exposé, Bourdain also demonstrates his humanity when he acknowledges these class differences and his privilege in the restaurant world. This burgeoning social and community consciousness seems somewhat incongruous with his gruff, rough-around-the-edges persona, but shows a spark of community concern that is later developed as he becomes more well-traveled.

Bourdain on the Value of Reality over Appearance

Just as Bourdain's humanity transcends class differences, so too his emphasis on community transcends social influence. Referring to the influence of what he called "Capitalist" society, in Season Two, Episode 6 of *A Cook's Tour*, Bourdain referred to the worldview of such a society as "corporate commodified darkness." In his infamous *Society of the Spectacle* (§168) Guy Debord wrote that "Tourism, human circulation considered as consumption, a by-product of the circulation of commodities, is fundamentally nothing more than the leisure of going to see what has become banal. The economic organization of visits to different places is already in itself the guarantee of their equivalence." This kind of philosophy against the social worldview conditioned by Capitalism was present throughout Bourdain's style of moving through the world. In fact, the social worldview conditioned by Capitalism is exactly what Bourdain understood as the worldview of the tourist.

In 2006, Bourdain and his crew visited Lebanon, for an episode of *No Reservations* (Season Two, Episode 14) when the city came under siege by bombings. While waiting to be evacuated with the crew at a hotel north of the capitol, Bourdain remarks with a pained look on his face, "You know, we're sitting around the pool getting tan, you know, watching a war. If there's a single metaphor in this entire experience, you know, that's probably it. Not a flattering one." (*Roadrunner*, 35:46). This comment can be understood as a critique of the sense in which one group of individuals can take a tour of another group of individuals' experience, even when that experience may be the violence of war. Yet, after a particularly close call with a landslide on a mountain road, Bourdain (perhaps unknowingly) quoted Søren Kierkegaard, remarking: "It is considered enlightening and therapeutic to think about death a few minutes a day." (Bourdain actually echoed this idea from Kierkegaard multiple times in his monologues.) Bourdain seemed acutely aware of the value of reality over appearance. The reality of mortality seemed to trump the pleasure of getting to treat the realities of others like objects in a giftshop.

At the same time, in a world without Capitalism, humans would still need to eat, and Bourdain valued the global human reality that is the necessity of food. Locally, shared practices inevitably develop, creating cultures and communities as humans find themselves together with one another and together with shared concerns. The uniqueness of how these communities navigate their locale and cope with their shared concerns and realities makes for experiences that are not banal. With director Darren Aronofsky, Bourdain traveled to the edge of the eastern Himalayas to the Buddhist Kingdom of Bhutan. The two explore the mountain kingdom, tucked between China and India, which has managed to stay relatively invulnerable to excessive influence from the West. Only a certain number of tourists are allowed at a time, and all visitors are assigned a tour guide.

Recalling both his celebrated distinction between traveler and tourist and the Debord quote above, throughout the journey, Bourdain appeared fixated on how Bhutan remains isolated and unaffected by mass tourism. While enjoying the local fare, Aronofsky and Bourdain spend the entire episode waxing philosophical about their different views of the world. The food remains a way to contemplate things on a deeper level. After finding momos (dumplings) particularly delicious, Bourdain jokes, "It's enlightenment—it's your third eye opening, man." As they eat sautéed yak hide, sample yak butter, and sip Bhutanese ara, the conversations start about food and move on to more complex topics, such as Buddhism, vegetarianism, and the potential impact of foreign social influence.

While speaking with an environmentalist about Bhutan's philosophy of "Gross National Happiness," Aronofsky and Bourdain discuss the fundamentally different ideas of "happiness" in the Eastern and Western worlds. Again, this distinction may be philosophically punctuated as the difference between the Bhutanese communal way of life and a more Western social worldview. Aronofsky likens the Bhutanese concept to the American "pursuit of happiness," while Bourdain chimes in with "We don't actually believe that." Elsewhere he referred to the "un-American propensity for high quality of life" (*The Layover*, Season Two, Episode 2). And, even more explicitly, Bourdain once quipped of concierge-type "catering to all your basic human needs as determined by fiendish marketers, merchandisers, and franchisers" that it may be either "the realization of the American dream or a candy-colored night-mare" (*A Cook's Tour*, Season Two, Episode 6).

Sitting by a river with Aronofsky, they discuss the future of the country. Aronofsky wonders, as Bhutan becomes more developed, if people will stay committed to happiness or will be seduced by consumption. Bourdain answers "First comes electricity, then comes a television, then come pop stars and materialism . . ." This sentiment from Bourdain repeats another idea from Debord's 1967 *Society of the Spectacle* (§40). "Economic growth has liberated societies from the natural pressures that forced them into an immediate struggle for survival; but they have not yet been liberated from their liberator . . . This economy has transformed the world, but it has merely transformed it into a world of economy." Bourdain concluded his conversation with Aronofsky, noting, "I know Bhutan is beautiful—I'm glad it hasn't been fucked up yet by the world."

Understanding Bourdain's differing attitudes toward consumer society and genuine community allows us to make sense of his trademark jaded and anti-establishment tirades against vegans, brunch, Yelp reviews, celebrity chefs, and McDonald's. On the one hand, Bourdain didn't temper his critique of the influence of Western society's worldview. It appeared that offending anyone was never his concern. On the other hand, he repeatedly acknowledged the value of encountering the reality encountered by the local community, especially through food. In his 2011 interview with *Playboy* he observed, "The notion that before you even set out to go to Thailand, you say 'I'm not interested,' or you're unwilling to try things that people take so personally and are so proud of and so generous with, I don't understand that—I think it's rude. You're at Grandma's house; you eat what Grandma serves you."

Bourdain's Food-Based Ethics of Community

Bourdain visited over eighty countries and became an emissary of global culture while promoting an aspirational style of authentic travel. He did so by examining what and how people eat. Bourdain still inspires foodies with wanderlust to travel and not fear discomfort. As travel blogger Jaron Gilinsky put it in "Why People Loved Bourdain," "Tony stood for more than mere writing, traveling, and eating . . . he became a cultural icon for the three isms of humanism, pluralism, and globalism . . . Bourdain had a trademark formula for human connection that is so simple, so replicable, and yet so lost in today's world . . . when you sit down and share a meal with someone . . . you have a better chance of understanding them." In an interview about his Beirut experience with the Television Academy Foundation, Bourdain stated, "Food's super important. It's the way we get people to say things to us."

With food as the medium for encountering their context and lived experience, Bourdain was able to make contact with the humanity of others. This is his food-based ethics of community. His sitting down to break bread and chat led his TV viewers to do the same. He managed to tell individual stories of tragedy and triumph through food and helped shed light on marginalized people and controversial political situations. His interviewees ranged from kings and political figures to home-cooking grandmas and fishermen, and he shared meals with people who span all cultural, political and socio-economic spectrums. He even dove into the Israeli-Palestinian conflict using food to find common ground. Over a meal, he always managed to put people at ease, even as he asked difficult questions. Bourdain once noted, "I'd begun to believe that the dinner table was the great leveler, where people from opposite sides of the world could always sit down and talk and eat and drink and if not solve all the world's problems, at least find, for a time, common ground."

In regard to her own travel writing, Jill personally notes:

> Bourdain was the reason I was captivated by my South Asian tuk tuk driver's harrowing story of escaping a tsunami, why I converse with my graffiti-artist bartender about his long commute and ailing mother over martinis at my Milan hotel; why I try (in my terrible Spanish) to ask questions to a local woman making tortillas on a piping hot griddle in a back alley of Tepoztlán, Mexico. Anthony Bourdain, troubled yet charming curmudgeon, left a legacy to an entire generation of traveling foodies, by leading us all to contemplate the moral and ethical implications of travel through the search for interactive cultural culinary experiences.

Across his many shows, Bourdain repeatedly referred to local establishments as "authentic." From the point of view of a typical tourist, Bourdain's advice regarding Rome might seem odd: "If you do one thing in Rome, one thing, forget about Vatican City, all the rest; one thing, find a place that is guaranteed by locals to make good *cacio e pepe*, get yourself a nice jug of wine, and eat." (*The Layover*, Season One, Episode 3). In an episode filmed in Sicily, Bourdain expresses frustration on camera when a fishing scene is staged with an already dead octopus. Bourdain always disliked the idea of "TV Magic," and worried that anything which smacked of inauthenticity damaged the integrity of the stories he was attempting to tell. As long as he made a true human connection with locals, though, the experience was authentic.

This again brings to mind the prescription from the original tagline to Bourdain's show *No Reservations*, "Be a traveler, not a tourist." To take a tour is to look at scenes from outside, like at a zoo. Whereas, to travel through a space is to be there, as much as one can, just as the locals are there. To be with the locals in their way of being, rather than to merely look at them as exhibits is to encounter the reality they encounter. For Bourdain, the value of participating in the shared practices of a community, which developed through their natural coping with the local environment, transcends all consumer-influenced social worldviews of environments.

In *The Nasty Bits*, Bourdain writes "Travel changes you. As you move through this life and this world you change things slightly, you leave marks behind, however small. And in return, life—and travel—leaves marks on you. Most of the time, those marks—on your body or on your heart—are beautiful. Often, though, they hurt." This is the human aspect of travel. When visiting New Orleans (*A Cook's Tour*, Season Two, Episode 2) Bourdain described the philosophy behind his intentions by noting, "One thing I'm not interested in is the whole French Quarter thing. No beads, no boobs, and no Bourbon Street. I want to check out the culinary margins, so I decide to head out into the sticks."

Just as a traveler differs from a tourist by way of emphasizing relationality and lived experience, so too the communal differs from the social. In his book *No Reservations: Around the World on an Empty Stomach*, Bourdain nicely summarized this distinction. "There's a harsh and simple rule to live—or at least eat—by: If you see more than two people from your own country or home state in a restaurant, you are in the wrong place" (p. 278). To truly experience the space, we need to relate to what is happening in the space. This is, of course, in contrast to spaces that have been converted into locales merely catering to tourists. In an episode titled, "The Struggle for the Soul of America," he referred to such tourist traps as the "generic uniformity of chains and franchises" (*A Cook's Tour*, Season Two, Episode 6).

Authentically traveling, not being a tourist, Bourdain expertly modeled how to make contact with the beauty, vast depth and deliciousness of the locals' communal dwelling. In this way, Bourdain's food-based ethics of community philosophically exemplifies a kind of humanism. The quirks and eccentricities of localities are not viewed from a distance and judged through the lens of an ideal (consumer) society. Rather, by placing the food and the culture of the space through which we travel first, a respect for otherness emerges along with the ability to experience true depth on our journey. It is in this way that the authenticity of Anthony Bourdain's "anti-social humanism" can function as an ethics for travelers.

14

Did Bourdain Go #MeToo Far?

Margot Finn

In what turned out to be the final years of his life, Anthony Bourdain was hailed as "one of the strongest #MeToo allies" (Rao 2018). When celebrity chef Mario Batali was accused of workplace abuses including sexual assault, Bourdain publicly criticized him and distanced himself from his former friend (Severson 2018a).

Bourdain also reflected with characteristic candor and humility on his own role in fostering the "bro culture" that dominated many restaurant kitchens, including some of his own as described in *Kitchen Confidential.* In a 2017 interview published in *Slate*, he said, "I guess I'm looking back on my own life. I'm looking back on my own career and before, and for all these years women did not speak to me. . . . I had to ask myself . . . : Why was I not the sort of person, or why was I not seen as the sort of person, that these women could feel comfortable confiding in? I see this as a personal failing" (Chotiner 2017).

Bourdain attributed his self-described vehemence on the issue of #MeToo to partner Asia Argento, and to hearing her experiences of rape and harassment in the movie industry and witnessing the criticism and scrutiny she experienced after becoming one of the women to accuse Hollywood director Harvey Weinstein of rape. In October 2017, when *The New Yorker* published Ronan Farrow's article first publicly indicting Weinstein and naming Argento among his victims, Bourdain tweeted @Argento: "I am proud and honored to know you. You just did the hardest thing in the world" (Marcus 2018). When asked for *Slate*, "what is it that's gotten you so passionate about the issues of harassment and assault recently . . . ?" Bourdain began, "I've been seeing up close—due to a personal relationship—the difficulty of speaking out about these things,

159

and the kind of vilification and humiliation and risk and pain and terror that come with speaking out about this kind of thing. That certainly brought it home in a personal way that, to my discredit, it might not have before." In December 2017, Bourdain tweeted, "I ain't woke. I was lucky enough to meet one, truly extraordinary woman" (Lange 2021).

Do you find yourself cheering? As a feminist, I do. So far, so good, right? Bourdain emerged as a champion of survivors in the very earliest days of #MeToo. He expressed unequivocal belief in women's accounts of assault and hostile workplaces and regret for his participation in the crass talk that too often elided with unwanted sexual advances, groping, manipulation, and rape. He took responsibility for his role in perpetuating the culture where assault thrived and for not having been the kind of colleague or boss women he had worked with would tell about it. When people applauded him, he gave all the credit to a woman.

But the story has a flummoxing coda, which became public only after Bourdain's death. In November 2017, a month after Farrow's article made Argento arguably more famous in America for having been raped by Weinstein than for being romantically linked to Bourdain or for her film career, an actor and musician named Jimmy Bennett sent Argento a letter of intent to sue for $3.5 million in damages including emotional problems and lost wages caused by her sexually assaulting him when he was seventeen years old in May 2013 (Severson 2018b). Argento ultimately agreed to pay Bennett $380,000 to prevent him from suing or releasing photos of the two of them half-naked in bed on the day of the alleged assault, seemingly at Bourdain's insistence and expense (Marcus 2018).

What should we make of this sordid postscript to Bourdain's support for #MeToo? In the documentary *Roadrunner* and Charles Leerhesen's *Down and Out in Paradise*, which portray Bourdain's relationship with Argento as obsessive, the Bennett payoff and Bourdain's #MeToo advocacy as a whole are primarily taken as proof of Bourdain's unhealthy infatuation and willingness to do anything for her. This story has a certain narrative coherence and plausibility, and yet, paying off your girlfriend's rape accuser is not typically among the forms of "support" expected of even the most avowed feminists and male allies. In addition to minimizing Bourdain's #MeToo allyship as merely another symptom of his supposedly addictive or codependent relationship with her, these stories implicitly discount Bennett's claims that what Argento did to him was rape.

Bennett's accusations dangle precipitously over the gap between the legal reality of rape, which currently depends on consent, and its social reality. That gap is the subject of Catherine MacKinnon's 2016 *Harvard Law and Policy Review* article "Rape Redefined." According to MacKinnon, the kind of rape by statute alleged by Bennett, which also prohibits sex between prisoners and guards or therapists and patients, is generally seen as a "lesser crime," if it is considered criminal at all (p. 463). If Bennett and Argento had met at a hotel in her native Italy, where the age of consent is fourteen, or Las Vegas, Nevada, where it is sixteen, them having sex would have been no crime. But would it still have been rape?

It might be seen that way, especially if Bennett were a woman and Argento a man. Argento's alleged rape of Bennett offers a useful test of how well MacKinnon's redefinition of rape as *sex compelled by inequality*, instead of *sex without consent*, corresponds to the social reality of rape in the #MeToo moment. Bourdain's insistence on settling privately with Bennett offers a further test of what it means to *believe* and *support* sexual assault survivors, as the #MeToo movement demands we do.

Who, Where, and When Is a Consenting Adult?

When rape law depends on consent, whether a crime has occurred depends on victims' subjective mental state of willingness at the time. We must believe victims because only they can know what was in their minds. The standard of consent perversely makes rape, that most embodied of violent crimes, an entirely disembodied legal concept: "rape occurs in the mind of B if it was nonconsensual, or in the mind of A if he wrongly thought B consented [for instance when she was too drunk to do so legally], *not by or in or on anyone's body in the world*" (p. 453, emphasis added). The need for legally objective expressions of this subjective mental state is how we get the refrain of "No means No" and attempts to cultivate a culture of "affirmative consent" and also, MacKinnon argues, why rape trials become inquiries into the victim's mental state based on clues like what she was wearing, how much she drank, and her sexual history (2016 p. 452). Immigrants intimidated into having sex by means of threats of deportation, women induced to perform oral sex under threat of imprisonment by police officers, and "a woman who insisted that a strange man who climbed through her window brandishing a knife use a condom before he raped her because she feared HIV infection" were all found to have consented to sex by U.S. courts (*ibid.* p. 446-7).

The role of consent in determining when sex becomes rape is also the reason *believing* women and victims regarding their accounts of sexual harassment and rape is one of the primary demands of #MeToo and feminist politics more broadly. But what is it exactly that we are required to believe? There's no question that the popular mandate to believe victims means we must believe, exclusively because Argento says so now, that any sex acts that occurred between her and Weinstein at Cannes when she was twenty-one were non-consensual and therefore rape. Why, then, should we not believe Bennett when he says sex acts occurred between him and Argento in 2013 in California, and furthermore, that he was harmed by them?

Surely Argento's victimization by Weinstein nearly two decades ago does not somehow require that we still believe her in perpetuity about other matters exclusively because she says so now. For one thing, her account is inconsistent. First, she said that she did not know Bennett was seventeen when they had sex and later, that she "never had any sexual relationship with Bennett," and was "deeply shocked and hurt by having read news that is absolutely false" (Marcus 2018). We must believe victims' experiences of assault because otherwise assault can never be said to have happened. The mandated credulity does not extend beyond the alleged assault, however, and certainly cannot be said to encompass defenses of harm they've been accused of causing to others.

Argento has implied that Bennett was just trying to get money out of her because of her connection to Bourdain. In the public statement denying that she had had sex with Bennett, Argento said, "Bennett knew my boyfriend, Anthony Bourdain, was a man of great perceived wealth and had his own reputation as a beloved public figure to protect." However, texts published by the celebrity gossip site *TMZ* that it claims were written by Argento to a friend read, "I had sex with him it felt weird. I didn't know he was a minor until the shakedown letter" (Marcus 2018).

According to Bennett's account of their meeting in May 2013, Argento invited him to a hotel and asked the family member who drove him to leave so they could be alone. She gave him alcohol, kissed him, performed oral sex on him, and then climbed on top of him and they had intercourse. They took photographs together with their unclothed torsos exposed, one of which was included in the letter of intent to sue. After returning home to his parents' house, he began feeling "extremely confused, mortified, and disgusted." The requested damages were based on Bennett's earnings, which were $2.7 million in the five years before his encounter with Argento but subsequently dropped to an average of $60,000 per year, which he attributes to the trauma. A public statement prepared by Bennett's lawyer says his "trauma resurfaced as she came out as a victim herself" and he was moved to "seek justice in a way that made sense to me at the time because I was not ready to deal with the ramifications of my story becoming public" (Severson 2018b).

When rape is defined as a crime of violating consent by statute, whether Bennett was assaulted depends on the legal determination of whether he could meaningfully consent to sex with anyone at the time. As MacKinnon points out, "It is a common refrain that children cannot consent to sex, hence intergenerational sex is rape by statute, but it is never said whether this means that children cannot give a meaningful yes (at age sixteen? seventeen?) or cannot enforce or be expected to sustain the consequences of a meaningful no. Nor is it explained whether and why whatever it is changes at age seventeen plus 366 days" (p. 462). The legal construct of an "age of consent" invents a chronological moment when all people become suddenly capable of consenting to sex in all situations and with all imagined partners when a day previously they could consent in and with none.

Rape by statute due to age may be where the law is the most out of step with the social reality. Few people would question Bennett's ability at two weeks past his seventeenth birthday to consent as meaningfully as anyone ever does to sex with an eighteen-year-old girlfriend. As MacKinnon notes, the genuinely wanted intimacy pursued by girls and boys close in age to eighteen "might be the most equal sex they will ever have in their lives" (p. 471). But rape law currently makes no distinction between teenage fumbling across the age of majority and powerful industry leaders exploiting aspirants in their field.

The law also has nothing to say about the sexual relationship between Argento and Weinstein subsequent to him raping her, which Argento described in *The New Yorker* as a complicated situation in which she felt powerless: "After the rape, he won" (Severson 2018b). The notion that any sex a twenty-something Argento had with Weinstein after he'd raped her was *consensual* past the point where she had given up on saying "no" is an excellent illustration of the meaninglessness of consent in any relationship where one person has a significant hierarchical advantage.

As an example of where the law does recognize the role of inequality, MacKinnon cites the American Law Institute Council, who explain in their provision for rape that may occur via "imposition without overt coercion" that "consent cannot be considered effective when the actor's authority vis-à-vis the person consenting substantially impairs the subordinate individual's ability to choose freely" (ALI preliminary draft quoted in MacKinnon, p. 462). Statutory rape laws represent one attempt to address this problem, but MacKinnon argues they don't go far enough: "The same recognition is at once made and elided in statutes that prohibit sex between prisoners and guards, teachers and students, patients and therapists, and lawyers and clients. The point they all recognize in what they do, yet fail to say in their rationales, is that *when power is unequal, consent to sex is unlikely to be meaningful, or it becomes impossible to tell*" (emphasis added).

Defining rape as sex compelled by inequality instead of as a violation of consent would narrow the gap between the current legal and social realities of rape. Whether Argento said yes to Weinstein is a poor indication of whether he was exploiting his advantages over her to manipulate or coerce her into having sex. Similarly, whether Bennett was on one side or another of the Nevada state line does not determine the social meaning of what happened between him and Argento. His age remains relevant wherever he's located, as is the fact that Argento was at the time a thirty-seven-year-old multiple David di Donatello–award winning-actress and recording musician whose Instagram posts subsequent to their May 2013 hotel meeting included: "Happiest day of my life reunion with @jimmybennett xox" and "jimmy is going to be in my next movie and that is a fact, dig that jack" (Severson 2018b). The standard of coercion by inequality might recognize what Argento did to Bennett as rape while allowing that seventeen-year-olds routinely say yes to sex that no one considers rape with people more nearly their social equals. MacKinnon's redefinition recognizes that what matters when it comes to distinguishing between sex and rape is not simply age, and not simply gender, but *power* in all its dimensions.

From Ransom to Reparations

When using the standard of consent, the fact that Bennett was seen as capable of consenting to sex with Argento in 38 US states and anywhere in Europe at the time of the alleged assault means he may have been *legally* raped by her in

California but few people would consider it a genuine assault. If there was no real crime committed, that makes the payoff by Bourdain essentially a successful bribe, which is more or less the framing put forward by the movie *Roadrunner* and the book *Down and Out in Paradise*. Both attribute Bourdain's eagerness to settle the matter privately to his obsession with Argento. Neither address the merit of Bennett's accusations, implicitly treating Bennett's request for money as a form of opportunism, exactly as Argento suggests. MacKinnon's redefinition of rape, which acknowledges any kind of sexual activity between Argento and Bennett as potentially exploitative and harmful due to the significant power imbalance between them offers another possible path.

Paying off an accuser is typically seen as a tacit admission of guilt. In statements denying any wrongdoing, Argento has explained why Bourdain would insist on paying Bennett, despite her insistence that she did nothing wrong: "Anthony was afraid of the possible negative publicity that such a person, whom he considered dangerous, could have brought upon us. We decided to deal compassionately with Bennett's demand for help and give it to him. Anthony personally undertook to help Bennett economically, upon the condition that we would no longer suffer any further intrusions in our life" (Marcus 2018). The state of California does not allow nondisclosure agreements in civil contracts involving allegations like Bennett's, so neither he nor Argento were ever barred from speaking publicly about it. However, in exchange for the $380,000, Bennett agreed not to sue Argento, publish any of the revealing photos, disparage her, or bother her for more money.

We have a phrase for payments like this, designed to purchase silence about something shameful: *hush money*. Elsewhere in this volume, I applauded Bourdain's unflinching integrity, his refusal to cater to social expectations and defiance of suffocating bourgeois norms. Quietly arranging to pay someone a mid-six-figure sum to keep a difficult truth out of the public eye seems like quite a departure from a persona ordinarily characterized by irrepressible authenticity. It was also a short-lived silence Bourdain managed to purchase. In August 2018, an unidentified party forwarded Bennett's letter of intent to sue and documents detailing the subsequent arrangement for payments to the *New York Times*, which published most of the details included above under precisely the kind of headline one imagines Bourdain would have most hated to read: "Asia Argento, a #MeToo Leader, Made a Deal With Her Own Accuser" (Severson 2018b).

The payment to Bennett might seem more consistent with the Bourdain many fans felt they knew and loved if we had a way to acknowledge what happened to Bennett as a genuine assault requiring some kind of redress. The notion of one's clan compensating someone wronged has a long history, although it has not been the dominant mode of justice in the modern West. Jesuit missionaries scandalized seventeenth-century European readers with stories about the indigenous inhabitants of New France among whom there was "no punishment which is inflicted on the guilty, and no criminal who is not sure that his life and property are in no danger." According to the 1644 account of Father Lallemant quoted at length in David Graeber and David Wengrow's *The Dawn of Everything*, instead of punishing criminals themselves, "the Wendat insisted the culprit's entire lineage or clan pay compensation. This made everyone responsible to keep their kindred under control." Similarly, among other nations he encountered in the Great Lakes region, "if a Huron had killed an Algonquin or another Huron, the whole country assembled to agree the number of gifts due to the grieving relatives, 'to stay the vengeance that they might take'" (p. 42).

Lallemant and other missionaries remarked on how well this system appeared to work, despite requiring no violence or force. Those who contributed when compensation was needed appeared to do so willingly, even bragging and vying among each other to outdo each other with contributions seen as being for the public welfare. Furthermore, Lallemant observed: "this form of justice restrains all these peoples, and seems more effectually to repress disorders than the personal punishment of criminals does in France," despite being "a very mild proceeding, which leaves individuals in such a spirit of liberty that they never submit to any Laws and obey no other impulse than that of their own will" (p. 42). Without any evidence or indication that Bourdain *intended* his payment to Bennett to be seen in this way, I wonder if we might nonetheless think of it as a sort of vengeance-staying gift in the tradition of the Wendat, Huron, and Algonquin.

Bennett claims to have been harmed, with one of the harms he specifically named being financial loss. Responding as Bourdain did, if he can be seen as representing Argento's clan, and giving Bennett what he asked for, if not precisely as much as Bennett requested, could be seen as an entirely appropriate form of redress, after which Bennett would be expected not to seek any other form of revenge. The duration of the silence purchased also matters less if the money is seen as less a bribe for privacy not long maintained than a kind of fine for damages Bennett suffered.

Writing for British newsweekly *The Week*, Jeva Lange also argues that *Roadrunner* got Bourdain's "#MeToo devotion all wrong." In contrast to the movie's suggestion that his "fervor was somehow a sign of his too-far-gone romantic intoxication," Lange says, "*Roadrunner* would have done well to see it as exactly what made Bourdain, Bourdain. Caring about victims of sexual misconduct and assault wasn't out-of-character or a red flag; it was an extension of the deep empathy and compassion he had for others." Argento also described Bourdain's insistence on paying Bennett as an attempt to address the situation *compassionately*. Seen as a form of amends to another victim of sexual assault, paying off Argento's accuser seems entirely consistent with Bourdain's otherwise unassailable support for #MeToo. Perhaps no response to Bennett's accusations could be more in keeping with the thoughtful, empathetic listener audiences who loved Bourdain believed they knew.

15

The Subtle Persuasion of Culinary Adventure Programs

Andrew Wahnsiedler

I was never a fan of Anthony Bourdain. However, this is not to say that I actively disliked him. I just never really watched any of his television shows or read any of his books. Admittedly, this is largely due to the fact that I am not a fan of memoirs or docuseries. I tend to prefer other television genres, and when I do read for pleasure (which is an increasingly rare feat these days), I crave fiction and fantasy, pure escapism.

At the same time, though, I've always found Bourdain's type of television show rather troubling. The idea of a white man traveling to an African or an Asian country, only to then discuss how different they are, has always seemed to me somewhat distasteful, especially considering the global legacy of European colonialism. I know Bourdain routinely traveled to locations outside of Africa and Asia, including various locations across the United States, and that alone should be reason enough not to dismiss him outright.

The question, then, is how does Bourdain view these non-European countries, these former colonies, when he visits? Perhaps more importantly, how does his approach to these countries affect us when we watch his shows?

Culinary Adventure Programs

My initial concern over Bourdain's television shows comes from the subgenre of television that he represents. Over the years, Bourdain has produced and starred in numerous shows, including *A Cook's Tour* (2002–2003) on the Food Network and *The Layover* (2011–2012) on the Travel Channel. However, his best-known shows remain *Anthony Bourdain: No Reservations* (2005–2012) and *Anthony Bourdain: Parts Unknown* (2013–2018). These two award-winning shows ran for over twenty seasons collectively, meaning that while Bourdain has at times participated in various cooking competition shows, the bulk of his television output consists of what we might call "culinary adventure programs."

Culinary Adventure Programs (CAPs) are a unique subgenre of documentary television that blends travel journalism with food criticism. The format of these shows is largely the same across the various examples: a celebrity chef or food critic travels to different destinations in order to sample a unique culinary culture, one that is markedly different from the presumed audiences' native tastes.

Culinary Adventure Programs are of course entertaining. They are essentially a modern form of the classic adventure stories that have long excited audiences with their depictions of faraway lands. However, critics of this subgenre point out that while Culinary Adventure Programs have the potential to bridge cultural divides, maybe even to challenge racist preconceptions, the individual examples often fall short of this ideal.

The ratings for these shows are usually driven by the perceived exoticism of the destination in question, which for a predominantly Western audience tends to mean a focus on African and Asian countries. This becomes especially problematic when the foreign cultures are presented without any sense of history or political context, including the brutal legacy of colonialism many of these countries endured under the various European powers. Under the colonial system, the native inhabitants of these countries were dehumanized, so when CAPs treat the local population as a voiceless backdrop, it immediately recalls how these people were once viewed as objects rather than human beings.

Perhaps it's too much to ask Culinary Adventure Programs to take the legacy of colonialism into account, though. After all, while these shows may have the side effect of educating their audience, their primary purpose is to entertain. I can certainly appreciate how many, if not most people, when relaxing with a little primetime television before bed, would not want to be confronted with the atrocities of the past. Still, CAPs present us with an interesting ethical dilemma: are we tuning in to observe and learn, or are we tuning in to gawk and judge? Perhaps more importantly, does the show in question somehow encourage one of these approaches over the other?

Bourdain Flips the Script . . .

Giving Bourdain the benefit of the doubt, I sat down for a weekend binge of the first season of *Parts Unknown*, after which I was pleasantly surprised. In the premiere episode of the series, Bourdain visits Myanmar following the dissolution of the military junta and the liberalization of the formerly oppressive regime. Rather than focusing on the novelty of his access as many Culinary Adventure Programs might, Bourdain actually opens the episode with a narration outlining the country's tumultuous history. This attempt at historicizing the present situation is already unique, as many CAPs would likely overlook the fact that the impoverished state of their destination is the result of a legacy of war and colonialism. But Bourdain continues, filling the remainder of the episode with philosophical musings on the virtues of democracy and freedom of the press.

This episode ultimately sets the tone for the remainder of that first season. Throughout the following episodes, which feature trips to Morocco and Libya as well as several other countries, there remains a noticeable difference between the average Culinary Adventure Program and the way Bourdain approaches his material. The host of any CAP is inevitably an outsider passing judgement on a foreign culture, a situation that has historically proven a breeding ground for racist stereotypes.

However, while many hosts seem blissfully unaware of this, Bourdain actively takes steps to mitigate it. The underlying mantra of *Parts Unknown* seems to be 'When in Rome,' and rather than 'civilizing the native,' the series instead utilizes the 'going native,' trope. Bourdain doesn't stand removed from the culture he visits, nor does he act as the 'white savior' trying to teach them a better way. Instead, he seeks to understand by practicing cultural immersion, by following in the locals' footsteps and eating what they eat. Rather than hiring a guide or some third-party mediator, Bourdain speaks directly to the local population, empathizing with them as they share their stories. In doing so, he not only gives the native population a voice on an international platform, he also gives his series an air of credibility that many CAPs otherwise lack.

Parts Unknown thus presents a refreshing change of pace, not only from other Culinary Adventure Programs, but also from Bourdain's earlier television series. Early in his broadcasting career, Bourdain drew criticism for trafficking in negative stereotypes. Most notably, the "Cambodia" episodes of *A Cook's Tour* were criticized for being "filled with tawdry stereotypes" (Mai, "Humble Pies"). While we might argue that Bourdain was simply describing what was directly in front of him, the point is that he actively chose to focus on the "abject

poverty in the city, comparisons to the Stone Age in the coun-
tryside, dirty hovels for hotels," rather than what arguably
should have been his focus: "Cambodian cuisine? Barely mentioned." Still, this was earlier in Bourdain's television career,
when he was less established and possibly more inclined to
confirm his audience's preconceptions rather than challenge
them. It's entirely possible that his overall approach in *Parts
Unknown* was his means of atoning for these past mistakes.
But if this is indeed the case, then how might we account for
the first season finale of *Parts Unknown*?

. . . Or Just More of the Same?

In closing the first season of *Parts Unknown*, Bourdain visits
the Democratic Republic of the Congo. Inspired in part by
Bourdain's love of Joseph Conrad's *Heart of Darkness*, the
episode plays a documentary of the Congo's fall from grace:
with discussions focused on the violence and corruption of their
former rulers, Bourdain's narration continually invokes a
sense of perennial desperation, concluding that there's "a lot
more hope here than there's any right to expect" (*Parts
Unknown*, "Congo"). Unlike previous episodes in the season,
Bourdain is passing this judgment as an outsider. He does not
discuss the persistence of hope with the local population at any
great length. In fact, he actually abandons his usual 'going
native' approach. Instead, direct interaction with the locals is
limited, and cultural space is negotiated through a white mediator. Meanwhile, Bourdain seems more preoccupied with re-
enacting the boat trip from *Heart of Darkness* with himself as
the main character, clearly oblivious to the fact that this puts
him in the role of the white colonizer.

In all fairness, Bourdain does present the current state of
Congo as the result of nearly a century of colonialism. Over the
course of the episode, he provides a brief overview of the atrocities committed under King Leopold II of Belgium, and then he
explains how Congolese independence was subverted when the
United States and Belgium both backed the Mobutu dictator-
ship. However, Bourdain continually speaks fondly of the past,
demonstrating a sense of nostalgia for the first half of the
twentieth century when the Congo was Africa's premier tourist
destination. Bourdain claims that Belgian rule made the Congo
the "envy of Africa," and at one point, when surveying the city
of Kisangani, he remarks wistfully, "If you blur your vision a
little bit, you can see the way it used to be" (*Parts Unknown*,
"Congo"). These statements come as Bourdain is lamenting the

fate of a luxury hotel once frequented by Humphrey Bogart and Katharine Hepburn during the filming of *The African Queen* (1952). The irony here is that this display of nostalgia directly follows a discussion of the apartheid-like system that dominated the Congo until the 1960s.

Bourdain's overall approach in the "Congo" episode might be best characterized as a type of "colonial nostalgia," a longing for the "better days" of European colonialism or the belief that colonialism was actually better for the subjugated peoples. This is immediately apparent from Bourdain's constant references to *Heart of Darkness*. In his book *Joseph Conrad and the Fiction of Autobiography*, cultural theorist Edward Said argued that Conrad's writing reflected the colonial desire to "civilize" native peoples. If Said is correct, then Conrad's novella is indeed a troubling example for Bourdain to follow. Granted, it might be tempting to say that Conrad is really to blame for creating the story and inspiring Bourdain, but I'm not sure we can absolve Bourdain of all responsibility when he actively chose Conrad's novella as a guide.

Bourdain's colonial nostalgia continues through the final interview of the episode. In speaking with the caretaker of a now defunct research facility in Yangambi, Bourdain asks the man if he remembers the Belgian rule. The man responds that the period before Congolese independence was a much better time. Of course, Bourdain does not challenge this claim, and understandably so. After all, he is a guest and probably does not want to appear disrespectful. However, neither does Bourdain challenge this claim in his narration. Instead, he offers a rhetorical question: "What do you say to someone who suggests that Belgian colonialism might have been the good times?" (*Parts Unknown,* "Congo"). This open-ended question, coupled with the state of disrepair showcased throughout the episode, allows the audience to entertain the possibility that Belgian colonialism might not have been the worst thing to happen to the Congolese. This obviously presents a challenge to Bourdain's fans who are thus forced to reconcile the "Congo" episode with their view of the man they have come to love as a benevolent crusader for cross-cultural awareness and respect. My concern, however, lies in the impact that this particular episode might have given Bourdain's position as a public intellectual.

Bourdain and Gramsci, A Tale of Two Tonys

It might seem odd at first to categorize Bourdain as an intellectual. Sure, his intelligence is readily apparent, and his television shows are filled with his own philosophical musings. Still, he's more of a rock star than a nerd. However, while Bourdain may not fit our common understanding of an intellectual, he easily fits the definition outlined in the political philosophy of Antonio Gramsci. Gramsci is best known for his *Prison Notebooks*, so named because he wrote them as a political prisoner during Mussolini's fascist regime. Gramsci wrote prolifically during his incarceration, ultimately filling more than thirty notebooks with his analyses of history and culture. Thanks to a network of close friends, the notebooks were smuggled out of prison and eventually published, and they remain a landmark addition to the field of political philosophy and cultural theory.

Gramsci's philosophy was formulated during a time of defeat, and not just in terms of his imprisonment. As a founding member of the Italian Communist Party, Gramsci was a dedicated Marxist, and like many other Marxists of his generation, he had been led to believe that the communist revolution was inevitable. All across Europe, though, labor movements were losing ground, and Gramsci had personally witnessed the crushing of the Italian workers' movement, first by the factory owners and then by Mussolini's Fascist Party. Gramsci questioned why the revolution had failed, and throughout the *Prison Notebooks*, he works to develop an explanation. His answer has since become his most enduring philosophical legacy: cultural hegemony.

The concept of hegemony originated in Ancient Greece, where the term "hegemon" referred to a state that held a significant military advantage over the others. The hegemon was therefore in a position to make demands, and if the weaker states didn't comply, the implication was that they might be annexed or possibly even destroyed. The historical concept of hegemony thus implied the threat of physical domination. Gramsci, however, believed that this definition needed to evolve to better reflect our modern world. Rather than a political structure with an implied threat of physical domination, Gramsci saw hegemony as a form of cultural domination.

Much like how it was used in Ancient Greece, Gramsci's understanding of hegemony is about control, but rather than occurring between states, he saw it as occurring between the different social groups within society. Gramsci argues that because of their political and economic power, the dominant social group is in the unique position to determine society's overarching cultural values. These values could be political and economic ideals, or they could be racial and gender ideals, but all of them will reinforce the dominant group's position at the top of the social hierarchy. The dominant group then works to normalize these values throughout the whole of society as a means of legitimizing their dominance.

We might consider as an example the fact that many newspapers and media outlets are owned by the incredibly wealthy. Because of the wealthy owner's editorial control, these newspapers and media outlets will present wealth inequality not as one possible economic system, but rather as the natural order. Gradually then, the idea that some people will be incredibly wealthy while others live in abject poverty will embed itself in society, even to the point that those who are actively harmed by this idea will accept it, because that's just the way things are. Cultural hegemony, then, is the idea that power is reinforced not through physical dominance, but rather through the images we create and the stories we tell.

Gramsci notes that in some cases, this acceptance of the supposedly "natural" order may be the result of resignation. Members of society's subordinate groups might feel there is no viable alternative to the existing social order or that the cost of rebellion is too high. However, he also argues that acceptance more readily comes in the form of active consent, and for Gramsci, this is the true source of hegemonic control. If you can convince people to willingly agree to the same values as the dominant group, then they will be less likely to try to change things. According to Gramsci, the cultivation of such consent is the responsibility of public intellectuals, a collection of individuals he calls the "deputies" of the dominant group (*Prison Notebooks*, p. 306). According to Gramsci, intellectuals are responsible for giving society its homogeneity, meaning they are the ones who convince people to accept the status quo.

Bourdain as the Gramscian Intellectual

Throughout the *Prison Notebooks*, Gramsci never offers a definitive list of these intellectuals. It seems likely that if he had, that list would include not only politicians, but also prominent media personalities like Bourdain. This is because the intellectual, according to Gramsci, is not defined by some mental or academic characteristic, but rather by a social function. As he colorfully explains, "everyone at some time fries a couple eggs or sews up a tear in a jacket, but we do not necessarily say that everyone is a cook or a tailor" (p. 304). In other words, just because someone is capable of deep thought doesn't mean that they perform the social function of an intellectual.

Let's consider then how Bourdain fits Gramsci's definition of an intellectual. Gramsci argues that an intellectual is determined by two attributes. The first of these is that the person must be a specialist of some kind, meaning that they have some sort of expertise in a particular field. More importantly, this expertise must be recognized by other people. Ironically, Bourdain never claimed to be an expert, and as his longtime producer Tom Vitale illustrated in his own memoir *In the Weeds*, there were several instances in which Bourdain was just flat-out wrong. For example, while filming an episode of *The Layover* in Hong Kong, Bourdain was raving about the best Peking duck he'd ever eaten. He was then informed that he was actually eating suckling pig, to which Bourdain could only reply, "Well, this is awkward" (*In the Weeds*, p. 247). Still, Bourdain is regularly upheld as an expert, as the voice of authority. In 2017, CNN partnered with the independent journal *Roads and Kingdoms* to create a digital guide for recreating Bourdain's international journeys, thereby positioning Bourdain as an authority on world travel. Even today, this attributed expertise is reinforced through the routine publication of articles featuring "important lessons learned from Anthony Bourdain" (Natalie Compton). So even though Bourdain never claimed to be an expert, he is still considered one by the general public, and for Gramsci, that's really all that matters.

The second attribute that Gramsci identifies is that an intellectual must have political capabilities. This doesn't necessarily mean the ability to successfully campaign for public office, but rather the ability to act as a social or community organizer. As Gramsci explains, "He must be an organizer of masses of men; he must be an organizer of their 'confidence'" (p. 301). In other words, an intellectual must have the ability to get people to change either their beliefs or their behaviors.

While this might not have been his intent, Bourdain's ability to do just that is on full display in what many food and travel industry professionals have dubbed the "Bourdain Effect." Rachel Avila, a general manager for ICS Travel Group, has noted that customers respond positively to any mention of Bourdain's name, and as a result, the company has been marketing several tours as "Bourdain-endorsed" with great success (Beisiada, *Travel Weekly*). Even at home, Bourdain's influence is widely recognized. José Coto, whose bakery was featured on the "Bronx" episode of *Parts Unknown*, experienced a dramatic increase in sales following Bourdain's visit (West and Passy, *Wall Street Journal*). These are, of course, only a couple of examples of the degree to which Bourdain has influenced public opinion, and there are many more available. Even today, he continues to be a major point of reference regarding which foods and travel destinations we should like and which ones we should avoid.

Bourdain's demonstration of these two attributes places him squarely among the ranks of other politicians, writers, and social media influencers who might likewise be considered intellectuals. As such, we need to consider that the views he expresses on his shows are never just an expression of personal opinion. Rather, there is a deeper social implication, as they have the capacity to reshape public opinion and reinforce our existing cultural hegemony.

Bourdain, Agent of Hegemony

The way Gramsci describes it, cultural hegemony is almost like Stockholm Syndrome, where victims come to empathize with their captors and end up supporting the same goals. If Gramsci is correct here, then it would certainly explain some things. It might explain why people living in poverty would actively vote against welfare expansion or why the children of immigrants would actively support anti-immigration political candidates. More to the point, it might explain why the man Bourdain interviews at the close of the "Congo" episode would support Belgian colonialism, despite the fact that under Congolese apartheid, he would have been restricted from certain areas or from even being on the street after dark. For Gramsci, cultural hegemony explains both the failure of the Italian workers' movement and Mussolini's rise to power. Simply put, the workers were not able to overcome the cultural hegemony of the capitalist factory owners, whereas Mussolini was able to manipulate it to his own ends. Gramsci thus argues that any potential communist revolution must begin by establishing a sort of "counter-hegemony," one that opposes the dominant group's existing hegemony and unifies all of society's subordinate groups in the process.

In many ways, *Parts Unknown* seems to be working towards a type of counter-hegemony. Throughout the series, Bourdain challenges longstanding assumptions of American and European cultural superiority. Rather than presenting African and Asian countries as naturally inferior, he recognizes how their current situations are largely the result of long-term Western interference, and he encourages his audience to do the same. This directly contradicts the existing hegemony, which

sees the United States and Europe at the top of a global hierarchy. This hierarchy is continually reinforced by more conser-
vative media figures who will imply that African nations are
incapable of governing themselves, or who will reframe slavery
and colonialism in a positive light. While Bourdain openly challenged this view throughout most of his career, it is still worth
considering how his colonial nostalgia in the "Congo" episode
may similarly be reinforcing this status quo.

Consuming Media Responsibly

This is in no way meant to be an indictment of Anthony
Bourdain. While there are some moments of his career that are
troubling, when considering his overall ability to promote
cross-cultural awareness and respect, I would argue that his
career was filled with significantly more hits than misses. It's
true that those misses are indeed concerning, but in the specific example of his colonial nostalgia in the Congo, it's worth
asking how much blame can we reasonably assign to
Bourdain? He's certainly not the first to express this viewpoint,
and we could argue that he is merely following in the footsteps
of those that came before him. It's entirely possible that
Bourdain's own views of the Congo were shaped by previous
generations of Gramscian intellectuals, making him just as
much a victim of cultural hegemony—and can we really blame
the victim? The answer to this question speaks to a larger
philosophical debate surrounding the possibility of agency,
whether or not we can actually act independently or are merely
acting out roles forced upon us, but that is a discussion for
another day.

In the end, the "Congo" episode of *Parts Unknown* carries
two important lessons. First, it illustrates the problems with
mythologizing our celebrities. Even though we treat them as
heroes, our celebrities are not infallible. They are human and
just as prone to making mistakes, maybe even holding personal
opinions that we the audience would normally find detestable
(recent years have seen numerous celebrities "cancelled" when
their private lives were made public). As inspirational as he
was to many, Bourdain was just as human as the rest of us, and
he would have been the first to admit his own flaws. When
Bourdain returned to Cambodia in the seventh season of *No
Reservations*, he acknowledged that his original presentation of
the country was unfair and hurtful, and it's entirely possible
that were he still with us, Bourdain would have also apologized
for the approach he took in the Congo. Unfortunately, this is no

longer a possibility, and so the "Congo" episode stands as an important reminder to take what Bourdain said (and please pardon the pun) with a grain of salt.

Second, and perhaps more importantly, the "Congo" episode reminds us that media consumption is not without its political implications. We might watch Anthony Bourdain to be informed or entertained, but given his status as a Gramscian intellectual, there is inevitably more at stake. Bourdain wasn't just providing us with a glimpse of a foreign culture. He was modeling the ideal approach to that culture, one that we the audience assume we should likewise adopt.

The "Bourdain effect" has already been demonstrated through the many people who travel to foreign countries, or even eat at certain restaurants, simply because Bourdain went there first. It's already worth considering the way that media can normalize certain behaviors, even something as mundane as the way characters interact with each other on a sitcom, but with Bourdain being lauded as an expert, this effect becomes much more profound. Bourdain thus reminds us that even the most mindless television is never only entertainment, leaving us with the task of determining how to consume such media responsibly.

16
Fine Dining with Children Starving

WALTER BARTA AND CANDACE MIRANDA

Anthony Bourdain's lifelong project was a philosophical one: he pursued the good life. On the one hand, in an obvious way, he was an advocate of living well, exploring the experiences that the world has to offer, tasting and traveling; on the other hand, and more subtly, he was an advocate of doing good, showing a mostly western and well-to-do audience how the rest of the world was living and showcasing their humanity, both in celebration of multiculturalism and consternation over human suffering.

But in this duality lies a kind of dilemma that many Bourdain fans may be only vaguely aware of: shall we indulge ourselves or assist others? For example, should you dine at Michelin star restaurants, or should you give to charity to feed the starving children of the world? At first glance, this may seem like the fallacy of a false dichotomy: only two options given when more options are available. However, you can spend the same dollar amount on either option (or on innumerable other options), and in this sense every consumer choice is itself a zero-sum moral decision: where should you best spend your dollar? Indeed, Anthony Bourdain himself describes precisely such a question while filming an episode of his television show *No Reservations* in Haiti in the aftermath of flooding and famine:

> We are often shooting in countries that are very poor, where there are many people standing around . . . who are really, really hungry, and our cameras alone represent a year's income or more—you know, more money than they could ever imagine. I'm there talking local cuisine, and that means I'm there stuffing my face with food that a lot of these people can't afford. How do you deal with that? What do you do? ("Anthony Bourdain on the Haiti episode of *No Reservations*", 0.01 to 0.37)

Bourdain's dilemma in this scenario may seem highly local and specific to Haiti during hard times, but it has been generalized into a famous thought experiment known as the "Shallow Pond Argument" in philosopher Peter Singer's famous article, "Famine, Affluence, and Morality." Singer asks us to imagine the following scenario, similar to Bourdain's: you are walking in your nicest shoes and suit when you see a small child drowning in a shallow pond, and you can easily rescue the child without any great risk to yourself, but in the process you will assuredly ruin your clothes. According to Singer's (and most people's) intuitions, you would have to be a moral monster not to jump into the shallow pond; your clothes are simply not worth the life of a child. But then, Singer asks us to make the following realization: rather than buying the fancy clothes in the first place, a first-world citizen could donate the same amount of money to charity and thus save a child in a third-world country from starvation. At the time of publication, Singer was thinking about an actual famine transpiring in East Bengal, but similar such famines continue to this day—in Haiti, for instance, to give one example amongst many others. In other words, according to Singer, in a globalized world with extreme wealth inequality, we are always standing beside a shallow pond, we are always in our best shoes, and there is always a drowning child that we could rescue—if only we would just donate some money.

With these considerations in mind, a twenty-first century first-world person, like Bourdain, finds himself in an omnipresent moral dilemma: many of us live in a world where we can afford ourselves fantastic luxuries, and even feel justified in buying these for ourselves; and yet, almost everywhere we go in the world there are people less fortunate than ourselves whose material conditions and quality of life we have the affluence to improve. There is a direct tradeoff between doing good in the world and living well ourselves. Furthermore, as the world becomes smaller through communication and transportation technologies, the circle of moral consideration becomes wider, extending far beyond our own immediate proximal domain of influence. In other words, in modern times we no longer can appeal to ignorance or distance when declining to help the less fortunate. Not only do we both know about world suffering through international news coverage, but we can act upon it through reputable and effective relief agencies. This is especially true for a celebrity like Bourdain, who sees the whole world first-hand and has the powers of celebrity at his disposal to make a difference; but it is even true for his viewers (ourselves), who view Bourdain's adventures secondhand, are thus aware of world problems, and may have the time and money to give.

So, with such considerations in mind, how is it ever justifiable to eat at a fancy French restaurant, like Anthony Bourdain's Les Halles, when you could instead charitably donate the same amount of money to a starving family? For some insights into these questions we can turn to some theories from philosophy.

Living Well

Anthony Bourdain himself would surely defend the pursuit of some luxuries: good experiences for their own sakes. He describes his most valuable lesson from culinary school as: "how to cook for *ourselves,* for the pure pleasure of eating" (*Kitchen Confidential*, Chapter 2). For example, when Bourdain eats at The French Laundry, a Michelin star restaurant in California run by Thomas Keller, a chef Bourdain deeply respects, Bourdain unapologetically enjoys the experience in spite of its exorbitant expense, describing it as "driving a Rolls Royce in mink underpants—it's just so over the top luxurious" (*A Cook's Tour*, "The French Laundry Experience"). Admittedly, living Bourdain's lifestyle seems like an extravagant dream, and living vicariously through him is a close second, which surely accounts for at least part of the reason we watch him in the first place.

But, with Peter Singer's "Shallow Pond" in mind (with children starving in the world), is this kind of luxury *ever* justifiable? And are moral people thus doomed to meager bread and water? Various philosophers have offered reasons that the affluent can use to justify (or rationalize) their luxuries in the face of egregious poverty. Many of these philosophers are utilitarians, moral philosophers who think that we ought to pursue the happiest consequences—which, interestingly, is a school of thought that Singer himself embraces. Because these notable thinkers and others (like Bourdain) could be construed as advocates for living well, it's worth considering their views, to see whether and where Singer's critique of wealth may go astray.

Jeremy Bentham was one such utilitarian philosopher. In his most famous work, *Principles of Morals and Legislation*, Bentham outlines his utilitarian justifications for morals and laws. Bentham also offers a method for making moral decisions according to different quantifiable variables: he suggests that sensation has both "intensity", the magnitude of sensation for the individual person, and "extent", the number of persons experiencing the sensation (*Principles*, p. 22). In other words, pleasures and pains may be mild or extreme and felt by only one person or by many. According to Bentham's account, it's conceivable that a dinner at The French Laundry might be of such extreme intensity that a single bite would be worth many bowls of tasteless porridge. Thus, Bentham might ultimately be indifferent to a decision like whether it is ethical to eat at a restaurant like The French Laundry: both options, luxury and charity, optimize happiness by different variables. A world-class meal is optimal in intensity; donating the money that meal would cost to those who are hungry is optimal in extent. Indeed, Anthony Bourdain was certainly a defender of intensity and seems euphoric with every bite of his French Laundry experience.

John Stuart Mill, famous for his works *Utilitarianism* and *On Liberty*, offers a more qualitative utilitarianism. Mill suggests that there are "lower pleasures" and "higher pleasures", qualitatively different kinds of pleasures (*Utilitarianism*, p. 5). The former kind includes animal cravings whereas the latter kind includes fine arts and philosophical contemplation (as might be expected from a philosopher). To quote one of Mill's most famous remarks, "It is better to be a human being dissatisfied than a pig satisfied; better to be Socrates dissatisfied than a fool satisfied" (*Utilitarianism*, p. 7). This belief directly counters the more eclectic view of Bentham, who famously suggested that "all else being equal, pushpin [a simple children's game] may be as good as poetry" ("The Rationale of Reward," p. 206). According to Mill's account, a dinner at the French Laundry may be a higher pleasure and charity donations may result in lower pleasures. Thus, Mill might argue that these pleasures are simply incommensurate. The Michelin star dinner is more like contemplating philosophy; the charity dinner is more like a pig's trough. Like Mill, Anthony Bourdain certainly occasioned higher pleasures, dining on gourmet dishes at upscale restaurants around the world, working at one for much of his life, even going so far as to describe the French Laundry as "absolute perfection."

Henry Sidgwick, a philosopher whom Peter Singer himself greatly admires, has a different view. In the book, *Methods of Ethics*, an attempt at a comprehensive formalization of ethical systems and principles, Sidgwick offers a more dualistic utilitarianism, suggesting that there is a "dualism of practical reason": there are two equally rational and irreconcilable ethical systems (*Methods of Ethics*, p. 498). These two systems are egoism and universalism (utilitarianism): according to the former, it is rational for an ethical agent, like Anthony Bourdain, to maximize his own individual good; according to the latter, to maximize the universal good, the aggregate goods of all people. Although a guy like Bourdain may have been humble, he certainly treated himself, living perhaps one of the most personally satisfying lives that one can imagine, maximizing self-exploration and self-indulgence and even getting famous doing it! On Sidgwick's account, there is no shame in this. A charity donation may maximize the universal happiness, according to utilitarianism; but, a dinner at The French Laundry may maximize an individual happiness, according to egoism. Thus, Sidgwick might argue that Bourdain would be reasonable in choosing either option. The Michelin star dinner and charity donation optimize different ethical systems. According to Sidgwick, we may choose one *or* the other—or even better *both*, when compatible, like at a charity gala—but no further moral principle obliges us to choose one *over* the other.

We can speculate that Peter Singer would probably object to the above defenses of luxuries, and Bourdain might even agree on some of Singer's finer points. Regarding Bentham's "intensity," first, we might say that although we might optimize for the intensity of one pleasure, we might also optimize for the extent of another. This gives us no positive reason to eat gourmet any more than give to charity. Second, although eating gourmet may be intense, it seems worryingly counterintuitive to say that it is that intense *enough* to warrant starving children.

Regarding Mill's "higher pleasures," first, we might point out that although we might straightforwardly classify some pleasures as higher and lower, Mill does not give us a clear way of drawing that line. At five stars? Four stars? Three stars? Two stars? Second, at least according to a naive higher/lower dichotomy, we're tempted to the counterintuitive result that no amount of lower pleasure could ever equal a higher pleasure. Thus, if we have to choose between rescuing Socrates in his fine toga and rescuing one million starving drowning squealing pigs, we should go with Socrates; ending world swine suffering would not be worth one minute of forgone well-attired philosophizing.

Lastly, regarding Sidgwick's "egoism," first, we might point out that we have no moral reason to choose egoism over universalism, or vice versa. Thus, the egoist cannot justify his actions any more than the utilitarian. Second, we might argue, against

Sidgwick, that egoism is ultimately not justifiably moral—a critique that Singer elaborates upon in his book *The Expanding Circle*.

Notably, Anthony Bourdain himself frequently makes such criticisms of the luxuriant mentality. He is sometimes disappointed that fine delicacies are not intense but "rather bland" (*A Cook's Tour*, "Dining with Geishas"). He is frequently skeptical of the mystique of the high pleasures of fine dining, often in favor of family food and street food, even on occasion admitting to the guilty pleasures of fast food (*A Cook's Tour*, "My Own Heart of Darkness"). Furthermore, he's notoriously self-deprecating as a writer and a chef, saying, "I wasn't that great a chef, and I don't think I'm that great a writer," which suggests to us that, although he enjoyed the finer things, Bourdain was hardly egotistical, frequently admitting his own ignorance and insecurity in print and on camera ("A Drunken Afternoon with Anthony Bourdain"). With these thoughts in mind, we perhaps might reconsider what Michelin stars are truly worth.

Doing Good

Anthony Bourdain himself probably would have cringed to be considered an apologist for luxuries. By his own admission, Bourdain frequently felt the guilt of not helping more people: He wrote that when he died,

> I will decidedly not be regretting missed opportunities for a good time. My regrets will be more along the lines of a sad list of people hurt, people let down, assets wasted, and advantages squandered" (*Kitchen Confidential*, Chapter 25).

In other words, Bourdain's own circle of moral consideration significantly extended beyond his own personal pleasures. According to Peter Singer's book, *The Expanding Circle*, the domain of proper moral consideration has expanded over time and continues to expand, far beyond Sidgwick's "egoism," towards universalism. According to Singer, the original organic impulse of things was towards self-preservation, which led to the survival and reproduction of life forms. Then, in addition to themselves, certain species began caring for their own offspring. As evolution and civilization progressed, humans extended their sphere of influence and moral consideration beyond the family: to tribes, city-states, and nations. Singer identifies at least three categories that the moral circle is expanding to encompass in the modern era.

The first category of the expanding circle is the poor. People in unfortunate conditions stand to benefit the most from the least and are therefore difficult to justify excluding from any relevant moral consideration, especially those involving wealth distributions. Of course, Anthony Bourdain himself was in the top percentile on a global scale of wealth. The second half of his career was spent as a best-selling food critic and television show host. Most of us will never have the opportunities, financial or temporal, to truly walk in his footsteps.

However, for a celebrity, Bourdain had a rough start. The first half of his career was spent job-hopping between numerous restaurants on the East Coast, working his way up from an entry-level kitchen hand. Eventually he became a chef at Les Halles, an upscale French brasserie on Park Avenue in downtown Manhattan; but only after having a one-off opinion piece published in *The New Yorker* magazine did he become a household name.

As he put it in one of his last interviews, "I'm having a really good time. I worked a blue-collar job for the first thirty years of my life. Now I have the best job in the world" ("Anthony Bourdain on food, travel and politics", 0:10 to 0:20). Furthermore, in his book *Kitchen Confidential: Adventures in the Culinary Underbelly,* Bourdain scandalously undercuts sacred considerations of prestige by breaking class boundaries: first, telling us that high-class cuisine is perhaps overrated, hinting at many of the dirty secrets that go into supposedly five-star menus; second, telling us that kitchen staffs are perhaps underrated, shining a spotlight on their personalities and humanity. In this manner, Bourdain focuses on the people who are paid too little to make the food for which you paid too much. In his television shows, Anthony Bourdain frequently features foods eaten by the lower classes alongside foods eaten by the higher classes. He further emphasizes that "low class" often does not mean "low quality". He also showcases authenticity over affluence, especially avoiding tourist traps and popular sites—for example, shunning Disney World like the plague. In the last television episode he ever made, Bourdain returns to his roots on the Lower East Side of New York and reflects upon the poverty there (*Parts Unknown,* "Lower East Side"). In this way, Bourdain expands the circle to those in unfortunate circumstances.

The second category of the expanding circle is the foreign. People in other nations have often been considered beyond the scope of moral consideration because they live geographically external to the jurisdiction of the governing bodies by which such considerations are made. And yet, with the advent of world trade and world travel, the boundaries between countries seem to become increasingly meaningless and unwarranted. Although his grandparents were immigrants, Anthony Bourdain was a westerner and a first-worlder. Even as a person who had lived the lower- and middle-class American experience, he never lived in the conditions of world poverty. Even when he traveled the world for his television shows, he never went to countries quite as immiserated as East Bengal, the place wracked by famine that Peter Singer used as an example in his "Shallow Pond" argument.

Yet Bourdain did venture far out of his comfort zones, expanding the range of mainstream tourist spots: he put his destinations on the world map, in 301 episodes of television, traveling to over eighty countries. Even at his own peril and discomfort, he went to places where humanity was suffering: aforementioned Haiti, during hurricane season; Libya, during the Benghazi uprising; and Beirut, as the Israel-Lebanon war broke out; and so on. This was self-consciously part of a greater project, to expand the sphere of cultural understanding, even, as he put it, to "parts unknown." As Bourdain explains, "All of my relationships with people around the world begin when I express an interest and a willingness to respect their traditions" ("Food May Not Be the Answer to World Peace, but It's a Start, Says Anthony Bourdain," 2:00 to 2:10). In this way, Bourdain expands the circle of first-world awareness into third-world countries where we might never venture, expanding our awareness and empathy.

The third category of the expanding circle is the non-human. Although humans have historically bestowed moral consideration exclusively upon other humans, in modernity there is increasing consideration for non-human animals as well. Singer himself is sometimes considered the father of the modern animal rights movement; his book *Animal Liberation* is a classic of that movement. With the dawning awareness that many non-human animals probably feel pain and discomfort like humans do, some of the more brutal techniques of animal husbandry, like factory farming, have become increasingly difficult to morally justify. Thus, Singer himself has long advocated for staunch veganism. In contrast, Anthony Bourdain himself had a complicated relationship with animals. Bourdain was an avid meat eater, famously had an outspoken scorn for vegans, and even once defended the practice of force-feeding ducks for foie gras—in the French tradition. Bourdain's general objection to veganism seems to have been about pleasure and culture: he believed in experiencing the full range of tastes and traditional cuisines, not limiting oneself to an incomplete palate. In this sense, veganism is a kind of deprivation, so Bourdain would strongly disagree with Singer's own dietary habits. And yet, although more than willing to eat most animals, Bourdain was not a friend to animal abuse. In his own words, "The cruelty and ugliness of the factory farm—and the effects on our environment—are, of course, repellent to any reasonable person" (*Medium Raw*, p. 103). Bourdain and Singer would seem to agree on this point: modern methods for mass-producing meat create great pain and suffering. Bourdain would prefer that we acknowledge, respect, and be kind to our animals, even as we are raising them to be eaten, admitting that meat "started out as a live creature. It still is . . . until just before dinnertime," and further expressing some guarded admiration for small farms and markets that do their dirty work in plain view, suggesting that "It seems like a panorama of cruelty at first, but in some ways it's more honest than our system" (*A Cook's Tour*, "Cobra Heart, Foods that Make You Manly"). To Bourdain this "raw" honesty is a virtue in itself, but an awareness of animal suffering may also have the added benefit of leading us to identify and question the cruel practices of the meat industry. In this small way, Bourdain expands the circle even to non-humans, even while maintaining a desire to eat meat.

Like Singer, Anthony Bourdain himself was a man who expanded the circle, if not in theory, in action, whether through considerations of the poor, the foreign, or the non-human.

More on Morals and Morsels

As you're reading *Anthony Bourdain and Philosophy*, you probably have enough education to have a prior interest in the higher pleasure of philosophy, you almost assuredly find yourself in the English-speaking world, and you are definitely human. In as many words, you have some affluence, at least enough to buy the small luxury which is this book, and you perhaps even bought yourself a modicum of good thereby. But, as Peter Singer shows us, any purchase, even a small purchase like this one, comes at the expense of a possible charitable donation towards someone else's bare necessities. With any luck, you may get intense, high-brow, personal pleasures from reading and viewing Anthony Bourdain's work (we authors can hope and humor ourselves). And yet, it is hard to compare our leisure reading to the hungry eating. If it makes you feel any less guilty, we authors are hardly off the hook either: the time we indulged in the guilty pleasure of writing could have been spent volunteering for humanitarian causes, or some such, in countries far off Bourdain's beaten path. Peter Singer does not quite exonerate us there, nor does Anthony Bourdain. In the theme song of *Parts Unknown*, the sentiment of the expanding circle seems to prevail:

> I took a walk in this beautiful world
>
> Felt the cool rain on my shoulders
>
> Found something good in this beautiful world
>
> I felt the rain getting colder.

The dueling lines contrast the beauty and good of the world with the coldness of the rain. On one interpretation, the juxtaposition of these pairings is suggestive of the ability for the world to have "beautiful" things, and yet a concomitant burden on our "shoulders," the moral responsibility to preserve and protect those things wherever we find them.

Having the weight of the entire world on our shoulders may understandably be too much for any given person to bear. This is one of the dominant objections to the seemingly self-denying demandingness of Peter Singer's morality: if we can't enjoy ourselves even a little, then what's the point of having a better world anyway? Wouldn't the best possible world have some luxuries, after all? This also seems like something Anthony Bourdain would surely point out, as even in the lowest moments of his journey of self-discovery and world-travel, Bourdain always made it a personal pleasure. Not only that but helping others can often be even harder than it seems at first glance. For example, during Bourdain's own misadventure in Haiti, he did indeed attempt to feed some of the hungry children, like Singer would oblige us to, but, quite tragically, the locals began fighting over Bourdain's handouts, and the situation spiraled into a riot ("Anthony Bourdain . . .", 0:37 to 1:48). As Bourdain learned, famine relief is not quite so simple as stepping into a shallow pond.

So, let's not be too hard on ourselves, lest we throw up our hands and shrug off the burden entirely; we have to start somewhere. As Anthony Bourdain says, "Food may not be the answer to world peace, but it's a start" ("Food . . .", 1:30 to 1:40). And yet, there are ways to work towards forgiving first-world excesses, so let's still consider what small things we can do to help, especially if, like Bourdain, we are very fortunate. Next time you go to a fancy restaurant, can you leave a bigger tip, can you give leftovers to a homeless man, or can you order cruelty-free animal products? Maybe some greater good can come out of your love and admiration of Anthony Bourdain (and reading this book). Surely this starts with acknowledgement of and gratitude for our privileged positions in the world and the attendant awareness that there may be people less privileged whom we can help.

17
Chef of the Future?

Marc Cheong

After the untimely death of Anthony Bourdain, director Morgan Neville sought to narrate his life in the documentary *Roadrunner* (2021). Many famous people have had documentaries made about them after their deaths, of course, but one key decision by Neville made *Roadrunner* stand out and generated a lot of hype.

You're watching *Roadrunner* and you suspect that a minor plot point in the movie is amiss, but you can't quite put your finger on what. Or, maybe you don't realize anything is amiss at all. That is, until you open up Roadrunner's IMDB page, or scroll through the user-generated commentary on Amazon Prime Video, or pick up a copy of the *New Yorker*.

The crux of the issue? Several snippets of speech in *Roadrunner* which sounded like Anthony were originally written by him, but, contrary to first impressions, were not actually vocalized by Bourdain. The moviemakers used an Artificial Intelligence (AI) Doppelgänger to simulate Bourdain's voice reading out sentences he never actually narrated in real life. When asked which lines contained the AI-synthesized voice of Bourdain, filmmaker Neville told the *New Yorker*'s Helen Rosner: "If you watch the film, . . . you probably don't know what the other lines are that were spoken by the AI, and you're not going to know . . . *We can have a documentary-ethics panel about it later*" (Rosner). On the Internet, this all proved to be a big deal: *Roadrunner*'s Wikipedia article has almost a quarter of its text dedicated to discussing this sole issue (Wikipedia Contributors 2023).

Reactions were mixed: Some people may find the use of a synthesized voice to be innovative and a way to bring Bourdain's personality to life in a new and engaging way.

Others may view the use of this as unethical and disrespectful to Bourdain's legacy, as it creates a false representation of him.

Consider this chapter the "documentary-ethics panel" invited by Neville. Why did Bourdain's synthesized narration get so much attention? Why is this technique ethically problematic? Is it possible that Bourdain (bless his soul) could suffer any harm from this? Or, on the contrary, did anyone gain from a richer understanding of Bourdain's life thanks to his AI Doppelgänger? To help us answer these questions and more, we must first uncover how AI managed to bring Bourdain's voice back to life.

Anthony Bourdain's Doppelgänger?

With the increase in computing resources in recent years, several Star Trek-esque technologies anticipated in the past have finally become a reality. Take the friendly voice assistant on your computer or phone: Siri for example (or Alexa, or Google Assistant). While jumping on your bike to beat traffic and the office-hour rush, you can ask it to read out, say, the most recent text from your partner: "See you for beer at 5 p.m.!"

How does software like Siri learn how to speak? The techies who build such systems first train its "voice model" with lots of samples of speech. Using techniques such as "hidden Markov models"—simply put, complex mathematical models adept at speech generation—Siri will then learn to associate parts of a word with the actual sound bite needed to reproduce it. So, when a voice actor supplies words to 'train' the AI—"**bee**," "**fear**," "**sat**," "**fi**nite," and "hi**ve**"—it learns enough sound characteristics to read the phrase "be-er at fi-ve."

Old versions of speech generation systems sound stiff and unlifelike, kind of an audio version of Mad Libs being played through the speaker. However, with advancements in technology, modern systems like Siri can modulate their voice, with the appropriate ebb and flow in pitch and intonation, as it speaks a sentence out loud. This is because it has been trained on large volumes of voice samples, and 'knows' the difference between, say, the last syllables of 'cough' and 'bough'.

To reproduce Anthony Bourdain's voice for a documentary, we would need a large amount of audio samples of Bourdain speaking, which would be used to train a deep learning model to mimic his speech patterns. Once the model is trained, it can be used to generate new audio recordings of Bourdain speaking any desired script.

In the case of Bourdain's voice AI, filmmaker Neville told Rosner that "about a dozen hours of recordings" were used to train it; "Neville and his team used stitched-together clips of Bourdain's narration pulled from TV, radio, podcasts, and audiobooks." Taking as input text snippets from Bourdain's writings, a voice model can convert that text into soundbites that mimic Bourdain's unique speech patterns rather convincingly. This is where it gets tricky.

Assembling Our Documentary-Ethics Panel

Alluding back to Neville's quote, we will probably not know about all of the lines spoken by Bourdain's AI doppelgänger. What we do know is that one of the lines spoken is found in the trailer to *Roadrunner*.

To put this in context, the vocalization was from an email Bourdain sent to his friend David Choe when Bourdain was feeling low; the movie uses this as a device to hint at Bourdain's emotional trajectory:

> . . . and my life is sort of shit now. You are successful, and I am successful, and I'm wondering: Are you happy?"
> (https://youtu.be/jpkNYsuZScA—specifically at the 1:24 mark).

Even to my untrained ear, the snippet in the trailer sounded a bit 'machine-like' to be organically spoken, and the same snippet received the most media coverage, confirming the fact.

Why then, are we engaging in our 'documentary-ethics panel'? Is it because Bourdain's voice was synthesized in the first place? Or the fact that we couldn't pick out which other sentences are synthesized? Or is there something deeply unsettling about hearing Bourdain 'say' something he did *not*, after his death?

AI technology is able to create convincing outputs that would trick an uninitiated human observer. Improvements in computing hardware support fancier techniques for computers to 'learn' and process the large swathes of data required for 'training' AI. Systems such as ChatGPT (which creates convincing passages of text from scratch), and DALL-E (which can create photorealistic images) can be used even without much technological know-how, programming prowess, or the latest computers. One needs simply to open a web browser and type in an input 'prompt' for the computer to work on. *Deepfake* generation—as in the case of Bourdain's AI Doppelgänger—might need a bit more in terms of computing resources and fine tuning of outputs; but as *Roadrunner* has illustrated, the line between real and fake is becoming blurrier with each passing day.

The point is that technology is sufficiently advanced that many ethical conundrums once considered mere 'hypotheticals' are now actual ethical issues. As fans and admirers of Bourdain, and as philosophy aficionados, let's reflect on what our 'documentary-ethics panel' will consider. Ethics involves evaluating what makes an action—and its consequences—a 'good' and 'moral' one. Years ago, the question 'Should we fake Anthony Bourdain reading a heartfelt, emotional passage to prove a point before his passing?' would be a 'thought experiment' in the minds of auteurs and filmmakers, as there was no way it could be done given the limitations of traditional film-making methods.

But now, as the adage goes, just because we '*can* do it', '*should* we do it'? In Bourdain's case, it was done. With *deepfake* technology—simply put, technology that uses machine learning algorithms to generate highly realistic digital media, such as videos and audio recordings, that can manipulate or replace real content with fake content—becoming easy to access, this question is no mere hypothetical. We will now consider who might be affected.

Firstly, let's focus on Bourdain himself. Assume that Anthony Bourdain is still with us today, looking at how he is portrayed by this documentary. How would he have taken to his voice being replicated by an AI? (Even though Bourdain might no longer be with us, we still have to consider how it would affect him and his legacy). Finally, how would the use of the AI Doppelgänger affect us, the viewers of *Roadrunner*, from the outside looking in? Is it merely an artistic device that we should accept, or would we be wronged or deceived? (And if we are deceived, does it matter how much or how little?)

Anthony Bourdain's 'Voice'

Watching *Roadrunner* and *Parts Unknown*, and reading *Kitchen Confidential*, we see how Bourdain takes great care to ensure that the people he interviews are given a chance to say things from their perspective. Bourdain honors his interlocutors' agency, uniqueness, and independence. From the kitchens of New York to the remotest corners of the globe, Bourdain respected his guests' personal 'voice' and expression.

This is where the AI Doppelgänger of Bourdain raises a potentially thorny question. Does the act of having this digital clone speak 'for' Bourdain on screen deny Bourdain his personal 'voice'? Did the decision to use AI to impersonate Bourdain deny *him* the very autonomy he was always at pains to protect in others?

Autonomy is one of four common principles in the field of applied ethics. Beauchamp and Childress introduced these principles in their landmark "Principles of Biomedical Ethics" to guide medical practitioners in navigating tricky ethical issues in their work. According to Beauchamp and Childress, "The autonomous individual acts freely in accordance with a self-chosen plan . . . In contrast, a person of diminished autonomy is substantially controlled by others or incapable of deliberating or acting on the basis of his or her desires and plans" (p. 58).

The act of deepfaking Bourdain's voice raises some thorny ethical and legal issues because the principle of autonomy above was not adhered to. To see this, consider the legal aspect. I'm not a lawyer, but the Ford Motor Company was sued for using a voice impersonator to portray Bette Midler's voice in an ad without her consent. Midler successfully took legal action against Ford for this violation of her autonomy; Ford was [not] "acting on the basis of . . . [her] desires and plans" (*Midler v. Ford Motor Co.*, 1988). In the same judgement, the court's opinion was somewhat philosophical: "What . . . [Ford] sought was an attribute of Midler's identity… A voice is as distinctive and personal as a face."

On the other hand, AI technology can allow us to celebrate our relationship with the deceased and cherish our memories about their life well-lived. Technology such as MyHeritage's "Deep Nostalgia" recently allows anyone—no tech skills required—to digitally-reanimate photos of their grandparents, simply by uploading any photos we have of them. Surely these boons will outweigh any hypothetical loss of the deceased's autonomy? After all, would we not want to be remembered—digitally or otherwise—by those who survive us?

What seems morally hazardous in one context (as in Midler's case) can be beneficial in another (as in MyHeritage). However, there are clear acts which belong in the 'morally hazardous' category: stealing from Bourdain's estate, for example, is a big no-no, both ethically and legally (you can go to jail for that one!). An equivalent 'no-no' in our case is when, say, Bourdain's script for a new book was published (or worse, read in a documentary via his doppelgänger) without his consent, violating his intellectual property rights postmortem. The use of deepfakes, especially for the deceased, are still being explored in legal circles; extant "legal frameworks are unlikely to be sufficient to address the fundamental challenge that deepfakes pose to society" (Talas and Kearns 2019). The jury is still out as to whether deepfaking a person's likeness post mortem can yield more harm than good.

For Bourdain's *Roadrunner* though, there is another issue to consider: Bourdain has no 'right of reply' to the use of his likeness. Specifically, he can't defend himself against any harms or backlash arising from its use! Take the two cases we discussed earlier. In the MyHeritage case, it is limited to a 3D animation of an existing portrait and is limited in its ability to mar our memory of the deceased (for example, it cannot be used to make our loved ones, post-mortem, perform an embarrassing dance or say something illegal or downright racist). In the Bette Midler case, the Doppelgänger is a voice impersonator who sounded like Midler; even if the impersonator said something that Midler would not say in real life, ultimately it is *not* Midler's very own words and speech. But if you combine the two—given enough 'training' on Bourdain's old voice clips, the AI Doppelgänger can say anything, even, hypothetically, things Bourdain would have vehemently disagreed with—our 'right of reply' issue becomes clearer.

This, dear 'documentary-ethics-panel', is another complex side to the issue of 'autonomy' that we need to consider. Unlike impersonators who are easily recognizable as not being the actual person, deepfakes create highly convincing and nearly indistinguishable recordings. Bourdain cannot give his own account of events, potentially causing harm to his reputation and legacy. Would Bourdain have wanted his most intimate emails to be read by his Doppelgänger (even if it merely consisted of a digital mélange of all his speech patterns)? What if the narrated sound bite was something that Bourdain would have kept a carefully guarded secret: would he have wanted his digital alter ego to say those words, and mar his reputation in eternity?

Let's assume that, for one, Bourdain would have consented to the inclusion of his email exchange with Choe post-death, but only using traditional filmmaking techniques, such as having it displayed on screen or clearly read by a narrator. Aside from the 'creepy' factor of having a dead person speak, would Bourdain have anticipated how the AI voice would affect the viewers of *Roadrunner*? What if his loved ones' opinion of him has changed after hearing those words in Bourdain's 'own' voice, where those words were hitherto never spoken by him before; in a sense, he no longer has a 'right of reply' once the AI voice has mouthed his words aloud.

Parts Unknown, Quite Literally

All the above questions, however, assume that we actually do know which words are voiced by the AI doppelgänger. However, as seen in the earlier quote, the mystery lies in the fact that we don't really know which of Bourdain's words are deepfaked; filmmaker Neville was rather mysterious about it in his *New Yorker* interview. Hence, we have to consider the potential deception of us, the viewers.

If we recall the email by Bourdain to Choe mentioned at the beginning of this chapter, the vaguely robotic voice can betray the fact that it was not really Bourdain's voice. However, the mystery behind not knowing what other parts of the script are digitized raises the potential for deception. Which other words in the movie are genuinely Bourdain's own words voiced by his own mouth, and which are not? Philosophers who study the ethics of Artificial Intelligence, such as Vincent Muller, claim that the use of deepfakes undermines trust in general regarding digital media. Muller's concern might be expressed this way: how can we be confident that we're really seeing or hearing Bourdain when 'his' words, ideas, and stories are accessed via advanced technology and audiovisual films vulnerable to manipulation and deepfaking?

Besides the Bourdain-Choe email exchange, I could not personally spot which other parts of the movie were deepfaked by the AI Doppelgänger. However, thanks to sleuths, experts, and fans of Bourdain (Simonite 2021; Rayzn1123, 2021), two other passages have been identified which are highly likely to be faked. One, at the 22:30 mark, goes "I love Vietnam. Maybe it's a pheromonic thing. Like when you meet the love of your life for the first time, and she just, somehow, inexplicably smells and feels right. You sense that given the opportunity, this is the woman you want to spend the rest of your life with."; the other at the 1:20:00 mark, "It's this relentless instinct to fuck up a good thing. I think it's something that people on TV, people who write, people who cook share: this difficulty in giving love and receiving love. They just don't quite know how to do it."

These snippets are believed to have been generated from Bourdain's written work, and they are meant to evoke emotions and increase our empathy towards him. In this case, the source text provides context and depth to Bourdain's character: hearing him recite these passages can create a more personal and intimate connection between Bourdain and the audience. I'm not the filmmaker, but my guess is that it ostensibly helps to reinforce the idea that Bourdain was a loving person, as it provides tangible evidence of his affection and compassion.

Upon listening to these two lines again, I was astounded as to how they eerily blended in without raising a suspicion on my first watching of the film. Put yourself in my position: you went through the movie the first time without batting an eyelid, read about the 'hidden' fakes for the first time and ended up knowing how to find them, and finally listened to these lines again to confirm the fact. How would you feel: Astonished? Surprised? Bamboozled? More than likely, you would also have thought to yourself, "I didn't know that was fake—sure fooled me!". That's why epistemologists—philosophers studying the concept of knowledge—regard the use of AI deepfakes as a "serious threat to knowledge" (Fallis 2021). Put in another way, because of AI Doppelgängers, our ability to acquire knowledge of the world—such as our knowledge of which words were really voiced by Bourdain—is diminished. Apart from being an epistemological issue, that's also an ethical issue, and one also related to autonomy. Our ability to deliberate and act is compromised if we can't trust the information at our disposal.

Where To?

As this mini 'documentary-ethics panel' has shown, using AI Doppelgängers (including Bourdain's, but not only his) raises serious ethical issues. Even recently these issues were not so salient because technological constraints, cost, and, ultimately, how convincing the end product was, all limited their deployment. Now, however, thanks to advanced digital technologies, these issues (and future ones, I'm sure!), will become increasingly common in ways that should concern us all.

What might Neville have done better in the movie? For starters, the audience of *Roadrunner* could have been informed about which parts (unknown) were not actually in Bourdain's own voice. As pointed out by *Wired* Magazine (Simonite 2021), the use of subtitles for "disclosing them in the film" instead of "boasting they were undetectable" might have made a difference.

And here is the ultimate plot twist, to jog the inner philosopher in all of us, dear reader. What if I told you that *every penultimate paragraph in each of the prior sections you've read thus far* was mostly written by ChatGPT, the text-generation AI alluded to earlier in this chapter? That's right: it has been written (mostly) by a program, pretending to write as if it was me: I just had to make the sentence flow by sprinkling words, segueing sentences, and my 'personal style' here and there.

I admit I'm guilty of faking bits of my writing—you thought it was me, but it turns out that it isn't. You might be astounded, confused, bamboozled, or feel somewhat tricked. How are you feeling right now? What if I had failed to disclose this important nugget of information, and pretended that nothing was amiss? Has this plot twist given you an appreciation as to the kinds of issues—ethical and epistemological—that I have been alluding to?

In our case, I am still fully aware of—and consented to—the use of my Doppelgänger typist, ChatGPT, to write those sentences. Unfortunately, a question that we may not have an answer to, is: what would Anthony Bourdain have thought about the use of an AI Doppelgänger? What we *do* have, though, is a better appreciation as to how philosophers and ethicists approach the deployment of such technologies in filmmaking, the potential impact to the subjects and the audience, and to how we can slowly unpack ethical issues of the same sort.*

---

* The title of this chapter, as some readers might have realized, is borrowed from Bourdain's *Kitchen Confidential*. My special thanks to Scott Calef, our editor, for suggesting this interesting angle on Bourdain's life and legacy, and for his kind suggestions and improvements to the manuscript. I'd also like thank Dr. Jo Byrne, my partner, for bearing with me while I was stealing time from our holidays to write this chapter over *vino* and *cervezas* at airports, European wine bars, and everywhere in between!

Finally, I'd like to dedicate this chapter to the memory of Anthony Bourdain, for being an inspiration to us all.

18
The Journey May Also Save Us

TRIP MCCROSSIN

An "angry and thinly veiled warning that we are destroying our planet," Anthony Bourdain tells us early in "Bhutan," the Season Nine finale of *Parts Unknown*, is the reason why he finds himself there in the first place. More precisely, the warning's author, filmmaker Darren Aronofsky, its form his controversial film, *Mother!*, a "masterpiece" Bourdain declares, in spite of the "unjustifiably horrified reaction" dogging it.

And just in case a cli(mate)-fi(ction) masterpiece and its author as pretext to explore Bhutan as "environmental wonderland" isn't provocative enough, the episode's premiere, on June 24th 2018, marks, however unintentionally, the thirtieth anniversary of a watershed moment in the history of such warnings.

Setting the episode in a broader context, this one and others, helps to make clear that Bourdain's doing more than just traveling with a "friend," plugging his new movie. (We already knew that he was doing more than just traveling around, eating scrumptious food.) They're fellow travelers not just the once, that is, to Bhutan, but a few years earlier already, for Season Five's "Madagascar," which premiered on May 17th 2015. And this, a little over a year after Aronofsky's earlier cli-fi film premiered on March 10th 2014, *Noah*, which Bourdain nicely quips is "appropriate to our location." All the clearer, then, they're fellow travelers not just literally, but politically, and not just generally speaking (see above), but as fellow environmentalists. Bourdain could just as easily have traveled with a more conventionally wonky climate-crisis rock star, however (he did share noodles and beer with Barack Obama in "Hanoi," after all)—Al Gore, Naomi Klein, and Bill McKibben come to mind. But he didn't.

He *chose* instead to travel with Aronofsky, a fellow *story-teller*, who touchingly called Bourdain in turn a "poet of life." Their two-part journey, reflected in the climate-change diptych that is "Madagascar" and "Bhutan" taken together, is a contribution not just to the climate-crisis conversation, but more importantly still to a novel *storytelling* strain of it. As such, in addition to undoubtedly changing them, per Bourdain's oft-quoted *No Reservations* wisdom regarding "the journey," *this one* may also help *save us*.

The Slow Road to Bhutan

From a scientific point of view, we've known of climate change as a burgeoning climate *crisis* for well over half a century now, since Charles Keeling began measuring in *1958*, at the Mauna Loa Observatory in Hawaii, atmospheric levels of carbon dioxide. Reporting his first findings two years later, in 1960, "a worldwide rise in CO_2 from year to year," what's come to be known as the Keeling Curve, we had to know we were in trouble. One of the most momentous scientific discoveries of the twentieth century, it was instrumental in Paul Crutzen's equally momentous identification forty years later, in 2000, of a new geological era. Our era is now known as the Anthropocene, that is, marked by human activity having become a bona fide, sadly destructive geological agent, which most now date to the precipitous post-war increase in fossil fuel consumption known as the Great Acceleration.

The Bourdain we know and love came to us that same year, on New Year's Day, catapulted by *Kitchen Confidential* from self-described "journeyman chef of middling abilities" to celebrated author and public intellectual. A fan of many things, healthy and otherwise, he was a fan of science, in general and with regard to the climate crisis in particular. This he made clear in "Antarctica," which premiered on June 4th 2017, roughly two-thirds of the way from "Madagascar" to "Bhutan." What he was surely *not* a fan of, however, any more than any of the rest of us should be, is the fact that it took our politics another thirty years, after Keeling's first observations, to begin even to catch up. The appearance of "Bhutan" marking the beginning's thirtieth was a welcome, albeit likely coincidental nicety.

As Philip Shabecoff reports on the front page of *The New York Times*, that is, above the fold, on June 24th 1988, thirty years to the day before "Bhutan" premiered, notable experts appeared before the US Senate's Energy and Natural

Resources Committee that day, regarding the growing threat of what we now know as the climate crisis. (They included, for example, the National Aeronautics and Space Administration's James Hansen, the National Oceanic and Atmospheric Administration's Syukuro Manabe, Woods Hole Research Center Director George Woodwell, and the Environmental Defense Fund's Michael Oppenheimer.) "It is time to stop waffling," they testified, "the greenhouse effect is here," and "planning must begin now for a sharp reduction in the burning of coal, oil and other fossil fuels that release carbon dioxide," together with "a vigorous program of reforestation." In response, presiding Senator Timothy Wirth rightly urged, "Congress must begin to consider how we are going to slow or halt that warming trend and how we are going to cope with the changes that may already be inevitable," where the "we" would clearly need to be not merely national in scope, but international.

By December 6th, the United Nations had established its Intergovernmental Panel on Climate Change, issuing since over three-dozen increasingly dire public reports. With its *Special Report on Global Warming of 1.5°C* in particular, released thirty years later still, on October 8th 2018, a little over three months after "Bhutan" premiered, the IPCC seemed finally to be getting the public's attention. As Coral Davenport reports on it for *The New York Times*, on December 7th 2018, surviving the crisis will require "transforming the world economy at a speed and scale that has 'no documented historic[al] precedent.'" Unless we change in altogether unprecedented ways, in other words, we will soon enough pass the climate-crisis tipping point, on the other side of which humanity becomes at best dystopian, at worst extinct. While the report's authors conclude that it's "technically possible to achieve the rapid changes required," however, Davenport continues, incredibly "they concede that it may be politically unlikely."

Lest we think we can't add still to the absurdity of the concession, we recall Bill McKibben's call to arms, *The End of Nature*, which appeared on October 8th 1989, less than a year after the IPCC breathes its first. With it arises an ever growing, increasingly clear-eyed academic and popular political climate-crisis movement, its most notable recent contribution Greta Thunberg's "Skolstrejk för klimatet" ("School strike for the climate"), which she began on August 20th 2018, a little less than two months after "Bhutan" premiered, and which sparked the worldwide Fridays for Future movement.

How in the world are we *still*, then, after *all* these years, barreling more or less headlong toward extinction? Probably not the only reason, but perhaps we've just not been watching "Madagascar" and "Bhutan" properly. One wonders.

The idea, cheeky as it may seem, is not without support. Amitav Ghosh might well agree, for example. In *The Great Derangement*, that is, which appeared on September 14th 2016, eleven days before the noodles-and-beer sit-down aired, he imagines provocatively a curious fault that future generations may find in us. "In a substantially altered world," he wonders, in appearance more akin to the already ravaged Madagascar than still bucolic Bhutan, what of those who "turn to the art and literature of our time [and] look, first and most urgently, for traces and portents of the altered world of their inheritance?" Finding such traces and portents few and far between, "what should they—what can they—do other than to conclude that ours was a time when most forms of art and literature were drawn into the modes of concealment that prevented [us] from recognizing the realities of [our] plight." Most, but not all. Enter Bourdain and Aronofsky.

Bhutan via Madagascar

A distance of seven thousand kilometers separates Madagascar and Bhutan, as the crow flies, spanning a large swath of the Indian Ocean and then much of India proper. So, not your typical lay-over. Still, in the present context, there's something interestingly prefatory in "Madagascar," vis-à-vis "Bhutan." This even notwithstanding the seemingly haphazard manner in which the episodes' locations were chosen, at least in the first instance, as Aronofsky describes the choice.

Ruminating on his "time with Tony in Madagascar and Bhutan," on the occasion of the "Bhutan" premiere, a little over two weeks after Bourdain passed, we learn that they met in 2014 through social media, and became regular texters thereafter. He had "just finished [*Noah*] and was exhausted . . . thinking a new idea [would] never come . . . need[ing] fresh eyes," and asked Bourdain if he could "tag along" as he prepared this or that episode. Surprised to be offered the choice of venue, "half-joking" he suggested Madagascar, a place he "couldn't imagine ever getting to," and they were off on what turned out to be a "sobering journey." The island is "in a precarious state," after all, "struggling with real poverty and deforestation." Still, he returned "re-energized to start a new idea," which, given the striking resemblance between the ruined landscapes reflected in the episode and in the film, must surely be *Mother!*'s "angry and thinly veiled warning," with which we began.

Precisely how they end up in Bhutan, however, three years later, on this Aronofsky's less forthcoming. They'd stayed in touch occasionally in the wake the Madagascar trip, picking up suddenly in the run-up to Patrick Radden Keefe's "Anthony Bourdain's Moveable Feast" profile for *The New Yorker*, in the issue for February 13 and 20, 2017. "They called me [and] I called Tony," he relays, and "the next thing I knew we were headed to Bhutan." While this has more the flavor of "tagging along" on a trip already planned than in the case of the Madagascar one, there's nonetheless a tension between this and the way Bourdain himself describes the genesis of the Bhutan trip early in the episode. "I'm here because of this guy," he tells us, unequivocally, "my friend, the film director Darren Aronofsky." How best to interpret?

Perhaps we take "because of this guy" to mean, on the one hand, that Aronofsky did in fact set Bhutan as the new episode's destination, as he set Madagascar as the earlier episode's? Having gone to the trouble of making clear that the earlier choice was Aronofsky's, however, why not go ahead now and make clear that the later one was his as well? Perhaps instead, then, on the other hand, Aronofsky set Bhutan as the new episode's destination *less directly*, by *having* set Madagascar as the earlier episode's, which became eventually Bourdain's inspiration for choosing Bhutan as the new one's? Again, though, having gone to the trouble of making clear that the earlier choice was Aronofsky's, why not go to the little bit of extra trouble now to make clear that the later one wasn't, but rather Bourdain's? Cli-fi auteur Aronofsky being along for both rides, there's surely something significant about the pairing. But what?

"Who gets to tell the stories?," Bourdain asks, as "Kenya" concludes, the posthumous final season's premiere episode—a heart-wrenching moment, as tragically he would no longer be telling them, this his final written narration. In the spirit of what he'd proposed regularly over the years, in one fashion or another (in the Field Notes to "Madagascar," for example), his "answer in this case, for better or for worse, is *I* do—at least this time." It's "*my* story," he concludes, "not Kenya's, or Kenyans'," whose "stories are yet to be heard."

It's easy enough to imagine him intending the point to apply more comprehensively in retrospect, as in "not this or that place's, or its people's"—in particular, "not Madagascar's, or Madagascans'," "not Bhutan's, or Bhutanese's." Taking "Madagascar" and "Bhutan" together as a climate-crisis diptych, however, what follows, as to what's been heard, would presumably differ. *That* story, after all, "Madagascar *and* Bhutan's, and Madagascans *and* Bhutanese's," reflecting as it does *our* story, in the end *is* Bourdain and Aronofsky's, however unintentionally.

What's surely not unintentional is that, over and above being diptychal in the first place, their story has additionally helpful structure, within and across its "Madagascar" and "Bhutan" panels. The former divides into six "acts," as Bourdain calls them, loosely separated by commercial breaks. The six are preceded by a three-part preface, prior to the familiar "I took a walk through this beautiful world" theme song and title sequence. Finally, two overlapping arcs connect the three and the six. The first and third parts of the preface, naturally paired, extend into the episode's first through fifth acts, and then into "Bhutan." The intervening second part of the preface, extends into the episode's final act, and again into "Bhutan."

The Madagascan's Tale

"Madagascar" begins with a minute-long Madagascan tale, the first part of the preface (and the beginning of the first arc).

> When I was kid, my grandparents teach that there are some people who live in Madagascar before. They were very little people [perhaps in terms of individual stature, but more provocatively population size], and they live in forest, and they respect the environment. But then comes many people from other countries—from Africa, from Asia, [from] Spain, from France. Many of us don't know their history.

The medium being what it is, what we see and hear in the background's presumably not unimportant. Only briefly at the outset do we see the teller of the tale, or a figure we presume to be, illumined by a small fire in an otherwise darkened setting, while we listen to the first of the four sentences above. This gives way to bucolic images of undeveloped portions of Madagascar, as we listen to his second, peaceful music and the sounds of nature in the background. This gives way in turn to more ominous music and, as we listen to his third, the imagery turns to a distinctly less flattering reflection of Madagascar as it has developed. Finally, we return to the image of the fire, peaceful music in the background, as we listen to his fourth and final sentence. Cue the familiar theme song. (Thank you, Queens of the Stone Age.)

Roughly four minutes into what ensues, Bourdain concludes the preface with its third part, a narration of the "many people" portion of the Madagascan's tale.

Madagascar was settled, best we can tell, around 700 A.D., by people from what is now Indonesia, later by Africans. In 1895, the French took it, killed off a substantial number of people in the process, and as they do, left behind beautiful buildings and the French language. When independence came in 1960, it was sudden and ill prepared for. Continuing political incompetence has left most of Madagascar's twenty-two million people living on less than two dollars a day.

The history of the "many people [come] from other countries" is the history of colonialism, of course, the French variety in this instance, and of its tragic aftermath, generally speaking and in term of the climate crisis. As the Mouse says to Alice, in *Alice's Adventures in Wonderland,* our Madagascan might want to say to us, "Mine is a long and a sad tale!"

Further narration comes in the first and second acts, as Bourdain and Aronofsky discuss the country's "big issues." First, with celebrated postcolonial singer-songwriter Paul Bert Rahasimanana, better known as Rossy, over dinner at a popular eatery called *Look's Chez Ramasy*. Later, with legendary chef Mariette Andrianjaka, her fame spanning both colonial and postcolonial times, at her considerably fancier *Chez Mariette*. Madagascar's "very rich," Rossy reports, citing oil in particular, "but our political leaders most of the time are crook[s]," so the "big issues not being taken care of [remain] poverty and not enough education." Conversation over the later meal confirms the sentiment.

"We have a lot of things that a lot of people want," we learn, "for example, the trafficking of rosewood, prospecting for oil, for gas, and they don't leave anything for the rest of the country," and so "a lot of our forests are being burned down because people don't have land [with] which to grow their crops." Still, Madagascar's an "island paradise," but one that, as Aronofsky interjects, is "disappearing very, very fast." We can't help but recall here his earlier question, to Rossy, whether "environmental issues matter to the people or is it just about survival?" His answer is sadly, also defiantly, no.

They don't care. The international community, they've paid a lot of money to protect the forest. You protect the monkey, you don't protect the people. I eat the monkey, if I'm hungry, I eat them. They don't care about the world is going more and more warm. Yeah, okay, it's warm, okay, it's warm. You are going to die, yes, okay, you're going to die. That's life, for them, just normal.

And in case the point isn't getting through to us properly—that the "they" invoked here, in "they don't leave anything" and "they've paid a lot of money," are akin to the "many people [who came] from other countries" in the tale at the outset, and those in his subsequent elucidation—Bourdain makes damn sure that we're clear. "A lot of people feel that the future should be ecotourism," he chides, but "That's just a return to *colonialism*, isn't it?" (A rhetorical question, if there ever was.)

The point's emphasized further still in the third through fifth acts. In the first, they explore Ramona National Park with primatologist, anthropologist, and conservationist Patricia Chapple Wright, including a celebratory feast with the Tenalla, the "people of the forest." In the second, they travel by ramshackle colonial-era train to the once major port, now "sleepy beach town" of Manakara. Finally, in the third, once there they experience "what it's like to wake up at the end of the world [facing] nothing but thousands of miles of Indian Ocean," including, of course, another feast. The compelling vision we're offered is of the "island paradise" that Madagascar *could have remained*, had it not been for colonialist and post-colonialist development resulting in, among other things, fully ninety percent of its forests having been "slashed and burned." It's a vision, as Bourdain describes the feast in Manakara, equally applicable it seems to the one with the Tenalla, of being able "for a little while anyway, [happy in the moment, to] forget about where we came from and where we might be tomorrow."

The moment can't last, however, reality reasserting itself inevitably, as happens just shy of twenty-four minutes in, transitioning from park to train. "We're at the edge of the park," Aronofsky reports, and "right on the edge, literally, is where they built the power lines and where they're slashing and burning," as has happened or is happening throughout Madagascar, producing to one degree or another what they see before them, which is utter devastation, a "post-apocalyptic wasteland." Granted, we're soon enough off the train, soon enough enjoying Indian Ocean vistas, feasting with local folk. Even so, reality again reasserts itself. "Before 2000," a local fisherman confides, "more fishes, but since then, smaller fish and the quantity as well, smaller."

"Madagascar" is only the first panel of a climate-crisis diptych, however, a more permanent consolation coming provocatively into view in the second, "Bhutan." A nation with a history also dating to the 700s A.D., while not without upheavals and other complications, Bhutan has, for all intents and purposes, eschewed colonialism. If Madagascar is either "exotic unspoiled paradise or microcosm for the end of times," as Bourdain offers in part two of the preface, and if these are the only choices, then it's surely the latter, due at least in part, perhaps in large part, to its colonialist history. If Bhutan is an "environmental wonderland," then, as he describes it, the conjecture seems inescapable that this is due in part, perhaps in large part, to the *absence* of colonialism in its history. And as colonialism has scarcely been eradicated, having become simply a more covertly complex "corporate colonialist" business model, then the conjecture is not only historical, but prudential.

There's a saying that folks think about who think about biblical parables, one in particular: Job's the question, Jesus the answer. (There're no doubt other, more secular versions, involving, say, characters from Russian novels, but Aronofsky's already got us going.) In this spirit, not as a biblical parable, but as a climate-crisis one, one might well think of our present predicament as: Madagascar's the question, Bhutan the answer.

Manufacturing Dissent

The "Madagascar, exotic unspoiled paradise or microcosm for the end of times" choice in part two of the preface is a more complicated one than first appears (which begins the second arc). It follows what seems to be a variation on Bourdain's familiar "who gets to tell the stories" refrain, though a bit more self-deprecating a one than usual, with what appears to be something of a truism in between. "Over the years, I've let a lot of extraordinary landscapes recede into a blur outside my windows," he confesses, "looked, maybe seen, maybe noticed, then gone." The truism that follows, preceding the choice, is in the form of a question, again, surely rhetorical. "We all carry different experiences inside us," it goes, "see things differently, don't we?" Then the choice.

What follows almost immediately is fashioned to set Bourdain and Aronofsky in good-natured opposition. (Ah, the miracles of the editing room.) "We're on an island in the Indian Ocean," Bourdain begins, on the Madagascar as "exotic unspoiled paradise" side of things, "with this amazing ethnic mix, incredible landscape, something like eighty percent of the animals here don't exist anywhere else," and so on. Cut to Aronofsky. "What does it mean when an ecosystem goes out of balance?," he asks in response (see above), on the Madagascar as "microcosm for the end of times" side of things. "Here you can see the blowback," he continues, as "people have been cutting down the forest [and] now suddenly you don't have soil anymore, and you can't grow anything anymore. It's a real situation." We all do see things differently, yes, or may be edited to, for effect.

In reality, they're far more like-minded than not. Granted, they've their witty repartee on the subject of vegetarianism (Aronofsky a practitioner since *Noah*, Bourdain not so much). Not to mention Bourdain's occasional devil's advocacy, though mostly intended, it seems, to set up the obvious retort. "Look, all the original fauna and flora in New York City and Chicago and Detroit and Los Angeles are gone," he challenges, for example, as they're looking out on the ruined landscape from the edge of Ramona National Park, but we "don't feel too guilty about that." The obvious retort being, from Aronofsky, that while "the argument of all these developing countries is 'you did it,' [...] didn't they teach us in the third grade that two wrongs don't make it right?" At the end of the day, though, notwithstanding their various differences, they stand shoulder to shoulder at the edge of park bemoaning the "post-apocalyptic wasteland" before them, in Madagascar and around the world, and, in light of the exception that is Bhutan, the colonial and other forms of social and political dysfunction that have given rise to it. Why, then, the manufactured opposition?

The effect is to undergird the general perspective that emerges over the course of "Madagascar," on the one hand, of the diptych more generally, including the colonialism conjecture. Also, on the other hand, to anticipate in the final act of the episode an extension of Bourdain's oft-repeated whose-story-my-story refrain that's unusual, if not unique in the annals of *Parts Unknown*. It's not his story, that is, or at least not *his version*.

Telling the story of "Madagascar, in many ways, through Darren's fresh set of eyes," he writes in the episode's Field Notes, is "a useful reminder, worth having, that what you see on the show is not the only angle," that "we are looking at the world out my window, but that there are other windows—that maybe I've omitted or shaded something, if only to present myself in a more flattering light." Delighted that Aronofsky wanted to tag along, and with the choice of where to tag along to, Bourdain's "only request was that he shoot some footage—with whatever device he wanted to use"—and that, "at some point, he give us his version of at least a portion of the show for which we have already seen my version." This Aronofsky does, providing the substance, indeed from all appearances the only substance of the episode's final act.

> It's an example of what may or may not be missing from the shows we make. An ugly, uncomfortable reminder that it's not just pretty pictures and neat, hopeful sum-ups. It does not, I'm pretty sure, portray me in the best light. Or any of us for that matter. But there it is. I thought it was important.

In the end, the reminders are at best modest, and Bourdain suffers no particularly unflattering light—not obviously at least. Aronofsky's version of the story does nonetheless bring a different light to things, one which shouldn't surprise us given the central storytelling motif of the cli-fi that preceded "Madagascar," which is *Noah*, not to mention the one that will come to precede "Bhutan," which is *Mother!* In this respect, his version is at least a little less sparing toward *us*.

Are You There God? It's Me, Madagascar

The final act, Aronofsky's alternate take, begins with a brief homage to Terrence Malick's film, *The Thin Red Line*, which appeared on December 25th 1998, the year Bourdain became executive chef at Brasserie Les Halles, which led to *Kitchen Confidential* and its storied aftermath. We can't help but hear echo in the background the film's initial questions—"What's this war in the heart of nature? Why does nature vie with itself, the land contend with the sea? Is there an avenging power in nature, not one power, but two?" We're prepared, then, for ensuing religious discourse.

Sure enough, the act's primary location is Église Rhema de Madagascar, three-hundred plus kilometers North of Manakara, where the Manampotsy River meets the Indian Ocean, its overarching story a series of snippets from its passionate preacher's sermon. Among the Hallelujahs and Amens, we make out that he's preaching on two parables from the Old Testament, first Jonah, briefly, and then, at greater length, Noah. In between we've Bourdain's "if you were editing this show, how would you tell this story?" invitation to Aronofsky, newly edited footage from the train ride to Manakara, and Aronofsky's rumination on what happens when we "want [to] make it all make sense," additional ruminations yet to come once we're again immersed (no pun intended) in the Noah sermon.

The portion of the train ride footage in play occurs toward the end of the roughly seven minutes reflecting the whole of it, depicting the highly anticipated stop to satisfy the "imperatives of food, any food." The results are, Bourdain chides, "somewhat suboptimal," but then again, it's "hard to complain about the lack of food options when you look around," which the camera is doing for us, showing us "lots of kids," looking at least as hungry as our hosts, and very likely chronically so. Still, while these "[f]lashes of everyday life, the struggle to live, to eat" are portrayed as urgent, they're not portrayed as *desperately* so. Aronofsky clearly intends to correct for this, with a newly anxious soundtrack, shots of kids clamoring, in seeming desperation now, for food from "foreigners on board," and finally, a brief moment, not included earlier, in which Bourdain asserts, as he looks directly into the camera, and so directly at us, "This is really [fucked] up."

The condemnation is more palpable, yes, clearly, but also immediately mitigated by Aronofsky's subsequent "make it all make sense" rumination, which, given its surroundings, we reasonably believe originates with the occasion of Bourdain's "how would you" request in the first place. One "always want[s] a simple answer to everything," he ponders, to "make it all make sense," but "it," as in everything, all of it, "seems to [be] just constantly surprising."

It's further mitigated by being set in between distinct biblical portrayals of divine justice, first Jonah's and then Noah's. Jonah, so the parable goes, is charged by God to travel to Ninevah to announce to its inhabitants that, as our preacher puts it, "[God] will destroy the city because all of [you] people are sinners." Jonah has little, if any faith that God will make good on the threat, out of mercy, which will fail to see justice done, he objects. He flees, then, is thrown overboard on his way from Jaffa to Tarshish, is swallowed by a giant fish, spit back out after three days and three nights, on God's authority, to take up again the original charge, which he does, to predictably merciful results. Noah before him, on the other hand, so his parable goes, famously has complete faith in divine justice. Again from our preacher, Noah having built the ark in anticipation of the flood, God made "all of the animals come inside," but no one else, except Noah and his family, and as a result, "all of the people are dead, but Noah's family are saved."

Mitigation notwithstanding, the moral of the episode's concluding act, for the preacher as for Aronofsky apparently, seems clearly to be what comes next. "*Here* is our ship," he pleads, arms spread wide, enveloping his congregation, Madagascans more generally.

> God will choose *us*, like he choose Noah. He save *Noah*. He protect *Noah*. He will save us too. *Hallelujah!* Pray for Madagascar. *Pray* for yourself. *Pray* for your family. *Pray!* God will save *Madagascar!*

A variety of images running in the background, in quick succession, from one end of the emotional spectrum to the other, we naturally imagine this to be Aronofsky's ending, as our preacher's last utterance gives way to visions of a windswept beachscape and a forest canopy. But then we're looking through the smoke of small-scale slashing and burning, and *then*, just before the episode fades to black, a *fourth* image appears to give us pause. Lo and behold, our Madagascan storyteller, who at the outset spoke to us of grandparental teachings, has returned, illumined by the fire as before, looking on in silence now, with others more visible around the fire, also more visibly diverse, maybe even including our preacher and his flock. Gives us pause indeed.

The broader moral, then, not our preacher's exactly, but Aronofsky's nonetheless, comes it seems in setting side-by-side the religious and the secular—the last bit of our preacher's sermon with what we're invited to imagine our storyteller may be thinking. If God does indeed save Madagascar, that is, and by implication the rest of us, it'll be because God will *have* saved us, and not because of some business about divine foreknowledge and the like, but by virtue of our having been gifted the ability to *think*! In this spirit, invited as we are to imagine what the storyteller may be thinking, as he looks on in silence, perhaps it goes something like this. "Mine is *still* a long and a sad tale, at least in part because *still* many of us don't know properly the history of those who lived in Madagascar before, so let's *think together* on *that!*" Enter "Bhutan."

Actually, God, If You're There, It's Bhutan

A remote, relatively rarely visited kingdom of myth and legend high in the Himalayas, known as "the Land of the Thunder Dragon," we learn at the outset of "Bhutan," until recently "Carefully and deliberately kept free of development, non-Bhutanese influences, and Western architecture, the tiny kingdom [of Bhutan] is caught between the old world and the new." The episode's primary concern, over and above delighting as always in local cuisine, is how well the Bhutanese may be able to extricate themselves.

The country's going to be "a very, very different place in five years," Aronofsky acknowledges in the episode's concluding act, in light of different sorts of modernizations under way, but "do they stay committed to happiness and not to consumption," that's the question. "We're finally seeing the effects of climate change in a terrifying way," he continues, which increasingly media-savvy Bhutanese "witness" along with the rest of us, and "I think people are really going to hold on to treasures like this," referring to their location at the time, in the Tang Valley, the sacred Burning Lake. As is his wont, Bourdain is more muted in his appraisal. What "I know [is that] it's beautiful," he answers, and "I'm glad it hasn't been fucked up *yet* by the world." That *still* it's *not* is what makes it the diptych's second panel. Again, with greater specificity now, Madagascar's the question, Bhutan the answer.

Much has been made of the episode concluding as and where it does, with Aronofsky and Bourdain's silent prayers at Burning Lake, reflecting the Bhutanese "death ritual" practiced there, given that it first aired shortly after Bourdain's passed. Solemn as the connection rightly is, we do well to resist it obscuring the episode's overall motif, its various cultural-religious dimensions in particular, and the way in which they interact provocatively with the secular, in the spirit of "Madagascar," its final act in particular, understood as above.

Early on, in search of a better understanding of the sort of Buddhism practiced in Bhutan, the "Middle Path, Mahayana Tantric Buddhism," Aronofsky and Bourdain turn to Bhutan's "godfather of environmental conservation," Dasho Paljor Jigme Dorjim, known simply Dasho Benji, with whom they experience their first Bhutanese cuisine. "Yes," Buddhists consider the next life, "and always it's your karma; whatever tragedies fall on you, that's, in the family, karma; it's all about an attitude, [to] pick up and move on," which he summarizes with a thought the Dalai Lama left him with once. "Every day when you rise up," he said, "you try to be as good a human being as possible," which is "more important than being religious," or, put another way, is its fundamental business, its most palpable reflection. Equally important, how being the best versions of ourselves as individuals is a function of Buddhism's fundamental respect of nature, within which we all live, on which we all depend, and of the Gross National Happiness we create and share all of us together.

The Sound of Silence

"Madagascar," the diptych's first panel, concludes in silence—our Madagascan storyteller, illumined, looking on, inviting us to imagine the wisdom of his internal monologue. Its second panel, "Bhutan," also concludes in silence. "These are called tsha-tshas," Aronofsky explains, of the "offerings" central to the Bhutanese "death ritual," which he and Bourdain perform as the episode concludes. "You're supposed to put them somewhere where they'll last for a while," Aronofsky instructs, which we see each of them do, their hands in close-up, "and make a prayer." Again, we're invited to imagine their prayerful internal monologues.

At the forefront of their minds, we can't help but imagine, Bourdain's daughter, Ariane, who'd turned eleven a day shy of eleven weeks before "Bhutan" premiered, and Aronofsky's son, Henry, twelve three weeks and three days before. We imagine as easily their kids' moms, Ottavia Busia and Rachel Weisz respectively, and their then partners, Asia Argento and Aglaya Tarasova. Family and friends as well, presumably, various and sundry. And of course, our Madagascan storyteller, whispering hopefully to them, in the peaceful quiet of the moment, something like this.

> Ours has been a long and a sad tale indeed—*ours*, not just Madagascans', having devastating our land, but humanity's, having devastated the Earth. But maybe, just maybe, it's a tale a little less long now, a little less sad, thanks to the history of the Bhutanese and the opportunity it affords. *Our* opportunity, that is, humanity's, here and there and everywhere, not to succumb to colonialism, any longer or anew, traditional or newfangled. Let's *think together* on *that*! Let's *do something together* about *that*!

"People talking without speaking," so the song goes, "hearing without listening," and, while we're at it, *acting without thinking*. Bourdain was rightly celebrated for his unfailing ability to *listen*, deeply and sincerely, to whomever he was talking to, and to speak then, not just talk, but *speak*, in ways that truly touched us. "I have rarely witnessed talent on his scale be so willingly present and real," Aronofsky confessed in his Note, as "just himself: humble, confident, authentic, mischievous, kind." In the final months of his life, he became known as well for thoughtful action, in the context of the Me Too movement in particular. "The news in the world was crushing," Aronofsky continues, but he "had rolled up his sleeves and was ready for the ugly fight." How better to honor him, his memory, than by, hopeful whispers in mind, rolling up our own sleeves and being ready now for *this* fight, however ugly it becomes.*

---

* I'm grateful to many for kindly cultivating in me the sensibilities that have led me here, the following in particular, for their various unabashedly dedicated and inspiring environmentalisms. To Marvin Roberson, first and foremost, the Sierra Club's Michigan Chapter's Forest Ecologist, for his lifelong commitment to saving us from ourselves, which has inspired me since we were college chums. To Deborah Greenwood, since my early years at Rutgers, for her inspiring commitment to what properly wise agricultural practices should look like
    <https://rucore.libraries.rutgers.edu/rutgers-lib/47371>.
More recently, to Rachel Devlin, Marina Sitrin, and Sue Zemka, for the inspiringly enlightened lives they live. Finally, I'm grateful, very grateful indeed, to the volume's editor, for offering the opportunity in the first place, and since for patience and understanding *far* above and beyond the call. Less personally, thanks to Lewis Carrol (aka Charles Lutwidge Dodgson), Edward Herman, and Noam Chomsky, Judy Blume, and Paul Simon (and Art Garfunkel), for inspiring the third through seventh subheadings. (Fun fact, Herman and Chomsky's *Manufacturing Consent* first appeared on September 12th 1988, twelve days shy of three months before the Energy and Natural Resources Committee testimony in play here.)

Bibliography

Alhamrani, Danya. 2018. I Hosted Anthony Bourdain in Saudi Arabia. He Changed How We Were Seen by the World. *Elle* (June 8th) <www.elle.com/culture/career-politics/a21237666/anthony-bourdain-saudi-arabia-danya-alhamrani>.

Aristotle. 2014. *Nicomachean Ethics*. Hackett.

Aronofsky, Darren. 2018. A Note from Darren Aronofsky. <https://explorepartsunknown.com/bhutan/anthony-bourdain-darren-aronofsky>.

Battin, Margaret Pabst, ed. 2015. *The Ethics of Suicide: Historical Sources*. Oxford University Press.

Beauchamp, T.L., and J.F. Childress. 2001. *Principles of Biomedical Ethics*. Oxford University Press.

Bentham, Jeremy. 1830. *The Rationale of Reward*. Robert Heward.

Bentham, Jeremy. 2022. *The Principles of Morals and Legislation*. <www.earlymoderntexts.com/assets/pdfs/bentham 1780.pdf>.

Biesiada, Jamie. 2019. Tour Operators Feed Travelers' Hunger for 'Bourdain Effect' Experiences. *Travel Weekly* (February).

Binelli, Mark. 2012. A Drunken Afternoon with Anthony Bourdain. *Men's Journal* (December 12th) <www.mensjournal.com/food-drink/a-drunken-afternoon-with-anthony-bourdain-20121212>.

Bissell, Tim. 2019. Xu Xiaodong Ordered to Apologize and Pay Damages after Insulting Tai Chi Grandmaster <www.bloodyelbow.com/2019/5/27/18641269/xu-xiaodong-ordered-apologize-pay-damages-after-insulting-tai-chi-grandmaster-mma-china-asia-news>.

Blye, Ericka. 2018. 25 Pics of Food That Anthony Bourdain Actually Ate. *The Travel* <www.thetravel.com/pictures-of-food-that-anthony-bourdain-actually-ate>.

Bourdain, Anthony. 1999. Don't Eat Before Reading This. *The New Yorker* <www.newyorker.com/magazine/1999/04/19/dont-eat-before-reading-this#main-content>.

———. 2000. *Kitchen Confidential: Adventures in the Culinary Underbelly*. Bloomsbury.

———. 2000. *Bone in the Throat*. Bloomsbury.

———. 2001. *A Cook's Tour: In Search of the Perfect Meal*. Bloomsbury.

———. 2006. *The Nasty Bits: Collected Varietal Cuts, Usable Trim, Scraps, and Bones*. Bloomsbury.

———. 2007. *No Reservations: Around the World on an Empty Stomach*. Bloomsbury.

———. 2010. *Medium Raw: A Bloody Valentine to the World of Food and the People Who Cook*. Ecco.

———. 2014. Chicken Fried Steak <www.reddit.com/r/bjj/comments/2aaqb1/chicken_fried_steak>.

———. 2015. Older Practitioners: How Old Were You When You Started, & How Far Have You Progressed? <www.reddit.com/r/bjj/comments/30z933/older_practitioners_how_old_were_you_when_you>.

———. 2015 <https://www.reddit.com/r/bjj/comments/2k50b9/who_started_bjj_over_50/>.

———. 2015. <www.reddit.com/r/bjj/comments/3b0qhf/steven_seagal_sambo_champion>.

———. 2017. On Reacting to Bad News. *Medium* (December 12th) <https://medium.com/@Bourdain/on-reacting-to-bad-news-28bc2c4b9adc>.

———. 2018. Field Notes <https://explorepartsunknown.com/collection/field-notes>.

———. 2019. *Anthony Bourdain: The Last Interview and Other Conversations*. Melville House.

Bourdain, Anthony, and Joel Rose. 2013. *Get Jiro!* Vertigo.

———. 2018. *Anthony Bourdain's Hungry Ghosts*. Berger.

Bourdain, Anthony, and Laurie Woolever. 2016. Appetites: A Cookbook. Ecco.

———. 2021. *World Travel: An Irreverent Guide*. Ecco.

Bourdieu, Pierre. 1984. *Distinction: A Social Critique of the Judgement of Taste*. Routledge.

———. 1986. The Forms of Capital. *Handbook of Theory of Research for the Sociology of Education*.

————. 2018. Cultural Reproduction and Social Reproduction. *Knowledge, Education, and Cultural Change*. Tavistock.

Brillat-Savarin, Jean-Anthelme. 1949. *The Physiology of Taste*. 1949.

Brunvand, Jan Harold. 1981. *The Vanishing Hitchhiker: American Urban Legends and Their Meanings*. Norton.

————. 2001. *Too Good to Be True: The Colossal Book of Urban Legends*. Norton.

Carter, Ian. 2022. Positive and Negative Liberty. In Edward N. Zalta, ed. *The Stanford Encyclopedia of Philosophy* <https://plato.stanford.edu/archives/spr2022/entries/liberty-positive-negative/>.

CBC News. 2017. Anthony Bourdain on Food, Travel, and Politics. *The National* (January 29th) <www.youtube.com/watch?v=IoQ7dU9Dq08&t>.

Chotiner, Isaac. 2017. Anthony Bourdain Wonders What He Could Have Done. *Slate* (October 24teeth). <https://slate.com/news-and-politics/2017/10/anthony-bourdain-on-weinstein-john-besh-and-meathead-restaurant-culture.html>.

Compton, Natalie B. 2020. 5 Important Lessons Travelers, Chefs, and Writers Learned from Anthony Bourdain. *The Washington Post* (June 25th).

Darwin, Alexander. 2022. The Lost Diary of Anthony Bourdain. *Rolling Stone*, (December 11th) <www.rollingstone.com/culture/culture-features/anthony-bourdain-jiujitsu-secret-reddit-posts-1268801>.

Dickey, Jack. 2015. 10 Questions with Anthony Bourdain. *Time Magazine*, August 6th) <https://time.com/3987009/10-questions-with-anthony-bourdain>.

Diogenes Laertius. 2022. *Lives and Opinions of the Eminent Philosophers* <www.gutenberg.org/cache/epub/57342/pg57342-images.html>.

Egerton, Owen. 2021. Greek Tragedy and Horror Part I: Horror's Great-Great-Great Grand Pappy. *Fangoria* <www.fangoria.com/original/greek-tragedy-and-horror-part-i>.

Fallis, D. 2021. The Epistemic Threat of Deepfakes. *Philosophy and Technology* 34:4 <https://doi.org/10.1007/s13347-020-00419-2>.

Felluga, Dino. 2002. Modules on Kristeva: On the Abject <https://cla.purdue.edu/academic/english/theory/psychoanalysis/kristevaabject.html>.

Foundation Interviews. 2016. Anthony Bourdain on the Haiti episode of No Reservations <https://www.youtube.com/watch?v=SBTVDhIHiiA>.

Freud, Sigmund. 2001 [1920]. *The Complete Psychological Works of Sigmund Freud. Volume 18: Beyond the Pleasure Principle*. Vintage.

Garcia, Ernesto V. 2015. The Virtue of Authenticity. *Oxford Studies in Normative Ethics* 5.

Garza, Daniela. 2018. Anthony Bourdain's Most Memorable Quotes. *Eater* (June 8th) <www.eater.com/2018/6/8/17441238/anthony-bourdains-most-memorable-quotes>.

Ghosh, Amitav. 2015. The Great Derangement: Fiction, History, and Politics in the Age of Global Warming. Berlin Family Lectures <https://berlinfamilylectures.uchicago.edu/amitav-ghosh-great-derangement-fiction-history-and-politics-age-global-warming>.

———. 2016. *The Great Derangement: Climate Change and the Unthinkable*. Chicago: The University of Chicago Press.

Graeber, David, and David Wengrow, 2021. *The Dawn of Everything: A New History of Humanity*. Picador.

Gramsci, Antonio. 2000. *The Antonio Gramsci Reader*. New York University Press.

Harris, Molly. 2021. Anthony Bourdain Producer, Tom Vitale, on Processing His Writing and Grieving. *The Manual* (October 22nd) <www.themanual.com/travel/tom-vitale-discusses-anthony-bourdain>.

Harris, Sam. 2012. The Pleasure of Drowning <www.samharris.org/blog/the-pleasures-of-drowning>.

Hesse, Hermann. 2010. *Siddhartha*. Bernard Grasset.

Hume, David. 1985. On the Standard of Taste. In *David Hume: Essays Moral, Political and Literary*. Liberty Classics.

Kant, Immanuel. 2015. *Critique of Judgment* <www.gutenberg.org/cache/epub/48433/pg48433-images.html>.

———. 2016. *Perpetual Peace: A Philosophical Sketch* <www.gutenberg.org/cache/epub/50922/pg50922-images.html>.

Keefe, Patrick Radden. 2017. Anthony Bourdain's Moveable Feast. *New Yorker* (February 5th).

Korsmeyer , Caroline. 2007. Delightful, Delicious, Disgusting. In Fritz Allhoff and Dave Monroe, eds., *Food and Philosophy: Eat, Think, and Be Merry*. Blackwell.

———. 2012. Disgust and Aesthetics. *Philosophy Compass* 7:11.

Lange, Jeva. 2021. The Anthony Bourdain Documentary Gets His #MeToo Devotion All Wrong. *The Week* (July 16th) <https://theweek.com/culture/1002676/roadrunner-anthony-bourdain-documentary-metoo>.

Leerhsen, Charles. 2022. *Down and Out in Paradise: The Life of Anthony Bourdain*. Simon and Schuster.

MacCallum, Gerald C., Jr. 1967. Negative and Positive Freedom. *Philosophical Review*.

MacKinnon, Catharine A. 2016. Rape Redefined. *Harvard Law and Policy Review* 10:2 (September).

Mai, Joseph. 2018. Humble Pies. *Mekong Review* (12th August).

Marcus, Stephanie. 2018. How Anthony Bourdain Was Involved in the Sexual-Assault Allegations against Asia Argento. *Insider* (23rd August) <www.insider.com/how-anthony-bourdain-is-involved-in-sexual-assault-allegations-asia-argento-2018-8>.

Maxwell, Samantha. 2020. The Craziest Things Anthony Bourdain Ever Ate. *Mashed* <www.mashed.com/231840/the-craziest-things-anthony-bour-dain-ever-ate>.

McKibben, William (Bill). 1989. The End of Nature: The Rise of Greenhouse Gases and Our Warming Earth. *The New Yorker* (September 11th) <http://www.newyorker.com/magazine/1989/09/11/the-end-of-nature>.

———. 1989. *The End of Nature*. Random House.

Midler v. Ford Motor Company. 1988. 849 F.2d 460. <https://law.resource.org/pub/us/case/reporter/F2/849/849.F2d.460.87-6168.html>.

Mill, John Stuart. 2022 [1859]. *On Liberty* <https://www.earlymoderntexts.com/assets/pdfs/mill1859.pdf>.

———. 2022 [1863]. *Utilitarianism* <www.earlymoderntexts.com/assets/pdfs/mill1863.pdf>.

Müller, V.C. 2021. Ethics of Artificial Intelligence and Robotics. In E.N. Zalta. ed., *The Stanford Encyclopedia of Philosophy* <https://plato.stanford.edu/archives/sum2021/entries/ethics-ai>.

MyHeritage Ltd. 2023. MyHeritage Deep Nostalgia, Deep Learning Technology to Animate the Faces in Still Family Photos <www.myheritage.com/deep-nostalgia>.

Neville, Morgan (director). 2021. *Roadrunner: A Film About Anthony Bourdain*. Focus Features.

Nichols, Tom. 2017. How America Lost Faith in Expertise. *Foreign Affairs* (March–April).

PBS NewsHour. 2016. Food May Not Be the Answer to World Peace, but It's a Start, says Anthony Bourdain <www.youtube.com/watch?v=AsUSyepx1Ho>.

Plato. 2002. *Five Dialogues: Euthyphro, Apology, Crito, Meno, Phaedo*. Hackett.

Plato. 2012. *The Republic*. Penguin.

Proust, Marcel. 2002. *Finding Time Again*. Penguin.

Rao, Sonia. 2018. How Anthony Bourdain Became One of the Strongest #MeToo Allies: 'I'm Reexamining My Life'. *Washington Post*, (8th June) <www.washingtonpost.com/news/arts-and-entertainment/wp/2018/06/08/how-anthony-bourdain-became-one-of-the-strongest-me-too-allies-im-reexamining-my-life>.

Rayzn123. (2021). I've identified the lines in "Roadrunner" that were A.I. generated . . . <https://www.reddit.com/r/AnthonyBourdain/comments/ozjltv/ive_identified_the_lines_in_roadrunner_that_were>.

Ridgway, Judy, and Sara Hill. 2004. *The Cheese Companion*. Second edititon. Philadelphia: Running Press.

Rose, Charlie, and Anthony Bourdain. 2014. Anthony Bourdain on Cooking and Jiu Jitsu. *Charlie Rose*. PBS. <www.youtube.com/watch?v=QjHXipJoAqU>.

Rosenstein, Greg. 2018. Renzo Gracie Calls Former BJJ Student Anthony Bourdain 'A Great Soul' <www.espn.com/mma/story/_/id/23979330/renzo-gracie-former-bjj-student-anthony-bourdain-great-soul>.

Rosner, H. 2021. A Haunting New Documentary about Anthony Bourdain. *The New Yorker*. <www.newyorker.com/culture/annals-of-gastronomy/the-haunting-afterlife-of-anthony-bourdain>.

Russell, Gillian. 2010. Epistemic Viciousness in the Martial Arts. In Graham Priest and Damon Young, eds., *Martial Arts and Philosophy: Beating and Nothingness*. Open Court.

Said, Edward. 2008. *Joseph Conrad and the Fiction of Autobiography*. Columbia University Press.

Severson, Kim. 2018. Disgraced by Scandal, Mario Batali Is Eyeing His Second Act. *New York Times*, April 2tend <https://www.nytimes.com/2018/04/02/dining/mario-batali-sexual-harassment.html>.

———. 2018. Asia Argento, a #MeToo Leader, Made a Deal with Her Own Accuser. *New York Times*, (August 19th). <https://www.nytimes.com/2018/08/19/us/asia-argento-assault-jimmy-bennett.html>.

———. 2022. The Last, Painful Days of Anthony Bourdain. *New York Times* (September 28th) <www.nytimes.com/2022/09/27/dining/anthony-bourdain-biography.html>.

Shaffer, Michael. 2007. Taste, Gastronomic Expertise, and Objectivity. In D. Monroe, ed., *Food and Philosophy*. Blackwell.

Sidgwick, Henry. 1962. *The Methods of Ethics*. Seventh edition. Palgrave Macmillan.

Simonite, T. 2021. Are These the Hidden Deepfakes in the Anthony Bourdain Movie? *Wired* (August 23rd) <www.wired.com/story/these-hidden-deepfakes-anthony-bourdain-movie>.

Singer, Peter. 1972. Famine, Affluence, and Morality. *Philosophy and Public Affairs* 1:3 (Spring).

———. 1975. *Animal Liberation*. HarperCollins.

————. 1981. *The Expanding Circle: Ethics, Evolution, and Moral Progress*. Clarendon.

Stone-Mediatore, John. 2009. The Ocean's Roar. In Scott Calef, ed., *Led Zeppelin and Philosophy: All Will Be Revealed*. Open Court.

Surber, Jere. 2009. New Shades. In Brandon Forbes and George Reisch, eds., *Radiohead and Philosophy: Fitter, Happier, More Deductive*. Open Court.

Talas, T., and M. Kearney. 2019. Diving into The Deep End: Regulating Deepfakes Online. *Communications Law Bulletin* 38:3 <http://www5.austlii.edu.au/au/journals/CommsLawB/2019/24.pdf>.

University Press. 2021. Anthony Bourdain: The Biography. University Press. Independently Published.

Varga, Somogy, and Charles Guignon. 2020. Authenticity. In Edward N. Salta, ed., *The Stanford Encyclopedia of Philosophy* <https://plato.stanford.edu/archives/spr2020/entries/authenticity>.

Vitale, Tom. *In the Weeds: Around the World and Behind the Scenes with Anthony Bourdain*. Hachette.

Wang, Stephen. 2006. Human Incompletion, Happiness, and the Desire for God in Sartre's *Being and Nothingness*. *Sartre Studies International* 12:1.

Werner, Laurie. 2022. Fulfilling Bourdain's Vision, A Singaporean Hawker Center Opens in New York. *Forbes* (September 29th) <www.forbes.com/sites/lauriewerner/2022/09/29/fulfilling-bourdains-vision-a-singaporean-hawker-center-opens-in-new-york>.

West, Melanie Grayce, and Charles Passy. 2018. From the Village to the Bronx, N.Y. Restaurants Touched by Bourdain Mourn His Death; Restaurateurs around the City Featured by the Late Television Personality Praised His Humble Persona and Effects on Their Businesses. *Wall Street Journal* (June 9th).

Woolever, Laurie. 2021. *Bourdain: The Definitive Oral Biography*. Ecco.

Workneh, Téwodros W., and H. Leslie Stevens. 2019. *Anthony Bourdain: Parts Unknown* in Africa: Cultural Brokerage, 'Going Native,' and Colonial Nostalgia. *International Journal of Communication* 13.

Kitchen Crew from the Culinary Underbelly

DOUG ANDERSON is former chair of the department of philosophy and religion at the University of North Texas. Now retired, his work has focused on American philosophy, the history of philosophy, and the relation of philosophy to cultural practices. He has published essays in several popular philosophy volumes including those dealing with the work of Bob Dylan, Bruce Springsteen, Jimmy Buffet, and Neil Young. He is author or editor of nine books and numerous articles. He is also a full-time Americana musician.

WALTER BARTA is a principal investigator for the Digital Research Commons in M.D. Anderson Library at the University of Houston and an instructor at Wharton County Junior College. He also eats food and is interested in the intersection between popcorn and falafel.

SCOTT CALEF is a professor of philosophy at Ohio Wesleyan University. He edited *Led Zeppelin and Philosophy: All Will Be Revealed* (2009) and has contributed to pop culture volumes on Pink Floyd, Metallica, Jimi Hendrix, South Park, Alfred Hitchcock, and numerous others. The weirdest thing he ever ate was camel hump for Thanksgiving on Crete with an eccentric Norwegian shipping magnate. He doesn't recommend the hump. Come to think of it, the Norwegian was a little off, too.

MARC CHEONG is a digital ethicist and senior lecturer in the School of Computing and Information Systems at the University of Melbourne, Australia. He looks at issues related to the personal (phenomenological), ethical, and social effects of technology. To the delight of his friends and family, Marc loves his food, but dislikes dessert: hence there's always more dessert and sweets to share around the dining table. (Most importantly: he can proudly confirm that this bio is fully written by himself without the help of ChatGPT and its ilk).

DARCI DOLL is a Philosophy professor at Delta College. In addition to enjoying a cold pint at a mostly empty bar at 4:00, Darci has written several chapters on pop culture and philosophy books, such as *Queen and Philosophy*, *Better Call Saul and Philosophy*, and *The Princess Bride and Philosophy*.

RYAN FALCIONI is a Professor of Philosophy at Chaffey College, in Southern California. His areas of specialization include philosophy of language, religion, ethics, and cultural theory. Ryan also teaches Jiu-Jitsu at Chaffey. He received his black belt in Brazilian Jiu-Jitsu under Ana Laura Cordeiro and Rafael Pinto in 2018, and the first degree on his black belt from Master Carlos Gracie Jr. in 2021. He enjoys teaching, traveling, writing, and fighting . . . ideally all together. At his best, Bourdain modeled how to pursue all of these passions with humility, authenticity, and with an insatiable curiosity.

MARGOT FINN teaches undergraduate courses on food, fatness, and liberal education at the University of Michigan in a program now named Applied Liberal Arts, an oxymoron she has never liked and will not defend. She is the author of *Discriminating Taste: How Social Class Anxiety Created the American Food Revolution* (2017), and her writing and speaking about abortion has featured in *Slate* and the NPR podcas *More Perfect*.

ERIC HOLMES is a writing instructor/doctoral student and has published chapters in *Stranger Things and Philosophy* and *Neon Genesis Evangelion and Philosophy*. Like Bourdain, he is a big fan of using cautionary tales to impart morality to his children. His favorites include how a plugged toilet caused *Titanic* to sink, that Archduke Franz Ferdinand was shot because he didn't brush his teeth, and that Amelia Earhart really got lost forever in a child's messy bedroom.

JILL KITCHEN is a teacher, school administrator and head of the World Languages department at a large public high school in Brooklyn, New York. While spending two years in central China after college, she fell in love with exploring food, culture and language whilst attempting to live like a local. She is a self-proclaimed "dog-loving travel-obsessed foodie" who is always planning her next international adventure.

MICHEL LE GALL, former associate professor of Middle Eastern history at St. Olaf, co-taught several classes and has co-written a number of articles in popular philosophy with Charles Taliaferro. Le Gall's life-long love of cooking began when he served his first omelets to family members at age twelve. In time, he honed his skills and learned a number of tricks of the trade from Anthony Bourdain's books, including "mise en place" and the use of butter to emulsify and enrich sauces. He now lives in Manhattan's Upper West Side, enjoys fine dining, and works in executive and corporate communications.

SAMANTHA MAURO is a seasoned traveler and lover of art and food. She has been a follower of Bourdain's work for over a decade, turning to his wisdom abroad and at home when it comes to matters of trying new foods, savoring the good, and being open to experiences. Her career is reflective of her ever-growing epicurean passion; a journey that's led to working for Martha Stewart, on a cacao farm in Hawaii, and for chocolate makers in New York. She is currently a small business owner and craft chocolate maker, and enjoys educating on the importance of transparency, mindfulness and eating local when possible.

TRIP MCCROSSIN teaches in the Philosophy Department at Rutgers University, where he works on the nature, history, and legacy of the Enlightenment, in philosophy and popular culture, and where, without a doubt, the journey has changed him.

CANDACE MIRANDA is a graduate of English certified in creative writing from the University of Texas. She was born to a chef father who made reading *Kitchen Confidential* and watching *A Cook's Tour* a nightly family bonding ritual and a dentist mother who cleaned up the damages. Candace is also the owner of a small baking business selling baked goods to an organic grocer in Houston, Texas, and moonlights as a perioperative nurse to pay for her gourmet food escapades.

CHRISTOPHE POROT, like Anthony Bourdain, is an American of French heritage whose first exposure to culinary life came through travels to France during his youth. He is now a PhD candidate writing his thesis at the Sorbonne University Paris 1, who received his BA from St. Olaf College and has pursued his postgraduate studies at the University of Oxford and Harvard University. He has been a Deans Fellow recipient at Harvard and a Managing Editor, along with Dr. Charles Taliaferro, for a series on Philosophy of Religion in *Religious Studies Review*. He has edited for the Stanford Encyclopedia of Philosophy, the *Ashgate Companion to Theism*, and has published many articles including: "Mr. Robot and Philosophy" and "The Limits of Naturalism."

In addition to producing open-access philosophy through The Philosophemes Channel on YouTube, FRANK SCALAMBRINO works in the hospitality industry in Old Colorado City, Colorado, where he recommends local venues to travelers visiting the Garden of the Gods.

MICHAEL J. SHAFFER is currently a visiting Associate Professor of philosophy at Gustavus Adolphus College in Minnesota. He is also an external member of the Munich Center for Mathematical Philosophy and a fellow of the center for formal epistemology at Carnegie-Mellon University, a fellow of the Rotman Institute for Science and Values at the University of Western Ontario, and a Lakatos fellow at the London School of Economics. His research interests include epistemology, logic, and the philosophy of science; he has published several books and more than sixty articles and book chapters. He is also an accomplished cook, a serious collector of bootleg vinyl LPs, and a lover of wine and cheese.

ALLEN SIMON earned his Master of Theological Studies (MTS) degree from Harvard University and holds a BA in Religion from Rice University. Allen has ghostwritten a book on common themes across religions and works as both a writer and content strategist. He loves to cook at home and would like to some day follow in the path of Anthony Bourdain a bit by traveling more and trying cuisine from different parts of the world.

CHARLES TALIAFERRO, Emeritus Overby Distinguished Professor, St. Olaf College, has co-authored with Michel Le Gall chapters in popular philosophy volumes on topics from the Olympics and Sherlock Holmes to Stephen Spielberg. While Charles's ambition to be an adventurous chef was inspired by Anthony Bourdain, he has had to temper his ambition by realizing his best cooking can't hold a candle to the culinary genius of Max Evans, a nephew who seeks to follow Anthony to the Culinary Institute of America. Even so, Charles is connected to food, namely the Taliaferro apple, cultivated in Virginia which Thomas Jefferson described as producing "unquestionably the finest cyder we have ever known, and more like wine than any liquor I have ever tasted."

ANDREW WAHNSIEDLER is a lecturer at George Mason University, where he works with both the Integrative Studies and Cultural Studies departments. While he primarily focuses on the politics and sociology of mass media, his first love will always lie with his very first degree: philosophy. A long-time reader of the Popular Culture and Philosophy series, and its successor, Pop Culture and Philosophy, Andrew is thrilled to finally be making his own contribution. However, he found writing about Bourdain particularly challenging, given his self-described "gutter palate."

Index

Anyone Can Taste Wine

You Just Need This Book

Cees van Casteren

"It is the *best 'learn to taste wine' book I have ever come across . . . This is the book, hands down, which I would give to someone who came to me saying, 'I want to learn more about wine, where do I start?'"*

—JANCIS ROBINSON, wine advisor to King Charles III

"For anyone who loves wine, this book is a delight to read. Very educational with beautiful easy to understand tasting methods and color graphics . . . An excellent read for wine students and wine lovers alike."

—DR. LIZ THACH, PH.D., President, The Wine Market Council

"Cees is a brilliant taster, but just as importantly, he knows how to communicate his knowledge clearly and with real insight. New students of wine will love this book, but I learnt a lot from it too—and I've been tasting wine professionally for thirty-five years."

—TIM ATKIN, Master of Wine, award-winning wine writer

"In this thoughtful and highly original book, Cees van Casteren presents his structured and very practical framework for blind tasting wine. This isn't just for students of wine, but will be invaluable for anyone who tastes wine on a regular basis."

—JAMIE GOODE, PH.D., acclaimed wine columnist and lecturer

"I wish this book had been available when I was doing my own Master of Wine study! Cees has done an excellent job of clarifying what can be a complicated process and, on top, injected a sense of fun and pleasure into it."

—EMMA JENKINS, Master of Wine, international wine judge and wine journalist

CEES VAN CASTEREN is a brilliant scientist, author, and international wine competition judge, as well as one of the global super-elite (less than 500 top experts worldwide) who have been able to earn the supreme title, Master of Wine. Cees (it's pronounced 'Case') has written twelve books and more than a thousand articles on wine and food. He is a correspondent for Meininger's Wine Business International and partner of the blog, thestoryofmywine.com.

ISBN 978-1-63770-034-1 (hardback)

For more information on Open Universe books, visit us at

www.carusbooks.com

Cees van Casteren Master of Wine

Anyone Can Taste Wine

You Just Need This Book